Study Guide

THIRD EDITION

ADVERTISING
PRINCIPLES AND PRACTICE

Study Guide

ROBERT FIELD
St. Mary's College

THIRD EDITION

ADVERTISING

PRINCIPLES AND PRACTICE

WILLIAM WELLS
University of Minnesota

JOHN BURNETT
University of Denver

SANDRA MORIARITY
University of Colorado

Prentice Hall, Englewood Cliffs, New Jersey 07632

Project manager: *Cathleen Profitko*
Supervisory editor: *Benjamin D. Smith*
Production coordinator: *Ken Clinton*
Acquisitions editor: *David Borkowsky*
Assistant editor: *Melissa Steffens*

 © 1995 by Prentice-Hall, Inc.
A Simon & Schuster Company
Englewood Cliffs, New Jersey 07632

Printed in the United States of America

10 9 8 7 6 5 4 3 2 1

ISBN 0-13-723230-6

Prentice-Hall International (UK) Limited, *London*
Prentice-Hall of Australia Pty. Limited, *Sydney*
Prentice-Hall Canada Inc., *Toronto*
Prentice-Hall Hispanoamericana, S.A., *Mexico*
Prentice-Hall of India Private Limited, *New Delhi*
Prentice-Hall of Japan, Inc., *Tokyo*
Simon & Schuster Asia Pte. Ltd., *Singapore*
Editora Prentice-Hall do Brasil, Ltda., *Rio de Janeiro*

Contents

1 Introduction to Advertising

Chapter Objectives and Summary

- Define advertising and discuss its component parts.
- Understand the elements of great advertising.
- Identify the eight types of advertising.
- Explain the four roles of advertising.
- Identify the four players in the advertising world.
- Explain the impact on advertising of the invention of media forms such as print, radio, and television.
- Relate key figures in the history of advertising to their contributions to the field.
- Comprehend the future direction of advertising.

What makes advertising great? Good ads work on two levels: they engage the mind of the consumer while at the same time they deliver a selling message. Three broad dimensions characterize all great advertising: strategy, creativity, and execution. Great ads (1) are strategically sound, (2) have an original creative concept, and (3) use exactly the right execution for the message. Classic successful ads have used music, humor, action, sex, spokespersons, celebrities, fantasy characters, emotional appeals, children, animals, cartoons, drama, and inspirational ideas. Three broad dimensions are typical of great advertising: strategy, creativity, and execution. Strategy is directing the message to a certain audience, having a specific objective, and making every aspect of the ad contribute to that end. Creativity is an idea that sticks with the audience. Execution is paying attention to every detail to make sure that the strategy and the great idea are carried out with precision. Great ads are ads that (1) are strategically sound, (2) have an original creative concept, and (3) use exactly the right execution for the message.

Advertising is paid nonpersonal communication from an identified sponsor using mass media to persuade or influence an audience. The many types of advertising include: brand, retail, political, directory, direct-response, business-to-business, institutional, and public service. Advertising can also be explained in terms of the four roles it plays in business and society: marketing, communication, economic, and societal. Advertising can also be analyzed in terms of its objectives. Product advertising aims to sell a particular product. Institutional advertising tries to create a positive attitude toward the seller rather than sell a product. Direct-action advertising tries to produce a quick response while indirect advertising tries to stimulate demand over a longer period of time. Primary advertising aims to promote demand for a general product category. Selective advertising tries to create demand for a particular brand. Finally, commercial advertising promotes a product with the intent of making a profit, while noncommercial advertising is used by organizations who are not necessarily in business to make money.

The world of advertising has four major players: the advertisers, advertising agencies, the media, and the vendors. The first player, the advertisers, fall into four major categories: manufacturers, resellers, individuals, and institutions. Advertisers are usually involved in the advertising process in one of two ways: (1) through an advertising department or (2) through an in-house agency. The advertising department is the most common organizational arrangement chosen by large businesses. The actual advertising work may be carried out by an outside agency or departmental staff. Manufacturers tend to rely more on ad agencies. Companies that need closer control over advertising use an in-house agency. Most in-house agencies are found in retailing. Only about five percent of all advertising is done by in-house agencies. The second key player in the advertising world is the ad agency. The agency-client partnership is the dominant organizational arrangement in advertising. The strength of the agency is its resources, primarily in the form of creative expertise, media knowledge, and advertising strategy. The third player is the media, the channels used by advertisers to carry messages from the advertisers to the audience. Media must deliver advertising messages in a way that is consistent with the creative effort. Vendors represent the fourth player. Vendors are the wide range of service organizations that help advertisers such as freelancers, consultants, and self-employed professionals.

Advertising has been transformed by the development of the major media: print, radio, and television. The culmination of the age of print was the development of the newspaper. In the 1800s advertising played a pivotal role in the development of the mass market. While increased productivity resulted in excess production, customers had to be found beyond the local markets. Newspapers and magazines played key parts in reaching the first national markets. The emergence of radio as an inexpensive form of entertainment provided advertisers with the first pervasive national medium. When television married sight, sound, and motion, advertising's most powerful medium stepped onto the national stage.

In the twentieth century, advertising went through a series of transformations from hard to soft sell approaches. John Kennedy and Albert Lasker developed what Kennedy called "salesmanship in print." This "hard sell" approach emphasized "reason-why" arguments. Theodore MacManus devised a "soft sell." MacManus emphasized "image" that tried to penetrate the subconscious with a slow accumulation of positive images. Three creative geniuses, Leo Burnett, David Ogilvy, and William Bernbach inspired a revolution of creativity. Burnett, the leader of the "Chicago School" of advertising, looked for the "inherent drama" in every product. Ogilvy was a paradox because he represents both the image approach of MacManus and the reason-why approach of Lasker. He believed in research and copy testing, but he had a tremendous sense of image and story appeal. Bernbach's advertising focused on feelings and emotions. He believed that advertising is an art, not a science -- the art of persuasion. Economic turmoil brought an era of accountability. Ad agencies focused more on immediate sales increases rather than on developing brand equity. Many consumer products companies led a trend away from traditional advertising to sales promotion to generate short-term sales gains. The biggest trend in the 1990s is and will continue to be integrated marketing communication. Integrated marketing communication places a focus on working from the consumer back to the strategy and message of advertising -- what is termed outside-in planning. Advertising will have to work with all areas of marketing communication to maximize results. Another trend is the globalization of advertising. The challenge to advertising will be to accommodate the needs of both global and local advertising simultaneously. Along with globalization is a trend toward tighter and tighter niche marketing to market segments and even to individuals. The byword for advertising in the future will be accountability.

Key People, Terms, and Concepts

advertising department	Most common organizational arrangement for handling advertising in a large business.
advertising manager	Has the primary responsibility for advertising in a large business.
advertising	Paid nonpersonal communication from an identified sponsor using mass media to persuade or influence an audience.

Bernbach, William	Considered to be the most innovative advertiser of his time.
brand advertising	Focuses on a particular product that is manufactured and distributed nationally; concentrates on developing a distinctive brand image for that brand.
brand manager	In the typical multiple-brand, consumer-products company, this is the business leader who has ultimate responsibility for sales, product development, etc. as well as advertising.
Burnett, Leo	Leader of the "Chicago School" of advertising and believed in finding the "inherent drama" in the product. His most famous campaign is the Marlboro Man.
business-to-business advertising	Includes messages directed at other advertisers such as retailers, wholesalers and distributors as well as industrial purchasers and professionals.
Calkens, Ernest Elmo	Created a style of magazine advertising that resembled original art and was the first example of image advertising.
direct-action advertising	Intended to produce a quick response.
direct-response advertising	Tries to stimulate a sale directly.
director of advertising	Advises the brand manager; a specialist in recognizing and supporting advertising.
directory advertising	Used by people to help find out how to buy a product or service.
Gutenberg, Johannes	Invented movable type around 1440.
Hopkins, Claude	Sometimes called the greatest copywriter of all time, he pioneered in copy testing.
indirect-action advertising	Intended to stimulate demand over a long period of time; inform customers that the product exists.
institutional advertising	Tries to establish corporate identity or to win people over to the corporation's point of view.

integrated marketing communication	The concept or philosophy of marketing that stresses bringing together all the variables of the marketing mix, all the media, all the actions with which a company reaches its publics, and integrating the company's strategy and programs.
Kennedy, John E.	Started the "sales" approach to advertising with his reason-why copy style.
MacManus, Theodore	Originated the "soft sell" image approach to advertising..
marketing	The strategic process that a business uses to satisfy the consumers' needs and wants through goods and services.
Palmer, Volney	First "adman," in 1841 in Philadelphia.
political advertising	Used by politicians to get people to vote for them.
Powers, John	First well-known copywriter, employed by Philadelphia retailer John Wannamaker. He "journalized" advertising by making it newsy and informationally accurate.
primary advertising	Aims to promote the demand for the general product category.
product advertising	Aims to inform or stimulate the market about the sponsor's product; intent is to sell the product.
public relations institutional advertising	Tries to create a favorable image of the firm.
public service advertising	Communicates a message on behalf of some good cause.
Reeves, Rosser	Originated the concept of the Unique Selling Proposition.
Resor, Stanley	Developed the concept of account services.
retail advertising	Focuses on the store where a variety of products can be purchased or where a service is offered.
selective advertising	Tries to create demand for a particular brand.
target market	The particular consumers at which a company directs its marketing effort.

True/False

Circle the appropriate letter.

T   F   1.   The emotion that is the key to all great classic advertising campaigns is humor.

T   F   2.   The three dimensions that characterize great advertising are humor, visualization, and precision.

T   F   3.   The concept of integrated marketing communication implies that the marketing role and the communication role of advertising may be blending into one.

T   F   4.   Marketing is the strategic process a business uses to satisfy consumer needs and wants through goods and services.

T   F   5.   Primary advertising is intended to produce a quick response.

T   F   6.   The vendor is one of the categories of four primary players in the advertising world.

T   F   7.   The most common organizational arrangement in a large business is the in-house agency.

T   F   8.   Advertising provides information that helps match buyers and sellers in the marketplace.

T   F   9.   The value of an idea is measured by its originality.

T   F   10.   A good way to determine what is great advertising is to find out which ads were the most popular with consumers.

T   F   11.   The growth of retailing in the late 1800s played an important role in the development of advertising.

T   F   12.   The advertiser's brand manager is in charge of the total advertising program.

T   F   13.   An important fact of the 1990s and beyond is that marketers will expect more from advertising than they have.

T   F   14.   The key word for advertising in the future will be "accountability."

T   F   15.   A strategically sound ad is one that can speak to many audiences at once.

True/False Answers

1.	F	9.	T
2.	F	10.	F
3.	T	11.	T
4.	T	12.	F
5.	F	13.	T
6.	T	14.	T
7.	F	15.	F
8.	T		

Completion

Fill in the missing word or words in the blanks provided.

1. _____ is the remaining useful function of participating in advertising award programs such as CLIOs, New York Art Directors, etc.

2. Good ads work on two levels, _____ and _____.

3. The three dimensions of great advertising are _____, _____, and _____.

4. The four roles of advertising discussed in the text are _____, _____, _____, and _____.

5. The strategic process that a business uses to satisfy the consumers' needs and wants through goods and services is called _____.

6. The three primary players in the advertising industry are _____, _____, and _____.

7. The four major groups of advertisers are _____, _____, _____, and _____.

8. _____ is most likely to have the primary responsibility for advertising in a large business.

9. The three functions of advertising identified in your text are _____, _____, and _____.

10. In the _____ role of advertising, advertising mirrors fashion and design trends and contributes to our aesthetic sense.

11. _____ approach to copy emphasizes image and emotion.

12. Most in-house agencies are found in _____.

13. The definition of advertising has six elements: (1) paid communication, (2) _____, (3) _____, (4) using mass media, (5) _____, and (6) _____.

14. Albert Lasker is associated with the _____ approach to advertising copywriting.

15. The eight types of advertising are brand, _____, political, _____, _____, business-to-business, institutional, and _____.

Completion Answers

1. boosting the morale of creative staffs
2. engage the consumer's mind and deliver selling message
3. strategy, creativity, and execution
4. social, economic, communication, and marketing
5. marketing
6. advertiser, advertising agency, and media
7. manufacturers, resellers, individuals, and institutions
8. advertising director
9. advertising may be either direct or indirect, advertising can be either primary or secondary, and advertising can serve a commercial or noncommercial function
10. societal
11. soft sell
12. retailing
13. that is nonpersonal, from an identified source, to persuade or influence, an audience
14. reason-why
15. retail, directory, direct-response, and public service

Matching

Match the terms and concepts with the appropriate statements. Each term or concept may be used only once; there are more terms and concepts than statements.

Terms and Concepts

a. advertising manager
b. brand
c. brand manager
d. business-to-business
e. Claude Hopkins
f. developed ads that were informationally accurate

g. direct-response
h. inherent drama of the product
i. institutional
j. J. Walter Thompson
k. John Kennedy
l. Leo Burnett
m. retail

n. Rosser Reeves
o. selective
p. Stanley Resor
q. target market
r. Theodore MacManus
s. use of copy testing to improve advertising
t. Volney Palmer
u. Elmo Calkens
v. primary
w. public service
x. communication role
y. Bill Bernbach
z. David Ogilvy

Statements

_____ 1. Advertising that is local and focuses on price, availability and location.

_____ 2. Advertising that includes messages directed at other advertisers such as retailers, wholesalers and distributors as well as industrial purchasers and professionals.

_____ 3. Advertising that tries to establish corporate identity or to win people over to the corporation's point of view.

_____ 4. Has the primary responsibility for making sure that the ads that have been run are run in the right media.

_____ 5. Shares the responsibility for advertising decisions with the advertising director in the typical multiple-brand, consumer products company.

_____ 6. The particular consumers at which a company directs its marketing effort.

_____ 7. Advertising intended to create demand for a particular brand.

_____ 8. The first "adman."

_____ 9. Change in the approach to advertising devised by John Powers.

_____ 10. What Claude Hopkins is known for bringing to advertising copywriting.

_____ 11. He defined advertising as "salesmanship in print."

_____ 12. Man most closely associated with developing the "soft sell" copy style.

_____ 13. He developed the concept of account services.

_____ 14. He introduced modern marketing research to advertising.

_____ 15. He emphasized that effective advertising must have a USP ("unique selling proposition").

Matching Answers

1.	m	9.	f
2.	d	10.	s
3.	i	11.	k
4.	a	12.	r
5.	c	13.	p
6	q	14.	j
7.	o	15.	n
8.	t		

Multiple Choice

Place the letter of the answer you think is correct in the blank provided.

_____ 1.   All classic ads work on two levels: they engage the mind of the consumer and
_____.
a. generate interest on the part of the consumer.
b. at the same time deliver a selling message.
c. make the consumer laugh.
d. entertain the consumer.
e. all of the above

_____ 2.   The future of advertising will be strongly affected by which of the following ideas?
a. integrated marketing communication
b. rising expectations of marketers
c. accountability
d. globalization
e. all of the above

_____ 3.   When the advertiser uses just the right technique in producing the ad so that it delivers
the message precisely intended to affect the desired audience in exactly the desired
way, what dimension of great advertising is involved?
a. execution
b. strategy
c. selling
d. creativity
e. planning

_____ 4.   Which of the following is **NOT** one of the primary players in the advertising
industry?
a. government
b. vendors
c. advertisers
d. media
e. advertising agencies

_____ 5.   The Yellow Pages is an example of _____ advertising because people refer to
the Yellow Pages to find out how to buy a product or service.
a. direct-response
b. institutional
c. public service
d. directory
e. retail

_____ 6. Advertising is a form of _____ communication.
   a. personal
   b. mass
   c. interpersonal
   d. intrapersonal
   e. all of the above

_____ 7. What is the dominant organizational arrangement in advertising?
   a. advertising department
   b. in-house agency
   c. the advertising agency-client relationship
   d. integrated marketing communication arrangement
   e. none of the above

_____ 8. Which of the following is **NOT** one of the types of advertisers?
   a. wholesalers
   b. individuals
   c. institutions
   d. resellers
   e. manufacturers

_____ 9. What was the objective of early commercial messages?
   a. persuasion
   b. selling
   c. coercion
   d. information
   e. all of the above

_____ 10. Which of the following is **NOT** one of the reasons that most in-house agencies are found in retail organizations?
   a. shorter time frames in retailing
   b. smaller profit margins in retailing
   c. advertising materials provided by manufacturers to retailers
   d. retail advertising requires less creativity
   e. production assistance provided to retailers by media

_____ 11. To which of the following did Gutenberg's invention of movable type contribute?
   a. development of print media
   b. advertising
   c. mass literacy
   d. mass communication
   e. all of the above

_____ 12. Which of the following were important to the development of advertising?
   a. growth of retailing
   b. development of magazines
   c. invention of movable type
   d. mass marketing
   e. all of the above

_____ 13. _____ stress bringing together all the variables of the marketing mix, all the media, all the actions with which a company reaches its publics, uniting the company's strategy and programs.
    a. Marketing Communication
    b. Advertising
    c. Sales Promotion
    d. Integrated Marketing Communication
    e. Public Relations

_____ 14. Creativity is involved in what part of great advertising?
    a. research efforts
    b. strategic planning
    c. message development
    d. buying and placing ads in the media
    e. all of the above

_____ 15. Who do advertisers hire to plan and implement their advertising effort?
    a. freelance copywriters
    b. advertising agencies
    c. the media
    d. journalists
    e. vendors

Multiple Choice Answers

1. b	6. b	11. e
2. e	7. c	12. e
3. b	8. a	13. d
4. a	9. d	14. e
5. d	10. d	15. b

Career Exercise -- Job Inventory

For what area of advertising are you best suited? To make that determination you need to know what jobs are available, what attributes and experiences are needed for those jobs, and what attributes and experiences that you have or could develop. You can make a start by looking at the job inventory that follows and picking out the jobs that interest you the most.

You must get to know the job that you shoot for in fine detail, in the final analysis. However, you can start the process by finding the answers to the following and similar questions.

- What is the nature of the job? High pressure, job security, casual vs. serious, etc.
- What degree/education/special training is required?
- What special experience is needed -- at the entry-level? at the 10-year point? at 20 years?
- What special skills will be needed -- at the entry-level? second job? etc.
- What extracurricular activities would be helpful in preparing for the job?
- What salary levels prevail for the job -- entry-level? second job? etc.
- What kinds of organizations would be most likely to have the job available?

- What locations would be most likely to have the job available? (Would you need to go to New York to get started, for example?)

The following is a brief inventory of jobs in advertising broken down by the three major areas:

Advertiser/Advertising Department/In-House Agency

advertising manager	advertising director
copywriter	artist
researcher	production specialist
marketing director	marketing assistant
technical writer	technical illustrator
sales promotion manager	public relations specialist
house organ editor/writer	audiovisual manager
brand manager	graphic designer

Advertising Agency

account executive	account manager
account supervisor	management supervisor
creative director	creative department manager
art director	copywriter
media planner	media buyer
researcher	print production specialist
film and TV commercial producer	traffic manager
production manager	office manager
sales promotion specialist	audio-visual technician

Media

sales representative	sales manager
researcher	jingle creator
photographer	film and videotape producer/director
sales promotion specialist	copywriter
artist	production specialist
free-lance artist	free-lance copywriter
mailing list broker	illustrator

2   Advertising and Society: Ethics and Regulation

Chapter Objectives and Summary

- **Discuss the major issues that advertisers must address.**
- **Explain the current judicial position concerning the First Amendment rights of advertisers.**
- **Comprehend the role of the FTC in regulating advertising.**
- **List and understand the characteristics of other federal agencies governing advertising.**
- **Explain the remedies available to different groups when an ad is judged deceptive or offensive.**
- **Discuss the self-regulatory opportunities available to advertisers and agencies.**

    The advertising industry is worried that a consumer revolt against advertising is taking shape. Advertising's high visibility makes it particularly vulnerable to criticism. Recent surveys show that many people see advertising as deceptive; even though they also find it useful. While consumers say that advertising provides useful information about products and services, they also felt that advertising encouraged people to use products they don't need and that it increases the cost of products. When advertising decisions are not clearly covered by a code, a rule, or a regulation, an individual must weigh the pros and cons and make an ethical decision. Three issues are central to an ethical discussion of advertising: advocacy, accuracy, and acquisitiveness. Beyond these general ethical issues are the many specific concerns such as puffery, taste, stereotyping, advertising to children, advertising controversial and sensitive products, and subliminal messages.

    Few elements of business have been more heavily legislated and regulated than advertising. The industry has sought the protection of the First Amendment. Although the Supreme Court has ruled that some very limited forms of advertising content merit First Amendment protection, it has not said that a business has the same First Amendment rights of expression as a private individual or a newspaper. Although the Court's interpretation of constitutional protection for advertising remains unsettled, it does appear to be moving in a direction that favors advertising.

    The federal government has taken a very active role in regulating advertising. The primary regulatory agencies governing advertising are the Federal Trade Commission (FTC), the Food and Drug Administration (FDA), and the Federal Communication Commission (FCC). The FTC is the leader in government regulation of advertising. The FTC is concerned with the following advertising issues: deception, comparative advertising, endorsements, and demonstrations. The current FTC policy on deception involves three basic elements: there must be a high probability that the consumer will be misled; deception is judged from the perspective of the "reasonable consumer"; and the deception must actually influence the consumers' decision making. The advertiser should have a reasonable basis for making a claim. This involves having data on file to substantiate the claim made in the advertising. Advertising that creates and reinforces false impressions will be judged deceptive when the consumers' perception of the truth of a claim and the truth of the claim are inconsistent. Comparative advertising claims must be based on fact; comparisons must involve meaningful issues; and the comparisons must involve meaningful competitors, or the comparative advertising will be judged deceptive. Endorsements must be qualified by experience or training to make the judgments made in an ad, and endorsers must actually use the product. Demonstrations must not mislead consumers, and a claim that is demonstrated must be accurately shown.

The FTC's remedies for deceptive and unfair advertising include consent decrees, cease-and-desist orders, and corrective advertising. A recent emphasis of FTC scrutiny of deceptive advertising is to hold the agency legally responsible. The FTC's policy requires that advertisers must substantiate a claim; it is not up to the FTC to disprove the claim. Other federal agencies that have responsibilities for advertising include the Food and Drug Administration, the Federal Communications Commission, the Postal Service, the Bureau of Alcohol, Tobacco, and Firearms, the Patent Office, and the Library of Congress.

In addition to governmental controls, the advertising industry has created a self-regulating mechanism to deal with such issues as deception. The rationale is for the industry to avoid confrontations with the government by policing itself. The most effective attempts at self-regulation have come through the Advertising Review Council and the Better Business Bureau. The main purpose of the Council is to negotiate voluntary withdrawal of national advertising that professionals consider to be deceptive. The National Advertising Division of the Council of Better Business Bureaus (NAD) and the National Advertising Review Board (NARB) are the two operating arms of the National Advertising Review Council. At the local level, self-regulation centers on the Better Business Bureau, which has no legal power. The media also attempt to regulate advertising by screening and rejecting ads that violate their standards of truth and good taste.

Key Terms and Concepts

accuracy	Ethical issue involved when a toy manufacturer implies that a whole environment is available with the purchase of a doll when in fact only the doll is being sold.
acquisitiveness	Ethical issue that centers on the argument that advertising symbolizes our society's preoccupation with accumulating material objects.
advocacy	Ethical issue involving the fact that advertising tries to persuade the audience to do something rather than just provide information about the product.
cease-and-desist order	Legal order requiring advertiser to stop unlawful ad practices.
consent decree	First step in regulation process after FTC determines ad is deceptive.
corrective advertising	Required by FTC in cases where consumer research determines that lasting false beliefs have been perpetuated by an advertisement.
Federal Communication Commission	Government agency formed in 1934 to protect the public interest with regard to broadcast communications.

Federal Trade Commission	Government agency responsible for regulating much of American business; established in 1914 to prevent business activities that were unfair, deceptive or anticompetitive.
National Advertising Review Council	Self-regulation organization that tries to negotiate voluntary withdrawal of deceptive national advertising.
puffery	Advertising or other sales representations which praise the item to be sold with subjective opinions, superlatives or exaggerations; vaguely and generally, stating no specific facts.
RICO suits	Lawsuits concerning deceptive advertising brought under the Racketeer Influenced and Corrupt Organizations Act; involves triple damages, legal costs; and being labeled a "mobster"
societal marketing concept	Careful balance between company profits, consumer-want satisfaction and public interest; organization must determine the interest of target markets and to deliver satisfaction more effectively than its competitors in a way that enhances the consumer's and society's well-being.
stereotyping	Presenting a group of people in an unvarying pattern that lacks individuality.
subliminal message	Messages transmitted in such a way that people are not consciously aware of receiving them.
Valentine v. Christensen	Case in which the Supreme Court ruled that a business does not have the same right of expression as a private individual.
Wheeler Lea Amendment	Gave FTC power to impose fines, to launch investigations without consumer complaints, and to order firms to stop questionable ad practices.

True/False

Circle the appropriate letter.

T   F   1.   Adese is advertising that praises the item to be sold using subjective opinions, superlatives, and other mechanisms that are not based on specific fact.

T F 2. A recent study of attitudes toward advertising co-sponsored by Advertising Age and the Roper Organization found that a large number of consumers don't care much about advertising one way or the other.

T F 3. The three issues that are central to an ethical discussion of advertising are accuracy, advocacy, and acquisitiveness.

T F 4. The most current questions of taste center on issues of sexual innuendo, nudity, and violence.

T F 5. Recent interpretations of the First Amendment suggest that the right of expression for advertisers is still being interpreted.

T F 6. The Supreme Court has found that all commercial speech is protected by the First Amendment whether it is truthful or misleading or deceptive.

T F 7. Data must be on file to substantiate claims made by advertisers.

T F 8. The FTC supports comparative advertising because it encourages competition.

T F 9. Corrective advertising is required when the FTC determines that an ad has created lasting false impressions.

T F 10. Self-regulation encourages voluntary withdrawal of deceptive advertising.

T F 11. Media can refuse to accept advertising that violates standards of truth or good taste.

T F 12. In general, the public and many advertisers feel advertising is unethical.

T F 13. The primary legal protection available to advertising is the First Amendment.

T F 14. The text suggests that the advertising industry's efforts at self-regulation have been very effective in controlling cases of deceptive or misleading advertising.

T F 15. An ad agency cannot be held legally liable even if the agency was an active participant in the preparation of the ad and knew or had reason to know that it was false or deceptive.

True/False Answers

1.	F	9.	T
2.	T	10.	T
3.	T	11.	T
4.	T	12.	T
5.	T	13.	T
6.	F	14.	F
7.	T	15.	F
8.	F		

Completion

Fill in the missing word or words in the blanks provided.

1. Three issues critical to the ethical discussion of advertising are: _____, _____, and _____.

2. Advertising or other sales representations which praise the item to be sold with subjective opinions, superlatives or exaggerations; vaguely and generally, stating no specific facts is called _____.

3. According to the text, current questions of taste center around the issues of _____, _____, and _____.

4. _____ is presenting a group of people in an unvarying pattern that lacks individuality.

5. A message transmitted below the threshold of normal perception so that the receiver is not consciously aware of having received it is called _____.

6. The _____ is a government agency responsible for regulating advertising as a form of unfair competition.

7. High probability to deceive, judged from a "reasonable" _____, and _____ are the three basic elements of the FTC's current policy for determining whether or not an ad is deceptive.

8. Under current FTC guidelines, having _____ on file to _____ the claim is considered a reasonable basis for making a claim in an ad.

9. _____, _____, and _____ are the most common sources of complaints concerning deceptive or unfair advertising practices.

10. The first step in the regulation process after the FTC determines that an ad is deceptive is the _____.

11. The landmark case involving corrective advertising was _____.

12. _____ requires a careful balance between company profits, consumer-want satisfaction and public interest. In this the organization must determine the interest of target markets and to deliver satisfaction more effectively than its competitors in a way that enhances the consumer's and society's well-being.

13. Comparative advertising is considered deceptive unless comparisons are based on _____.

14. _____ is required by the FTC in cases where consumer research determines that lasting false beliefs have been perpetuated by an advertising campaign.

15. The medium that would be seriously affected, even devastated, by a total ban on cigarette advertising is _____.

Completion Answers

1. advocacy, accuracy, acquisitiveness
2. puffery
3. sexual innuendo, nudity, violence
4. stereotyping
5. subliminal
6. FTC
7. consumer's perspective, must influence decision making
8. data support
9. competitors, public, FTC monitors
10. consent decree
11. Warner-Lambert vs. FTC
12. societal marketing concept
13. fact
14. corrective advertising
15. magazines

Matching

Match the terms and concepts with the appropriate statements. Each term or concept may be used only once; there are more terms and concepts than statements.

Terms and Concepts

a. accuracy
b. acquisitiveness
c. advocacy
d. bait advertising
e. cease and desist order
f. fantasy marketing
g. Federal Communication Commission
h. Federal Trade Commission
i. Library of Congress
j. patent office
k. puffery
l. subliminal advertising
m. Valentine vs. Christensen
n. Wheeler-Lea Amendment
o. National Advertising Review Council
p. consent decree
q. Warner-Lambert
r. avarice

Statements

_____ 1. In the discussion of ethics in advertising, the issue which involves the fact that advertising tries to persuade the audience to do something rather than just provide information about the product.

_____ 2. When a toy manufacturer implies that a whole environment is available with the purchase of a doll when in fact only the doll is being sold, this central issue of the ethical discussion of advertising is involved.

_____ 3. When critics argue that advertising promotes a society in which people believe they must have products in order to be happy, this issue of ethical discussion is involved.

_____ 4. Advertising or other sales representations which praise the item to be sold with subjective opinions, superlatives or exaggerations; vaguely and generally, stating no specific facts.

_____ 5. Messages that are transmitted in such a way that people are not consciously aware of receiving them.

_____ 6. The legislative action that extended the power of the FTC to include the power to impose fines, to launch its own investigations without complaints from consumers and to order companies to stop questionable advertising practices.

_____ 7. When a diet company offers a free diet assessment but fails to mention that special diet food must be purchased with the "free" diet program, this advertising problem is involved.

_____ 8. A legal order requiring an advertiser to stop its unlawful practices.

_____ 9. Established in 1914, this government agency is responsible for regulation to prevent business activities that are unfair, deceptive or anticompetitive.

_____ 10. Formed in 1934, this government agency is responsible for the protection of public interest with regard to broadcast communications.

_____ 11. Marketing directed at people caught up in the pursuit of greater life satisfaction while not wanting to give up material things.

_____ 12. The case in which the Supreme Court ruled that purely commercial advertising does not have the same protection under the First Amendment as a private individual's expression.

_____ 13. Extended the FTC's powers and made the agency more consumer oriented by adding "deceptive acts and practices" to the list of "unfair methods of competition."

_____ 14. This federal agency that oversees the registration of trademarks, which include both brand names and corporate or store names as well as their identifying symbols.

_____ 15. This federal agency provides controls for copyright protection. Legal copyrights give creators a monopoly on their creations for a certain time.

Matching Answers

1.	c	9.	h
2.	a	10.	g
3.	b	11.	f
4.	k	12.	m
5.	l	13.	n
6.	n	14.	j
7.	d	15.	i
8.	e		

Multiple Choice

Place the letter of the correct answer in the blank provided.

_____ 1. Which of the following is an issue central to an ethical discussion of advertising?
   a. avarice
   b. acquisitiveness
   c. competition
   d. fairness
   e. none of the above

_____ 2. Stereotyping in advertising has affected which of the following groups?
   a. blacks
   b. elderly
   c. women
   d minorities
   e. all of the above

_____ 3. Opponents of the ban of TV and radio cigarette advertising use what as the primary basis of their argument?
   a. economic harm to country
   b. economic harm to workers in the tobacco industry
   c. First Amendment rights of advertisers
   d. lack of fairness
   e. corporate legal rights of tobacco producers

_____ 4. In what case did the Supreme Court rule that purely commercial advertising does not have the same protection under the First Amendment as a private individual's expression?
   a. Virginia State Board of Pharmacy vs. Virginia Citizens Consumer Council
   b. New York Times vs. Sullivan
   c. Posadas de Puerto Rico Associates vs. Tourism Company of Puerto Rico
   d. Central Hudson Gas and Electric Corporation vs. Public Service Commission of New York
   e. Valentine vs. Christensen

_____ 5. Which of the following is **TRUE** about the regulation of advertising in children's television programming?
   a. most of the regulation has been left to self-regulation by advertisers
   b. the FTC established regulations for advertising in children's television programming in 1978
   c. the FTC banned certain techniques and strategies that were confusing and misleading with children
   d. the FTC established limits on the amount of advertising that could be used in children's television programming
   e. all of the above

_____ 6. A 1990 law limits the amount of time devoted to commercials in children's television programming to:
   a. 15 minutes on weekends and 20 minutes on week days.
   b. 10.5 minutes on weekends and 12 minutes on week days.
   c. 20 minutes on weekends and 15 minutes on week days.
   d. 12 minutes on weekends and 10.5 minutes on week days.
   e. 12.5 minutes on weekends and 20 minutes on week days.

_____ 7. What is the current position of the Supreme Court concerning the First Amendment rights of advertisers?
   a. commercial speech is not protected by the First Amendment
   b. the First Amendment protection of commercial speech is absolute and unlimited
   c. the First Amendment protects only commercial speech that is truthful and not misleading or deceptive
   d. the Supreme Court's position is the same as it has been for more than 100 years
   e. none of the above

_____ 8. What is the first step in the regulation process after the FTC determines that an ad is deceptive?
   a. issue a cease-and-desist order
   b. consent decree
   c. case is referred to trial before administrative judge
   d. FTC requests advertiser to correct ad
   e. FTC requests advertiser to substantiate claim

_____ 9. When is corrective advertising required by the FTC?
   a. in every case of substantiated deceptive advertising
   b. when the FTC determines that irreparable harm has been done by the advertising determined to be deceptive
   c. when an administrative judge rules that specific damages have been done by deceptive advertising
   d. when consumer research shows that lasting false beliefs have been caused by the ad campaign
   e. all of the above

_____ 10. Which of the following is a practical difficulty in using subliminal messages in advertising?
   a. there are no practical difficulties in using subliminal messages in advertising
   b. placing subliminal messages into advertisements
   c. perceptual thresholds vary from person to person and from moment to moment
   d. finding subliminal mesages that actually affect people
   e. convincing advertisers to allow the use of the subliminal messages

_____ 11. In which of the following did the Supreme Court decide that the First Amendment protects purely commercial speech?
   a. Virginia State Board of Pharmacy vs. Virginia Citizens Consumer Council (1976)
   b. Cincinnati v. Discovery Network (1993)
   c. Posadas de Puerto Rico Associates vs. Tourism Company of Puerto Rico (1986)
   d. Central Hudson Gas and Electric Corporation vs. Public Service Commission of New York (1980)
   e. all of the above

_____ 12. In 1971, the FTC initiated a major policy change concerning the reasonableness of claims. This change in policy was:
   a. the FTC became responsible for disproving a claim's validity.
   b. advertisers have responsibility for proving claim's reasonableness.
   c. an administrative law judge was given responsibility for determining the reasonableness of a claim.
   d. the National Advertising Division was given the ultimate responsibility for determining the reasonableness of a claim.
   e. none of the above

_____ 13. What federal agency is responsible for regulating deceptive advertising?
   a. Federal Trade Commission (FTC)
   b. National Advertising Division (NAD)
   c. Federal Commerce Commission (FCC)
   d. Federal Communication Commission (FCC)
   e. Food & Drug Administration (FDC)

_____ 14. Which of the following federal legislation is important to advertising?
   a. Wheeler-Lea Amendment
   b. Lanham Act
   c. Magnuson-Moss Warranty Act
   d. FTC Improvement Act of 1980
   e. all of the above

_____ 15. Which of the following is **NOT** a remedy for deceptive and unfair advertising used by the FTC?
   a. corrective advertising
   b. cease and desist order
   c. order advertiser not to use a particular strategy again
   d. consent decree
   e. fines

Career Exercise -- Approaches to Ethics

The following are the three most common approaches to the development of ethical positions. Using these approaches to ethics, try personally assessing the various issues that the text has discussed.

Absolutist Ethics There is a fixed set of principles or laws from which there should be no deviation. This position is sometimes referred to as "legalism." If it is wrong to lie, it is always wrong to lie. Consequences are irrelevant to the "rightness" of an action.

Antinomian Ethics This is the opposite end of the spectrum from the "absolutist" view. The term "antinomian" means against law. Actions in any situation are spontaneous and unpredictable. There is no predetermined standard of conduct nor moral rules. The antinomian approach is not concerned with motives, consequences or obligations. Every situation is different. There are no "principles" that can guide decision-making. It places faith in the individual to decide what is right in any given circumstance.

Situation Ethics This approach is between the two extremes of absolutist and antinomian ethics. Situation ethics does not hold that everything is relative as in antinomian. This approach knows, understands and accepts the standards of the community. Unlike the absolutist position, situation ethics is prepared to compromise or set rules aside if "unselfish love for one's neighbor demands it." Lying is unethical. However, if the consequence of telling the truth is to harm a fellow human being -- then lie. Human life, human values are the highest possible good. People always come first; rules second. Act in such a way that is good for the largest number of people. Always be concerned with human consequences.

For example, how do you feel personally about the portrayal of women in advertisements? Do you feel that that advertisers have a responsibility to avoid inaccurate portrayals of women because of a social or legal rule that should prevent inaccurate portrayals? In the current absence of such a rule, perhaps you feel there should be such a law? This is an absolutist position.

Maybe you find your position on the opposite end of the scale. Do you feel that advertisers should be free to do whatever seems right to the individual advertiser? There should be no ethical restrictions -- or legal restrictions for that matter -- on the behavior of advertisers. We should trust in the individual to do the right thing. This is an antinomian position.

Perhaps, you feel that while there may not be a law or rule that prohibits inaccurate stereotyping of women in ads, advertisers should be personally compelled to pursue accuracy because to fail to do so is harmful to women as human beings. Even if the law does not require it, advertisers should be compelled to treat women fairly because of the human consequences that could be involved if they fail to do so. This is a situation ethics position.

Repeat the process with each of the following ethical issues raised in the text: puffery, taste, stereotyping (in addition to portrayals of women, portrayals of minorities, the elderly, and other special groups such as "baby boomers"), children's advertising, advertising controversial products, and subliminal advertising. You can use the same process to evaluate your personal position on the regulation of advertising and such issues as deception, basis for making claims, comparative advertising, endorsements, and demonstrations.

3   Advertising and the Marketing Process

Chapter Objectives and Summary

- **Understand the concept of marketing, and the role of advertising within the marketing strategy.**
- **Appreciate the concept of the market and the four types of markets.**
- **Explain the marketing concept and its evolution.**
- **Explain and define the 4Ps of marketing and how they interface with advertising.**

Marketing is the process of planning and executing the conception, pricing, production, and distribution of ideas, goods, and services to create exchanges that satisfy individual and organizational objectives. Advertising is a subset of the part of marketing called promotion or marketing communication. Advertising is only one aspect of marketing communication. The success of a particular marketing effort depends on whether a competitive advantage can be established in the minds of the customers. The process of creating an exchange revolves around a marketing plan. A marketing plan involves four stages: a research stage, a strategy stage, an implementation stage, and an evaluation stage. Advertising is one of the strategic alternatives available to the marketer.

A market is either a region where goods are sold and bought or a particular type of buyer. The four primary types of markets are consumer, industrial, institutional, and reseller. The marketing concept recognizes the fact that it isn't enough to produce a product efficiently and offer it for sale. In a competitive situation, it becomes necessary to identify consumers' needs and preferences. The marketing concept changes the focus in commerce from the seller's product to the buyer's needs. Companies should focus on consumer problems and try to develop products to solve them. The marketing concept means working from the customer backward rather than from the factory forward. Advertising is used to deliver information that will facilitate decision making. The goal is to produce advertising that is honest, useful, and matches the needs of the customer so that the customer is satisfied with the choices made.

The various marketing elements are classified into the following four categories known as the marketing mix and popularly referred to as the 4Ps: product, place, price, and promotion. The marketing mix consists of the design of the product including its package, pricing the product, as well as terms of sale; distribution of the product; and promotion of the product. Promotion consists of advertising, public relations, sales promotion, personal selling, packaging/point-of-sale, and direct marketing. The product is both the object of the advertising and the reason for marketing. It involves both tangible and intangible product characteristics. Stressing the most important attributes is the key to influencing customer choices and serves as the foundation for much advertising. The product's life cycle has four stages (introductory, growth, maturity, and decline). The point that the product occupies in its life cycle has a major effect on the advertising strategy. Package design is also very important to advertisers because it is such a vital part of brand image and product identity. Whether the marketer uses direct or indirect marketing, the place factor, which is the channel of distribution, is the basic mechanism for delivering the product to the customer. Depending on the market coverage desired, the marketer can choose exclusive, selective, or intensive distribution. The price the seller sets is based not only on the cost of making and marketing the product but also on the seller's expected level of profit. Psychological factors also affect the price. The marketer can choose from customary, psychological, prestige, or price lining. All elements of the marketing mix are coordinated to focus on satisfying the needs of the consumer rather than on the marketer's production capabilities.

Key Terms and Concepts

branding	Process of creating an identity for a product using a distinctive name or symbol.
brand equity	The reputation that the product name or symbol connotes.
channel of distribution	Individuals and institutions involved in moving products from producers to customers.
competitive advantage	When the consumer decides how close one product, service or idea comes to satisfying his or her needs versus a competitor's product, service, or idea.
cooperative advertising	When producers and retailers share in the cost of local advertising.
customary (expected) price	Pricing strategy which involves the use of a single well-known price for a long period of time.
direct marketing	Distributing a product without using a reseller.
exclusive distribution	Market coverage strategy in which only one distributor is allowed to sell the brand in a particular market.
generic product	Products that are marketed without any identifying brand.
indirect marketing	Distributing a product through a channel structure which includes one or more resellers.
intensive distribution	Market coverage strategy which places the product in every possible outlet (including vending machines) in order to attain total market coverage.
market	Region where goods are sold and bought; or a particular type of buyer.
marketing concept	Focuses on the needs of the consumer rather than on the marketer's production capabilities; means working from the customer backward rather than from the factory forward.

marketing mix (4Ps)	Product, price, place, and promotion; consists of the design of the product including its package, pricing the product, as well as terms of sale; distribution of the product; and promotion of the product.
marketing philosophy	General perspective or attitude the marketer has toward the consumer.
marketing	Process of planning and executing the conception, pricing, promotion, and distribution of ideas, goods, and services to create exchanges that satisfy individual (customer) and organizational objectives.
prestige price	Where a high price is set to make the product seem worthy or valuable.
price lining	When Sears, Roebuck and Company offers different types of tennis rackets on the basis of "good," "better," and "best," with prices that vary accordingly.
product life cycle	Perspective of product that treats products as people and assumes they are born (introduced), develop, grow old, and die; consists of four stages: introductory, growth, maturity, and decline.
promotion mix	Consists of advertising, sales promotion, public relations, and personal selling.
public relations	Set of activities intended to enhance the image of the marketer in order to create goodwill.
sales promotion	Element of the promotional mix; extra incentive to buy now.
selective distribution	Market coverage strategy which expands the number of outlets but restricts participation to those outlets that prove most profitable to the manufacturer.

True/False

Circle the appropriate letter.

T   **F**   1.   Integrated marketing communication requires a thorough understanding of the components of marketing.

T   **F**   2.   Marketing is the process of creating an identity for a product using a distinctive name or symbol.

T	F	3.	The package stimulates the purchase at the critical moment when the consumer is making a choice.
T	F	4.	Advertising helps the salesperson by laying the groundwork and preselling the product.
T	F	5.	Sales promotion activities are used to stimulate sales at a specific time in the future.
T	F	6.	What makes direct marketing unique from other forms of marketing and promotion is that it focuses on satisfying the needs of the consumer.
T	F	7.	The success of marketing is dependent upon whether a business can create a competitive advantage that results in an exchange.
T	F	8.	The marketing concept focuses on the predetermined goals of the marketer rather than the needs of the consumer.
T	F	9.	The product consists of a bundle of tangible components that satisfies the needs of the consumer.
T	F	10.	The two primary types of channel institutions are media and retailers.
T	F	11.	Advertising, sales promotion, and public relations make up the promotional mix.
T	F	12.	Brand equity is the idea that a respected brand name adds value to a product.
T	F	13.	The budget allocation for each promotional element is determined by the emphasis given to each element in the promotional mix.
T	F	14.	When a group of people share a need, can use a particular product to fill the need, and can afford the product, a competitive advantage exists.
T	F	15.	In terms of advertising expenditures, the reseller market is the largest of the four types of markets.

True/False Answers

1.	T		9.	F
2.	F		10.	F
3.	T		11.	F
4.	T		12.	T
5.	F		13.	T
6.	F		14.	F
7.	T		15.	F
8.	F			

Completion

Fill in the missing word or words in the blanks provided.

1. The stages of the marketing plan are: _____, strategy, _____, and evaluation.

2. Product, _____, place, and _____ are the components of the marketing mix.

3. Reseller, _____, industrial, and _____ are the four consumer markets.

4. Public relations, _____, sales promotion, and _____ are the activities of promotion.

5. In the modern marketing concept, marketing is _____.

6. Introduction, _____, maturity, and _____ are the stages of the product-life cycle.

7. The three distribution strategies discussed in the text are: _____, _____, and _____.

8. _____ markets buy products in order to make other products, while _____ markets buy products for their own uses.

9. The process of planning and executing the conception, pricing, promotion, and distribution of ideas, goods, and services to create exchanges that satisfy individual (customer) and organizational objectives is _____.

10. A state of felt deprivation, such as hunger, or a need for affection, knowledge, or self-expression is _____.

11. _____ is a region where goods are sold and bought; a _____ is a particular type of buyer.

12. The process of creating an identity for a product using a distinctive name or symbol is called _____.

13. The individuals and institutions involved in moving products from producers to customers are the _____.

14. An extra incentive to buy now is called _____.

15. _____ are markets which include a wide variety of profit and non-profit organizations, such as hospitals, government agencies, and schools that provide goods and services for the benefit of society at large.

Completion Answers

1. research, implementation
2. price, marketing communication
3. consumer, institutional
4. advertising, personal selling
5. consumer-oriented
6. growth, decline
7. intensive, selective, exclusive
8. industrial, consumer
9. marketing
10. human need
11. market
12. branding
13. channel of distribution
14. sales promotion
15. institutional

Matching

Match the terms and concepts with the appropriate statements. Each term or concept may be used only once; there are more terms and concepts than statements.

Terms and Concepts

a. bundles of satisfaction
b. competitive advantage
c. cooperative advantage allowance
d customary
e. decline
f. direct marketing
g. exclusive distribution
h. industrial
i. intensive distribution
j. line extensions
k. personal selling
l. public relations
m. reseller
n. selective distribution
o. strategic
p. consumer
q. product mix
r. indirect distribution

Statements

_____ 1. Stage of the marketing plan associated with developing objectives and strategies.

_____ 2. Markets which consist of companies that buy products or services to use in their own businesses or in making other products.

_____ 3. Markets which include wholesalers, retailers and distributors who buy finished or semifinished products and resale them for a profit.

_____ 4. An array of benefits, traits or values that are useful to the individual customer's needs and desires.

_____ 5. New or reformulated products that carry existing brand names that are introduced to try to take advantage of an existing brand's established reputation.

_____ 6. The stage of the product-life cycle in which advertising would be reduced or eliminated altogether.

_____ 7. When a company distributes a product without using a reseller.

_____ 8. When producers and retailers share in the cost of local advertising.

_____ 9. A market coverage strategy in which only one distributor is allowed to sell the brand in a particular market.

_____ 10. A market coverage strategy which expands the number of outlets but restricts participation to those outlets that prove most profitable to the manufacturer.

_____ 11. Placing the product in every possible outlet (including vending machines) in order to attain total market coverage.

_____ 12. The pricing strategy which involves the use of a single well-known price for a long period of time.

_____ 13. Face-to-face contact between the marketer and a prospective customer intended to create both immediate sales and repeat sales.

_____ 14. A set of activities intended to enhance the image of the marketer in order to create goodwill.

_____ 15. When the consumer decides how close one product, service or idea comes to satisfying his or her needs versus a competitor's product, service or idea.

Matching Answers

1.	o	9.	g
2.	h	10.	n
3.	m	11.	i
4.	a	12.	d
5.	j	13.	k
6.	e	14.	l
7.	f	15.	b
8.	c		

Multiple Choice

Place the letter of the correct answer in the blank provided.

_____ 1. Which of the following is an important idea to the concept of marketing?
   a. exchange
   b. consumer needs
   c. competitive advantage
   d. profit
   e. all of the above

_____ 2. Which of the following represents the four types of markets?
   a. industrial, reseller, institutional, consumer
   b. manufacturer, media, mass, local
   c. mass, local, regional, international
   d. consumer, retailer, international, government
   e. consumer, media, government, industrial

_____ 3. Which of the four types of markets is the largest in terms of advertising expenditures?
   a. reseller
   b. consumer
   c. industrial
   d. media
   e. institutional

_____ 4. Which of the following is NOT one of the stages of the product life cycle?
   a. maturity
   b. transition
   c. growth
   d. introduction
   e. decline

_____ 5. What are the 4Ps of marketing?
   a. product, price, packaging, and production
   b. product, profit, place, and publicity
   c. product, price, place, and promotion
   d. profit, packaging, production, and promotion
   e. price, production, place, and promotion

_____ 6. Customers view products as:
   a. bundles of satisfaction
   b. satisfying a specific need
   c. an irritating nuisance
   d. appealing physical things
   e. a utilitarian collection of benefits

_____ 7. What must marketing do to have success?
   a. create a product with multiple need satisfying qualities
   b. offer products at an appealing price
   c. create a competitive advantage
   d. bribe the distributors
   e. tell the consumers what they want to hear

_____ 8. What kind of product characteristic would warranty be considered?
   a. intangible
   b. invisible
   c. meaningful
   d. tangible
   e. non-specific

9. What are the two primary types of channel institutions?
   a. media and resellers
   b. media and retailers
   c. manufacturers and wholesalers
   d. wholesalers and retailers
   e. institutions and industry

10. What is the primary function of sales promotion?
    a. develop brand equity
    b. develop the image of the product
    c. generate immediate sales
    d. lay the groundwork for selling the product
    e. presell the product

11. What is the role of the marketing manager?
    a. maximizing profits
    b. creating a competitive advantage
    c. translating the product's characteristics into concrete attributes with clear benefits
    d. planning from the consumer's needs to the company's goals
    e. all of the above

12. What is the key value of branding?
    a. makes the product distinctive
    b. makes the price insignificant
    c. creates an image
    d. preventing cow theft
    e. all of the above

13. Which of the following is the least important to the marketing concept?
    a. consumer needs
    b. production efficiency
    c. profit
    d. competitive advantage
    e. research

14. Which of the following is **NOT** true about advertising when compared to other forms of promotion?
    a. has the ability to prompt an immediate behavioral change
    b. contact between advertiser and audience is indirect
    c. takes longer to deliver information to the target market
    d. takes longer to create a rapport with the target market
    e. greater ability to reach a large number of people simultaneously

15. What represents the last chance to affect consumer choice?
    a. sales promotion
    b. personal selling
    c. packaging
    d. advertising
    e. promotion

Multiple Choice Answers

1.	e	9.	d
2.	a	10.	c
3.	b	11.	e
4.	b	12.	a
5.	c	13.	b
6.	a	14.	a
7	c	15.	c
8.	a		

Career Exercise -- Career Marketing Plan

Orient your career plan around the marketing concept. You must become consumer-centered rather than product-centered. Because of the nature of the career marketing effort, it is easy to become product-centered. Being in college, working on student projects, working on internships, virtually everything you do is aimed at product development. You have to integrate consciously and forcefully the prospective employer's (the consumer's) needs into this process. Persistently asking what your future employer, who is probably unknown, wants from you is no simple process. It is, however, at the core of strategic planning in the marketing process.

With this consumer-centered marketing approach firmly in mind, a key step in developing a career marketing plan is to decide on your marketing objectives. The marketing objectives should be a marriage of what your future employers want from you and what you want from your future employers. The most important element in developing your career objectives is acquiring enough information to make sensible decisions. The typical marketing plan from Chapter 7 will serve as a good model for your plan.

Situation Analysis

Product

Recognition that you represent a product or at least a service that will be traded in an employment marketplace is important. The needs you satisfy in your personal marketing process may be diverse --- ranging from the simple tasks that you perform for your employers to the ego satisfactions that you may provide. In reality you will not be so different from any product or service which has both tangible and intangible characteristics that produce varying satisfactions for the consumers involved.

The first phase of the analysis of the product is determining what need-fulfilling qualities and abilities you have or could potentially develop. This process includes looking inside to find what your interests and native abilities are. Questions such as the following will point you in the right direction. What are your relevant features -- interests, abilities, traits? Do you have any distinctive features? Do you have a competitive advantage?

Next, you must identify as precisely as possible what will be expected. You must discover what experiences, skills, knowledge, personal qualities, salary expectations, personal connections, etc. will be expected. You also need to discover the nature of the product life cycle in your career area. While you are in college, you are engaged in a form of product development for the individual. Unfortunately, most students are involved in this process without a clear idea of what is needed for success in the job marketplace. Every decision about what course to take, what opportunities to take advantage of during college, what organizations to join, etc. should be based on their potential to enhance your marketability.

Marketplace

What is the size and nature of the market for advertising employment? Is the market expanding or shrinking or remaining constant? How many jobs are available in advertising? More to the point, how many entry-level positions become available each year? How many qualified advertising people are available to fill these entry-level positions? The marketplace is the employment arena of business and organizations within and outside of our society, depending on your personal desires.

Distribution

Where do employers buy the product? The distribution system for employment is not as straightforward as that for typical products. Nonetheless, there is a channel of distribution. Most of the time professionals engage in a form of indirect distribution whereby they act as their own personal sales agents. Of course, this is not the only channel available. The professional can hire an agent in the form of an employment agency or placement consulting firm. This channel becomes more important later in most career ladders, although acting as your own agent remains the main method.

Pricing

What is the most appropriate price in your career area? Is there a customary price, particularly at the entry level? Price is essentially salary -- but not exactly. Employees also receive payment in a wide array of benefits, such as insurance, retirement, company car, expense account, etc., that must be considered.

Marketing Communication

Is there any history of communication by you with the people in your career field? What is the nature of communication by your competition?

Consumer Behavior

Who will buy your product/service? How is the decision made? How are they likely to perceive you? How are they likely to perceive your competition?

Problems and Opportunities

After you have done your research in the Situation Analysis, the first step in developing your plan is to identify any problems or opportunities that may serve as the basis of objectives. For example, you discover that employers want people who are assertive and self-confident, and those traits happen to be two of your strongest qualities. That's an opportunity. On the other hand, employers may be looking for people with highly developed computer skills, and you have never used a computer. That's a problem. You can take advantage of the opportunity; you can correct the problem. Each can be incorporated into your career plan.

Objectives

Sales and share of market do not fit well with the realities of a career plan. However, there is only a small adjustment in terminology. In career planning it is still crucial to focus on what you want to accomplish. Key questions include the following. What kind of job do you want? What kind of work do want to do? What type of organization -- size, nature of business, etc. -- do you want to work for? Do you want to work for a Fortune 500 company, or would you be happier working for a small organization? What salary is necessary to satisfy you at various points in your career? What kind of job responsibilities do you want? Do you want to be a creative technician, a manager, etc.? What do you want to accomplish in your career, such as make a great deal of money, be well-known, be respected, be very good at your work, etc.? Do you have identifiable social or political aspirations? Do you want power -- social or professional? Do you want to be a community leader? Do you want to be a political leader?

Strategies

Strategy is developing the right mix of product characteristics, price, distribution, and promotion to satisfy the needs of the target market. Just as it is in any marketing situation, knowing the target market is a crucial aspect. In career planning as in most modern marketing, strategy begins with the identification of market segments from which target markets can be derived. You must identify a part of the advertising field that most closely matches what you have to offer and offers in return what you want. At the heart of the marketing strategy is the question, what will be the basis of exchange in your career field? What are the underlying needs that drive the employers in your career field? What personal traits, experience, skills, contacts, etc., do they look for when deciding who to hire? The following questions are important in formulating your career strategy. Who is important to achieving your career objectives? What would they need to know about you in order to get them to help you? What factors influence their motivation to help you achieve your career objectives?

Implementation and Evaluation

Schedule

Having a schedule laid out concerning the various steps that need to be taken to prepare for your career development can be one of the most crucial steps that you take. At a minimum, the schedule should help you see the sequencing of the various steps that must be taken so it is clear what steps must be taken before going to other steps.

Budget

The most neglected part of the career marketing process is budgeting. People seem to operate as if the financial end of the career plan will take care of itself. You must determine ahead of time how much various parts of the plan will cost and where the money will come from. Specific outlays such as producing a resume, developing a portfolio, clothing, costs of attending conferences, dues for professional organizations, costs of special training, etc., have to be budgeted. The ideal budget relates the expenditures to the ultimate objectives of the plan. The budget should allow you to see how much money will be required to meet each objective in the plan.

Start working on your career marketing plan by starting your research. You can start in the library. Look for general career planning books. You will also find that advertising textbooks can be a useful source of information since most have a chapter on the advertising career field. Books on the careers of successful advertising professionals can also be good starting points. In addition, check advertising professional publications. They can be excellent sources of salary information and current industry trends, not to mention the wealth of information on employers and names of professionals. Go to the career placement and counseling office on campus. The placement and counseling offices frequently have materials and tests for helping you identify the jobs for which you would be best suited by interest. Contact faculty and local advertising professionals for personal information. Finally, try drafting an initial marketing objective for yourself. Then, begin considering how you think you might land your first job in the advertising business. Do it in spite of the fact that you will change several times as you compile more information and develop personally. You will need to make these assessments and then later re-evaluate just as any planner would.

4   Advertising Agencies

<u>Objectives and Chapter Summary</u>

- **Understand the functions of an advertising agency.**
- **Explain how an agency is organized.**
- **Recognize the pressures for change in the business.**
- **Understand how agencies are paid.**
- **Comprehend the impact of technology in this sector as in other business sectors.**

     The essence of the advertising agency business -- the goal each agency strives to achieve -- is to add perceived value to the product or service of its client. In order to achieve consumer loyalty, advertising must do more than transmit data. Rather, it must tailor the product story to a potential customer. The advertising industry is in the process of evolving from the marketing plan concept of advertising to integrated marketing communication in which all of the communication functions of the marketing effort are coordinated under a single strategy. Integrated marketing communication has had difficulty in implementation both on the agency and the client side of the industry. Clients have had special problems understanding how the advertising agency fits into the integrated marketing communication approach. Advertising agencies have responded by becoming generalists in strategy design. They seek to guide strategy and coordinate execution.

     Companies hire advertising agencies to handle their advertising for a variety of reasons. The agency can more cost efficiently assemble and deliver a wider range of talents and experience and provide a more objective viewpoint in developing a client's advertising. In addition, clients hire agencies in the hope of building brand value, establishing better client-customer relations, and to make a special impression on the customer. Also, clients hire agencies and allow the agency to handle the problems of maintaining a staff with the diverse talents necessary.

     Advertising agencies range in size from one-person shops to giant businesses that employ thousands. The forms agencies take, the services they provide, and the types of agencies that exist are constantly changing. The full-service agency provides all of the four major staff functions: account management, creative services, media planning and buying, and research. The two key distinctions for the full-service agency are whether the personnel are full-time, as they will be in a full-service agency, and the extent of the services provided. Creative boutiques are usually relatively small agencies that concentrate entirely on preparing creative executions. The creative boutique differs from the free-lance creative person by the nature of employment and extent of service. There is no staff for media, research, strategic planning, or annual plan writing. Creative boutiques are usually not as long-lived as full-service agencies. There are also specialty agencies such as medical and minority agencies. In-house agencies are advertising agencies that are owned and operated by the advertiser. The reasons for using an in-house agency include: cost savings, specialized staff, priority service, and minimum staffing. Media buying services are similar to the creative boutique, only it specializes in media buying.

     Typically, the agency organizes around a client's account. Openness and flexibility are more important than organizational structure. The four primary functions of most agencies are account management, creative services, media services, and research. In addition, most agencies have internal support services such as traffic, print production, financial services, personnel, and direct marketing. Account management serves as the liaison between the client and the agency to ensure that the agency effectively focuses its resources on the needs of the client. Account management usually has four levels: management supervisor, account supervisor, account executive, and assistant account executive. The creative members of the agency typically hold one of the following positions: creative director, creative department manager, copywriter, art director, or producer. The media department must recommend the most efficient means of delivering the message to the target audience. The media buyer determines what media coverage is likely to be available at what costs. Buying involves ordering media on behalf of the client and according to the plan approved by the client. The emphasis in agency research is on assisting the development of the advertising message. When conducting original research, the agency concentrates on consumer attitudes and behavior.

Agencies derive their revenues from two main sources -- commissions and fees. The commission is a form of payment in which the agency receives a certain percentage of media costs. A 15 percent commission is the standard amount that most media allow agencies. In the 1980s clients began to squeeze agencies in an attempt to reduce expenses by getting agencies to accept a lower commission. The payment of a 15 percent commission by clients is rare today on large accounts and may be on its way out. Negotiated commissions are now common. Fees are a direct charge for services. With the squeeze on commissions and ultimately agency profits, it has become more common for agencies to ask clients to pay for services that were once free, such as marketing research. A variation on the fee system is incentive-based agency compensation. The incentive-base system pays the agency a basic amount and if the agency's work is judged superior, then the agency receives a bonus.

Many changes have occurred within the advertising industry in recent years, the most significant of which include megamergers of large international agencies, consolidation of large client account in a single agency, and the development of high-productivity agencies. For the future of the agency business, the organizational structure, methods of payment, and reasons for hiring agencies all appear to be changing. To survive, agencies are compelled to innovate by expanding services.

Key Terms and Concepts

account executive	Acts as the primary liaison between the agency and the client.
account management	Advertising liaison function between the agency and the client.
account supervisor	Member of agency management who is the key working executive of client's business and the primary liaison between the client and agency.
art studio	Once called the "bullpen," this part of creative department includes artists who specialize in presentation pieces, lettering, and paste-up.
assistant account executive	Normal entry-level position in the agency's account management department.
business unit	Units in a company that are focused around product lines, brands or specific services.

commission	Form of payment in which the agency receives a certain percentage of media charges.
creative boutique	Relatively small agencies that concentrate entirely on preparing creative executions.
creative department manager	Member of creative staff of an agency who is called "warden," "rabbi," and similar names because of the parental nature of the job.
creative director	Top manager of the creative side of the agency and creative conscience of the agency.
creative group	Part of the creative department which includes copywriters, art directors, and producers.
fee	Mode of payment in which an agency charges a client on the basis of the agency's hourly costs.
full-service agency	Type of agency that is staffed and managed to give service in all four areas of agency service.
in-house agency	Advertising agency that is owned and supervised by an advertiser.
integrated marketing communications	Promotional planning that focuses on integrated communications based on an analysis of consumer behavior.
management supervisor	Has the primary responsibility for noting and reporting to top agency management if agency started to lose money on a client account.
megamerger	Combination of large international agencies under a central holding company.
perceived value	The value that a customer or buyer intrinsically or subjectively attaches to a brand or service.
traffic department	Department that has job of making sure that work flow in agency is smooth and efficient.

True/False

Circle the appropriate letter.

T   F   1.   Creative management must be rigid in its organizational structure.

T   F   2.   Research should be a partner with the creative side, not a scorekeeper or judge of the creative department.

T   F   3.   The traffic department in many agencies has become a good place for entry-level people to get a start in the agency business.

T   F   4.   The traffic department is the life-line of the agency.

T   F   5.   Direct-marketing departments are still simply added on to existing agency departmental structure, in spite of their importance in integrated marketing communication.

T   F   6.   The media commission system has been under fire for a number of years.

T   F   7.   In addition to the standard agency commission, most media give an additional 2 percent cash payment discount.

T   F   8.   When functioning at their best, advertising agencies develop campaigns that enhance the value of the brands that they handle.

T   F   9.   Agencies have four basic functions: account management, the creative function, research, and support services.

T   F   10.   The creative function serves as the primary liaison between the agency and the client.

T   F   11.   Computerization has had a significant effect on the advertising agency business since the 1980s.

T   F   12.   Agencies typically receive a 10 percent commission from media placed.

T   F   13.   The economic climate of the 1980s and early 1990s contributed to increased competition for advertising agencies.

T   F   14.   Recently advertisers have reversed an earlier trend and are consolidating their advertising work with one agency.

T   F   15.   The only thing that seems to be constant in the advertising business is change.

True/False Answers

1.	F	6.	T	11	T
2.	T	7.	T	12.	F
3.	T	8.	T	13.	T
4.	T	9.	F	14.	T
5.	F	10.	F	15.	T

Completion

Fill in the missing word or words in the blanks provided.

1. The traditional advertising agency commission rate is _____.

2. Lance works for an advertising agency. He describes his work as serving as a liaison between the agency and the client. His job title is _____.

3. The four primary functions of the agency are: research services, _____, creative development, and production and _____.

4. The usual four levels of account management in a typical major agency are: assistant account executive, account executive, account supervisor, and _____.

5. _____ is the most likely job that an individual who is just graduating with an advertising degree would be offered in the account management department of a full-service agency.

6. The top manager of the creative side of the agency is called _____.

7. The Produce IT corporation placed an ad in a national magazine that cost $10,000 through the Bright Stars agency. Assuming the standard commission rate system was used, the agency would pay the magazine _____ for the ad.

8. When a company decides to appoint one agency to handle all its advertising, this is called _____.

9. A mode of payment in which an agency charges a client on the basis of the agency's hourly costs is called a _____.

10. In addition to the primary functions, agencies offer services such as traffic, print production, accounting and personnel. These would be in the category of _____.

11. The advertising liaison function between the agency and the client is known as _____.

12. The Creative Guys agency has placed an ad costing $1,000 in the "Basin State Rag." Assuming the standard commission system is used, the agency's commission will be _____.

13. If Creative Guys agency started to lose money on the Bark and Howl dog food company, the _____ would have the primary responsibility for noting and reporting this fact to top agency management.

14. Jane is seen by the client as the primary agency working contact and is responsible for preparing and presenting strategic plans. The position Jane is most likely filling is _____.

15. The average agency employee represents about _____ in billings, according to a study by the American Association of Advertising Agencies.

Completion Answers

1. 15%
2. account executive
3. media planning and buying; account management
4. management supervisor
5. assistant account executive
6. creative director
7. $8,500
8. consolidation
9. fee system
10. support services
11. account management
12. $150
13. management supervisor
14. account supervisor
15. $500,000

Matching

Match the terms and concepts with the appropriate statements. Each term or concept may be used only once; there are more terms and concepts than statements.

Terms and Concepts

a. account supervisor
b. art directors
c. business units
d. creative department manager
e. creative boutique
f. creative director
g. full-service
h. holding company
i. in-house agency
j. management supervisor
k. media research manager
l. megamerger
m. print production
n. traffic
o. assistant account executive
p. account manager
q. integrated marketing communications
r. art studio

Statements

_____ 1. The agency personnel who have responsibility for drawing ideas for print and television advertisements.

_____ 2. Within the traditional agency arrangement, the job of making sure that the work flow is smooth and efficient is the responsibility of this department.

_____ 3. The agency spokesperson for the client who is also responsible for delivering the agency's service and for providing an objective outside point of view.

_____ 4. The creative conscience of the agency.

_____ 5. Member of the creative staff of an agency who is referred to as "house mother," "warden," etc.

_____ 6. Prepares the media department's forecasts of future prices, ratings of television programs and audience composition.

_____ 7. Once called the "bullpen," this part of the creative department includes artists who specialize in presentation pieces, lettering, and paste-up.

_____ 8. Member of agency management who is the key working executive of the client's business and the primary liaison between the client and agency.

_____ 9. Department that takes a layout, a photograph or illustration, and a page of copy and turns them into a four-color magazine page.

_____ 10. Type of advertising agency that is staffed and managed to provide service in all four areas of agency service.

_____ 11. An advertising agency that is owned and supervised by an advertiser.

_____ 12. Organizational units in a company that are focused around product lines, brands or specific services.

_____ 13. Combinations of large international agencies under a central holding company.

_____ 14. Relatively small agencies that concentrate entirely on preparing creative executions.

_____ 15. Normal entry-level position in the agency's account management department.

Matching Answers

1.	b	9.	m
2.	n	10.	g
3.	j	11.	i
4.	f	12.	c
5.	d	13.	l
6.	k	14.	e
7.	r	15.	o
8.	a		

Multiple Choice

Place the letter of the correct answer in the blank provided.

_____ 1. Which of the following is **NOT** true about what the agency is striving to achieve for its clients?
a. set the product apart from its competition
b. create a memorable picture of the product
c. create a need for the product
d. give the product a personality
e. shape the basic understanding of the product

_____ 2. Which of the following is **NOT** usually a major function of a full-service agency?
a. account management
b. media planning and buying
c. public relations support
d. creative services
e. research

_____ 3. The value that a customer or buyer intrinsically or subjectively attaches to a brand or service is called:
a. perceived value.
b. brand equity.
c. a competitive advantage.
d. profit.
e. an image.

_____ 4. Which of the following is **NOT** an advantage of the advertising agency in terms of staffing and management for advertising campaigns?
a. availability of specialists
b. flexibility in adjusting to different staff requirements
c. having industry creative specialists for each client
d. trying out new job specialties
e. experience with managing creative people

_____ 5. Which of the following is **NOT** one of the primary types of organizations that make up the agency industry?
a. creative boutiques
b. media buying services
c. in-house agencies
d. direct-marketing agencies
e. full-service agencies

_____ 6. A department within a copmpany that functions as that company's advertising agency is called:
   a. a creative boutique.
   b. an in-house agency.
   c. an advertising department.
   d. a creative department.
   e. none of the above

_____ 7. What is the role of account management in the advertising agency?
   a. to create the client's advertising
   b. to serve as the agency's creative conscience
   c. to serve as a liaison between the client and agency
   d. to recommend the most efficient means of delivering the message to the target audience
   e. all of the above

_____ 8. Which of the following is **NOT** a service that could likely be provided by a creative boutique?
   a. media buying
   b. copywriting
   c. develop ad designs
   d. develop print media ads
   e. creative concept for ads

_____ 9. Which of the following was **TRUE** about most ad agencies in the 1990s?
   a. produced about $1 million in revenue per staff member
   b. increased their staffs
   c. saw revenues increase
   d. saw the standard 15% commission challenged by clients
   e. all of the above

_____ 10. Which of the following is a typical internal support department in an agency?
   a. account services
   b. creative services
   c. media planning and buying
   d. print production
   e. research

_____ 11. Which of the following is **NOT** a reason why advertisers hire agencies?
   a. professional expertise.
   b. objectivity.
   c. dedication and commitment.
   d. competitive price.
   e. specialized staffing.

_____ 12. Which of the following is **NOT** one of the usual levels of account management in a typical major agency?
   a. management supervisor
   b. advertising manager
   c. account executive
   d. account supervisor
   e. assistant account executive

_____ 13. An agency places an ad that costs $30,000. If the standard agency commission is paid, what will the agency be paid for placing the ad?
   a. $3,000
   b. $300
   c. $450
   d. $4,500
   e. $3,600

_____ 14. What are the main forms of payment for the advertising agency?
   a. bribes and kickbacks
   b. out-of-pocket costs and retainer
   c. commission and fee
   d. commission and retainer
   e. none of the above

_____ 15. Which of the following is a problem with the fee system of payment in the agency business?
   a. client must be able to trust that everyone working on the client's account is keeping accurate track of the time spent working on the client's business
   b. calculating exactly what the agency should charge for the hourly rate
   c. client must believe that the agency's hourly rate is fair
   d. client must be able to trust that the agency's staff can correctly apportion time to each client
   e. all of the above

Multiple Choice Answers

1.	c	9.	a
2.	c	10.	d
3.	a	11.	d
4.	c	12.	b
5.	d	13.	d
6.	b	14.	c
7.	c	15.	e
8.	a		

Career Exercise -- Career Progression

One of the most crucial steps in career planning is getting a clear fix on where you are going with your career. What do you want to accomplish? What you want to accomplish includes a recognition of how you will evolve over time. What jobs, experiences, skills, knowledge, etc., will you need in order to get the jobs that you want to hold over the course of your career? The task is a large one. You can look to your professors, professionals in advertising, and professional organizations to help you in this process. Seeing yourself as the product in terms of the product life cycle discussed in the text, may help you start to map out the phases of your development. The decline stage may not be especially appropriate for a career, but the introductory, growth, and maturity stages should help provide some useful insight.

At each phase of your career progression, you need to consider the four Ps of the marketing mix. For example, how will your characteristics vary from the introductory phase to later phases of development? What skills will be needed earlier in your career? What skills will be demanded later? What training will be necessary early versus later? As you develop and assume more responsibility, will you need different personality traits than earlier in your career? What salary and benefits can you expect in your first job? Later, as you grow what are your salary/benefit expectations? What distribution technique will be most appropriate in your first job? Will the methods you use to find subsequent positions be substantially different? Will the necessary promotional mix vary over time?

To start this process, you may want to refer back to your work for Chapter 1 where you considered the areas of advertising and began to evaluate which one would be most appropriate for your career. Different areas of advertising follow different patterns. While there will be similarities in necessary knowledge, skills, experience, etc., there will also be very marked differences in what will be expected, especially as you proceed to the later stages of the product life cycle.

To get you started, we will look at the career progression in the account management area of the agency business discussed in the text. You progress through a series of stages that match closely with the account management positions discussed in Chapter 4. The phases most often identified are the pre-professional (part-time jobs and internships prior to graduation from college), beginning professional (assistant account executive), staff professional (account executive), professional manager (account supervisor), organizational officer (management supervisor), and senior agency officer (vice president for client affairs). The time frame would be 0-2 years for the beginning professional, 2-6 years for the staff professional, 4-10 years for the professional manager, 10-15 years for the organizational officer, and 15-20 years for the senior agency officer level of the career progression.

Each level carries with it expectations in terms of experience, knowledge, and skills. Sometimes, there are additional attributes that are required, and sometimes there is only greater levels of the same attribute that is expected. The pre-professional and beginning professional levels stress technical skills. As the professional grows, more is expected in terms of planning and management at the strategic levels of advertising. The pre-professional and beginning professional might only be expected to produce a workable idea for an ad given the strategy. However, the idea would need to be polished by more experienced professionals. The staff professional would be expected to be able to produce a polished ad concept requiring minimal supervision and checking, but the staff professional would have only minimal expectations in terms of being able to monitor another pre- or beginning professional's work. The professional manager would be expected to supervise the work of other professionals. As a matter of fact, very little of the professional manager's time would involve direct work on developing ads. A major concern of the professional manager becomes the development of the underlying strategy from which the ads will emerge. The professional manager will also be involved in the development of budgets to support the strategic plans. The senior officers are more involved with the business of the agency than the creation of advertising. More businessman than advertising professional, the senior officer begins to turn the strategic marketing skills that once benefited clients to the interests of the agency.

Of course, this is only a cursory overview of even the account management area. The creative development area, the media buying and planning, and the support areas of the advertising agency have their own special career progression. There will be great variation to this pattern, especially as the size of the agency and the part of the country varies. The general time pattern will apply across many fields. A beginning professional level up to four years is very common. This is followed by 4-5 years of practice at the technical, production level. After 5-10 years of practical experience, a management stage begins that will last another 5-10 years, sometimes more depending on the individual. The final stage of organizational responsibility depends largely on the ability and the ambition of the individual.

Your individual career progression is significant because you must plan in order to be able to proceed from one phase to the next. First, you must seek out the answer to questions such as the following. What training is required for each level of development in the career area you have chosen? What skills are required at each level? What types of experience are required at each level? What personal qualities are needed at each level? What kinds of personal relationships will be needed at each level? Some attributes can be developed such as training, skills, experience, etc. Some such as personal qualities must simply be a part of you. One way or the other, the particular combination of attributes will be required at the point in time that you expect to move to a given level. To discover that patience is required and you do not have it, after putting in 20 years to reach an objective, would be unfortunate or even foolhardy.

5   The Consumer Audience

Chapter Objectives and Summary

- **Understand the different factors that affect the responses of consumers to advertisements.**
- **Define the concept of culture and subculture as it applies to advertising and consumers.**
- **Distinguish between psychographics and demographics and explain how advertisers use each.**
- **Relate such concepts as family, reference groups, race, and VALS to the practice of advertising.**

The goal of advertising is to persuade the consumer to purchase a product. There are actually two types of consumers: those who purchase the product and those who actually use the product. The distinction is not unimportant because the two groups can have very different needs and wants. If advertising is to succeed, advertisers must understand how consumers think and make decisions about products. Consumers are influenced by social and cultural, personal, and psychological factors. To cope with the complexity of the influences, the marketer uses market segmentation to divide the potential consumers into more manageable segments on these factors. A market segment can be based on geography, usage level of the product, and the type of consumer. The target market is the segment that is most likely to respond to what the marketer has to offer.

The social and cultural influences, the forces that other people exert on behavior, include culture, social class, reference groups, and family. Culture primarily reflects itself in consumer behavior through values and their resulting norms of behavior. Marketers and advertisers assume that people in different social classes behave differently for different reasons. Reference groups perform three functions: they provide information; they serve as a means of comparison; and they offer guidance for behavior. The family is our most important reference group because of its longevity and intensity.

Individual characteristics strongly influence consumer behavior. These characteristics can be divided into demographic and psychographic variables. Demographics are personal, social and economic characteristics such as age, gender, income, occupation, family status, education, income, and race and ethnicity. Geographic location is a very critical demographic characteristic to advertisers. Psychographics refer to psychological factors such as perception, learning, motivation and needs, attitudes, personality, self-concept, and lifestyles.

Perceptions are shaped by three sets of influences: the physical characteristics of the stimuli, the relations of the stimuli to their surroundings, and conditions within the individual. To the individual, all stimuli are not created equal. Some stimuli are selected, and others are ignored. The process of filtering out information that is not interesting is called selective perception. Selective perception mechanisms include selective exposure, selective distortion, and selective retention. One response to selective perception is the process of cognitive dissonance. Advertisers are interested in selective processes because they affect whether and how consumers will perceive an ad.

Perception leads to learning. If advertisers understand how learning takes place, they can design ads to optimize the learning of key elements in the ad. The theories of learning important to advertisers are cognitive learning, classical conditioning, and instrumental or operant conditioning. Advertisers using the cognitive perspective focus on the role of motivation in decision making and the mental processing consumers use to make decisions. Classical conditioning emphasizes developing associations among known need satisfying decisions and new products. Operant conditioning stresses the role of reinforcement in learning. All learning is based in the satisfaction of needs. Needs are the basic factors that motivate a person to do something. Attitudes are also important to advertisers because they influence how consumers evaluate products. All the personal and psychological factors interact to create personality. The individual's reaction to the world, formation of attitudes, and decision making are all reflected in the personality. Lifestyle factors are often considered the mainstay of psychographic research. Essentially, lifestyle research looks at the ways people allocate time, energy, and money. VALS -- Values and Lifestyles Systems is a widely used classification system that categorizes people by values for the purpose of predicting effective advertising strategies.

The process that consumers go through in making a purchase varies between low-involvement and high-involvement situations. There are six generally recognized stages in the decision process: need recognition, information search, evaluation and comparison, outlet selection and purchase decision, and postpurchase evaluation. Although it is impossible to know everything about the people with whom we communicate, the more we know, the more likely our message will be understood.

Key Terms and Concepts

attitude	Learned predisposition that we hold toward an object, person, or ideal.
classical conditioning	Pairs one stimulus with another that already elicits a given response.
cognitive dissonance	A tendency to justify the discrepancy between what a person receives relative to what he or she expects.
cognitive learning	School of learning that emphasizes the importance of perception, problem-solving, and insight.
connectionist	School of learning which argues that people learn connections between stimuli and responses.
consumers	People who buy or use products.
culture	A complex of tangible items (art, literature, buildings, furniture, clothing, and music) plus intangible concepts (knowledge, laws, morals, and customs) that define a group of people or a way of life.
customs	Overt modes of behavior that constitute culturally approved ways of behaving in specific situations.
decision process	Process consumers go through in making a purchase.

demographics	Statistical representation of social and economic characteristics of people, including age, sex, income, occupation, and family size.
discretionary income	Money available for spending after taxes and necessities are covered.
family	Two or more people who are related by blood, marriage or adoption and live in the same household.
gestalts	Meaningful patterns that enable people to solve problems.
habit	Limitation on or total absence of information seeking and evaluation of alternative choices.
high involvement decision making	Complex decisions that have high personal relevance and contain a high degree of perceived risk.
household	All of those who occupy a living unit, whether they are related or not.
innate needs	Physiological and includes the need for food, water, air, shelter, and sex.
instrumental conditioning	Depends on the voluntary occurrence of behaviors that are then rewarded, punished, or ignored.
lifestyle	Pattern of living that reflects how people allocate their time, energy, and money.
low involvement decision making	Simple decisions that require little information and virtually no evaluation.
market segment	Groups of consumers who share one or more significant characteristics that influence their response to a particular product or service.
market segmentation	Process of dividing a market into distinct groups of buyers who might require separate products or marketing mixes.
motive	Internal force that stimulates you to behave in a particular manner that results from an unfulfilled need.
norms	Boundaries each culture establishes for behavior.

perception	Process by which we receive information through our five senses and assign meaning to it.
personality	Collection of traits that makes a person distinctive.
postpurchase dissonance	Doubt or worry about the wisdom of a purchase even before the package is opened or the product is used.
primary gender differences	Physical or psychological traits that are inherent to males or females.
primary needs	Needs that are necessary to maintain life.
psychographics	People's psychological variables, such as attitudes, lifestyles, opinions, and personality traits.
reference group	Collection of people that you use as a guide for behavior in specific situations.
secondary gender differences	Traits that tend to be primarily associated with one sex more than the other.
secondary needs	Needs learned in response to our culture or environment, and not considered necessary to our physical survival.
selective exposure	Ability to process only certain information and avoid other stimuli.
selective perception	Process of filtering out information that does not interest us and retaining the information that does.
selective retention	Process we go through in trying to "save" information for future use.
social class	Position that you and your family occupy within your society.
social influences	Forces that other people exert on your behavior.
subculture	Divisions of the primary culture based on such factors as economic characteristics, social characteristics, beliefs, aesthetics, or language.
target market	Group of people who are most likely to respond favorably to what the marketer has to offer.

VALS	Conceptual models that categorize people according to their values and then identify the consumer behaviors associated with those values.
values	Source for norms, which are not tied to specific objects or behaviors.

True/False

Circle the appropriate letter.

T   F   1. Both marketers and advertisers look at people as an audience for messages.

T   F   2. Market segmentation allows the organization to design a marketing strategy that matches the market's wants and needs.

T   F   3. A target market is a group of people who have an interest in what the marketer has to offer.

T   F   4. Of the cognitive influences on people, the strongest and least changeable are values.

T   F   5. The forces that other people exert on your behavior are called demographic influences.

T   F   6. The benefits of purchasing by habit are saving time and facilitating decision making.

T   F   7. Perceptions are shaped by family background, culture, and stereotypes.

T   F   8. The cognitive school of learning stresses the importance of perception, problem-solving, and insight.

T   F   9. Consumers usually don't know when learning is occurring.

T   F   10. For advertisers, the operant conditioning school of learning means emphasizing repetition.

T   F   11. An attitude is a feeling that you hold toward an object, a person, or an idea.

T   F   12. Advertising tries to maintain existing positive attitudes and to change negative and neutral attitudes to positive ones.

T   F   13. The left hemisphere of the brain is concerned with nonverbal, timeless, and pictorial information.

T   F   14. The goal of advertising is to persuade the consumer to something.

T   F   15.   An advertisement or a coupon or other stimulus that triggers some kind of response in the consumer is called reinforcement.

True/False Answers

1.	F	6.	F	11.	F
2.	T	7.	F	12.	T
3.	F	8.	T	13.	F
4.	F	9.	T	14.	T
5.	F	10.	T	15.	F

Completion

Fill in the missing word or words in the blanks provided.

1.   The process of dividing a market into distinct groups of buyers who might require separate products or marketing mixes is called _____.

2.   A group of people (segment) who are most likely to respond favorably to what the marketer has to offer is called _____.

3.   A collection of people that you use as a guide for behavior in specific situations is called the _____.

4.   _____, _____, and _____ are the functions of reference groups for consumers.

5.   The statistical representation of social and economic characteristics of people, including age, sex, income, occupation, and family size is called _____.

6.   People's psychological variables, such as attitudes, lifestyles, opinions, and personality traits are called _____.

7.   The process by which we receive information through our five senses and assign meaning to it is called _____.

8.   The experiments of Ivan Pavlov, in which a dog was taught to salivate at the sound of a bell, is associated with the _____ school of learning.

9.   An internal force that stimulates you to behave in a particular manner that results from an unfulfilled need is called _____.

10. Abraham Maslow noted that needs exist in a hierarchy and that we tend to satisfy our primary needs before our secondary needs. _____, _____, _____, and _____ are needs which are not in Abraham Maslow's hierarchy.

11. A learned predisposition, a feeling that you hold toward an object, a person, or an idea that leads to a particular behavior is called _____.

12. A collection of traits that makes a person distinctive. How you look at the world, how you perceive and interpret what is happening around you, how you respond intellectually and emotionally, and how you form your opinions and attitudes is called _____.

13. Doubt or worry about the wisdom of a purchase even before the package is opened or the product is used is called _____.

14. _____ is defined as the pattern of living that reflects how people allocate their time, energy, and money.

15. _____ is defined as a basic force that motivates you to do or to want something.

Completion Answers

1. market segmentation
2. target market
3. reference group
4. information, comparison, guidance
5. demographics
6. psychographics
7. perception
8. classical conditioning
9. motive
10. physical safety, love, esteem, self-fulfillment
11. attitude
12. personality
13. postpurchase dissonance
14. lifestyle
15. need

Matching

Match the terms and concepts with the appropriate statements. Each term or concept may be used only once; there are more terms and concepts than statements.

Terms and Concepts

a. acquired needs
b. affiliation
c. discretionary income
d. family
e. habit
f. household
g. innate need
h. nurturance
i. primary needs
j. reinforcement
k. security
l. selective exposure
m. selective retention
n. social class
o. succorance
p. survival need
q. stimulation
r. independence

Statements

_____ 1. The position that you and your family occupy within your society.

_____ 2. Two or more people who are related by blood, marriage, or adoption and live in the same household.

_____ 3. All those who occupy a living unit, whether they are related or not.

_____ 4. The money available to a household after taxes and basic necessities such as food and shelter are paid for.

_____ 5. The process of seeking out messages that are pleasant or sympathetic with our views and avoiding those that are painful or threatening.

_____ 6. The process we go through in trying to "save" information for future use.

_____ 7. A limitation on or total absence of information seeking and evaluation of alternative choices.

_____ 8. The physiological need for food, water, air, shelter, and sex.

_____ 9. The needs we must satisfy in order to maintain life.

_____ 10. The needs we learn in response to our culture or environment including needs for esteem, prestige, affection, power, and learning.

_____ 11. The need for association with others; to belong or win acceptance; to enjoy satisfying and mutually helpful relationships.

_____ 12. The need to give care, comfort, and support to others; to see living things grow and thrive; to help the progress and development of others; to protect your charges from harm or injury.

_____ 13. The need to receive help, support, comfort, encouragement, or reassurance from others; to be the recipient of nurturing efforts.

_____ 14. The need to be free from threat of harm; to be safe; to protect self, family, and property; to have a supply of what you need; to save and acquire assets; to be invulnerable to attack; to avoid accidents or mishaps.

_____ 15. When a response to a cue is followed by satisfaction.

Matching Answers

1.	n	9.	i
2.	d	10.	a
3.	f	11.	b
4.	c	12.	h
5.	l	13.	o
6.	m	14.	k
7.	e	15.	j
8.	g		

Multiple Choice

Place the letter of the correct answer in the blank provided.

_____ 1. Which of the following is one of the types of consumers?
    a. testers
    b. shoppers
    c. users
    d. browsers
    e. all of the above

_____ 2. What is the function of marketing segmentation?
    a. design a marketing strategy to meet market's needs
    b. save money in marketing effort
    c. control production levels
    d. describe characteristics of market
    e. identify market's needs

_____ 3. Which of the following could be a reference group?
    a. social class
    b. family
    c. informal affiliation
    d. religious group
    e. all of the above

_____ 4. Which of the following resources does the family provide for its members?
    a. sexual
    b. ego
    c. economic
    d. power
    e. all of the above

_____ 5. An ad will be perceived only if it is:
    a. seen or heard by the consumer.
    b. new to the consumer.
    c. entertaining to the consumer.
    d. relevant to the consumer.
    e. all of the above

_____ 6. All of the following shape our perceptions **EXCEPT**:
    a. relation of the stimuli to their surroundings
    b. physical characteristics of the stimuli
    c. intensity of the stimuli
    d. conditions within the individual
    e. all of the above

_____ 7. Which of the following is **NOT** true concerning perception?
   a. we select stimuli that interest us
   b. our frame of reference changes what we perceive
   c. we perceive all the information to which we are exposed
   d. perception is a personal trait
   e. we perceive stimuli in ways that coincide with our view of reality

_____ 8. A target market is:
   a. a distinct group of buyers.
   b. potential customers of a particular product.
   c. a specific group to which the marketing effort is directed.
   d. a group of people who are most likely to respond to what the marketer has to offer.
   e. all of the above

_____ 9. The classical conditioning school of learning emphasizes:
   a. the discovery of meaningful patterns that enable people to solve problems.
   b. the importance of perception, problem-solving, and insight.
   c. trail-and-error process in which one behavior is rewarded more than another.
   d. the importance of people connecting a new stimuli with another that already elicits a response.
   e. all of the above

_____ 10. The forces that other people exert on your behavior are called:
   a. demographic influences.
   b. psychographic influences.
   c. cultural and social influences.
   d. personal influences.
   e. none of the above

_____ 11. Who is associated with the operant conditioning school of learning?
   a. Skinner
   b. Maslow
   c. Pavlov
   d. Jung
   e. none of the above

_____ 12. Which of the following is a stage in the decision process?
   a. postpurchase evaluation
   b. outlet selection
   c. evaluation and comparison
   d. need recognition
   e. all of the above

13. Which of the following is one of the cognitive components that influence consumer behavior?
    a. values
    b. beliefs
    c. attitudes
    d. all of the above
    e. none of the above

14. Complex decisions that have high personal relevance and contain a high degree of perceived risk are called:
    a. product decision process.
    b. low-involvement decision process.
    c. purchase decision process.
    d. high risk decision process.
    e. high-involvement decision process.

15. Which of the following would be part of a psychographic profile on consumers?
    a. age
    b. buying behavior
    c. family situation
    d. education
    e. all of the above

Multiple Choice Answers

1.	c	9.	d
2.	a	10.	c
3.	e	11.	a
4.	c	12.	e
5.	d	13.	d
6	c	14.	e
7.	c	15.	b
8.	d		

Career Exercise -- Employer Decision Process

The key steps in the decision process are the identification and recognition of needs to be fulfilled, the connection of the fulfillment of a need with a particular alternative, the delivery of knowledge of how the need will be fulfilled, the decision that a specific alternative is the best, the commitment to buy the preferred alternative, a trial purchase, and the commitment to repeat purchase. All of these phases of the decision process apply in the employment market just as they do with any other product.

All decision processes begin with the recognition of a need. This stage of the decision process is simply admitting that the existence of a need is not enough to start a purchase decision process. It is the drive state to fulfill the need that is important to the purchase decision process. A good example in the career marketing process is computer skill. Many employers do not effectively use the computer in their businesses. The fact that they do not use the computer does not mean they do not need it. The need is just as present; they just do not recognize the need. In the career plan, you must identify needs that are clearly perceived by employers and which motivate them in the hiring process. If you have a skill that is not recognized by employers, you will have to get them to recognize it first. Its mere existence as a relevant need will do you no good.

Next, you must establish awareness. Awareness has two components: one is the recognition of your existence as a possible employee and the other is the connection of you and the fulfillment of one or more of the employer's recognized needs. From a marketing standpoint, it does not help much that a potential employer simply knows who you are. If that employer does not also relate you to the fulfillment of employment or other relevant needs, you are not going to get hired. What is commonly referred to as networking is the key to developing awareness.

From this connection follows an accumulation of information about how you could satisfy the employment needs. The resume and the portfolio play significant roles in this part of the decision process. The most typical way for employers to do this is to determine if you have ever done the same kind of work before. If not, they must find information that would allow them to infer that you could do the work because you have the requisite qualities and skills to do so or have done similar work. All of this should be addressed in the resume and portfolio.

In this process of evaluating the likelihood that you could do or have done the job before, there comes a point at which the employer will compare what he knows about you to what he knows about other alternative employees. The employer will make a choice. The preferred alternative may still not be purchase. While the choice may be the best available, it still may not hold enough potential to satisfy the requirements to warrant a commitment to purchase -- called conviction. In the preference or conviction phases, references play the significant role. The employer needs confirmation from other sources.

Many people ignore the trial phase of the purchase decision process in the career planning process. They forget or ignore that the initial stage of employment is always a trial phase -- often referred to as probation. The trial phase has two important facets. One is that the trial phase is an information-seeking process in which the decision maker collects more information through experience and then reconsiders the entire decision process. The second facet is that the trial phase involves post purchase dissonance. The dissonance means that the decision maker will be experiencing second thoughts and will need reinforcement information to support the original decision to avoid reversing the decision. To proceed to a long-term commitment, the employer needs to see evidence that the decision was a good one. Often, new employees feel that the marketing communication process is over once they are hired. The fact is that marketing communication should peak in the trial and dissonance phases. The decision maker needs to be reminded of the reasons the employee was hired to see positive results of the hiring. The employee needs to work hard to avoid problems in the trial phase -- or at least to create a state in which the problems seem insignificant to all the positive information.

Start planning now to persuade your future employer to hire you. Where would you like to work? Try not to limit this to just one particular organization -- rather several similar jobs. Who makes the hiring decisions for these positions? Are any of these "hirers" aware of you? Do they know your name? Do they know anything about your abilities or personal traits? If they had a job opening for which you were qualified, would they hire you? Do you know anyone who could persuade these people to hire you? If you cannot answer yes to all of these questions, you need to get to work.

6   Strategic Research

Chapter Objectives and Summary

- **Explain the difference between qualitative and quantitative research.**
- **Identify sources of exploratory research in government departments, trade associations, secondary and primary research suppliers, and advertisers' and agencies' research departments.**
- **Develop a research program using the five parts of a strategy document.**
- **Distinguish between primary and secondary research.**
- **Understand how and when to use the six basic research methods: surveys, experiments, observation, content analysis, in-depth interviews, and focus groups.**
- **Understand how research is used in the development of the creative message.**

Information is the basic ingredient from which all advertisements and all media purchases are made. This information comes from two sources. The most important source is the collective business and personal experience of the advertiser and the advertising agency. The other source is formal research -- surveys, experiments, observation, content analysis, in-depth interviews, and focus groups. The information collecting begins with exploratory research which includes information from government organizations, trade associations, secondary research providers, and primary research providers.

Almost all large advertisers maintain marketing research departments. They collect and disseminate secondary research data and conduct copy tests, product tests, test markets, package and pricing tests, attitude and usage studies. In the 1950s all major advertising agencies featured large, well-funded and highly professional research departments. They did so because profits were high enough to allow the agencies to provide the research at no extra cost. Also, research departments of advertisers were underdeveloped. In the 1960s profit margins decreased so that agencies could not afford the service. In addition, advertisers moved aggressively in building their own research entities.

In the development of the campaign the problem usually is not too little information, but too much. In agencies with internal research departments, the task of making sense of the wealth of available information which will be in the form of both qualitative and quantitative data usually falls to the research department. In agencies without research departments, the task falls to the account group. In some agencies a new way of thinking about the role of research within the agency has emerged. The account planner becomes responsible for the generation, selection, and the use of research evidence at each stage of the advertising process. The account planner assumes this responsibility because he is responsible for the creation, implementation, and modification of strategy on which the advertising creative work will be based.

The outcome of strategic research usually reaches the agency creative departments in the form of the Strategy Document. The five major parts of the Strategy Document are the marketing objective, the product, the target audience, the promise and support, and the brand personality. The strategy document is usually prefaced by a brief strategy statement that distills the documents main points. The Marketing Objective section reviews the competitive situation and establishes a goal for the campaign. The Marketing Objective should be specific and realistic. The Product section would include consumers' perceptions of the brand and its major competitors and reactions to the brand's and competitors' advertisements and promotions. The Target Audience section provides demographic and psychographic descriptions of the campaign's target audience. The Promise and Support section documents what the product offers the consumer in the way of a reward for using the product and the most acceptable proof that the reward will in fact be delivered. The Brand Personality section describes what the product would be like if it were a person.

It is convenient to speak as though research contributes to advertising in a logical, systematic, and linear way. That impression is almost entirely wrong. Although facts do play important roles in many advertising campaigns, they are always filtered through a system of ideas, experiences, memories of past successes and failures, tastes, and preferences. What goes into the Strategy Document and how that information will be interpreted by the creative staff is never straightforward and simple.

Once creative work has started, the developing advertising may be checked against the intended audience in relatively qualitative and informal diagnostic research. Diagnostic research is used to choose the best approach among a set of alternatives. At first the research is rather loose and based on reactions to alternative creative strategies. Early feedback usually involves loose, unstructured interviews with members of the target audience concerning alternative creative strategies. Later, when advertising begins to approach a more finished form, diagnostic research becomes more clearly defined and uses techniques such as contact methods, surveys, experiments, direct observation, content analysis, in-depth interviews, focus groups, and communication tests. The problems of in-depth interviews and focus groups provide insight into the problems of qualitative analysis. In both cases the samples are very small and may not be representative of the whole target audience. Also, the research is done with the creative ideas in rough form in which some key element might be left out that would improve the audience reaction in the context of the entire campaign. Finally, a small minority of the members of the group can force their opinions on the rest of the group and distort the findings.

Key Terms and Concepts

account planner
Has the responsibility for the creation, implementation, and modification of the strategy on which creative work is based and the generation, selection, and interposition of the research evidence at each stage of the advertising process.

communication test
Research technique designed to answer questions such as did the ad convey the intended message or how did consumers react to the message; uses intensive interviewing and questioning about ads usually in research centers at shopping malls.

content analysis
Type of research that analyzes various dimensions of a message such as the length or the type of headline.

diagnostic research
Research used to identify the best advertising approach from among a set of alternatives.

direct observation research
Type of field research in which the researcher is in a natural setting where she records the behavior of consumers.

early feedback	Preliminary diagnostic research in which target audience reactions are sought to alternative creative strategies.
experimental research	Research method that manipulates a set of variables while controlling all other variables to test hypotheses.
exploratory research	Informal intelligence gathering such as reading everything that is available on the product, company, industry, sales reports, annual reports, complaint letters, and trade articles about the industry.
focus group	Qualitative research technique used to stimulate a group of people to talk candidly about some topic with one another; interviewer sets up a general topic and then lets conversation develop as group interaction takes over.
in-depth interview	One-on-one interview used to probe feelings, attitudes and behaviors such as decision making.
market research	Type of research used in the gathering of information about a specific market.
marketing research	Systematic gathering, recording, and analyzing of data that investigates all the elements of the marketing mix.
population	All of the individuals included in a designated group for research.
primary research	Information gathered from original sources through interviewing, observing, and recording the behavior of those who purchase, or influence the purchase of, industrial consumer goods and services.
qualitative data	Research that seeks to understand how and why people think and behave as they do.
quantitative data	Research that uses the numbers to describe consumers.
sample	Selection of people who are identified as representative of the larger population.
secondary research	Information that was originally collected by some other organization (and usually for some other purpose).
strategy document	Expression of the information compiled in the research for the advertising campaign that will be the basis of the creative process and includes the marketing objective, the product, the target audience, the promise and the brand personality.

strategy statement	Preface to the Strategy Document that distills the document's main points.
survey research	Research that uses structured interview forms to ask large numbers of people the same questions.
verbatims	Spontaneous comments of people who are being surveyed.

True/False

Circle the appropriate letter.

T   F   1.   The most comprehensive listing of primary research suppliers is Mediamark Research Inc.

T   F   2.   Verbatims are quantitative data.

T   F   3.   Simmons Market Research Bureau is a source of both product usage and media usage information.

T   F   4.   Direct observation is qualitative research.

T   F   5.   Diagnostic research is used to decide whether or not an advertising campaign will run.

T   F   6.   The biggest drawback to direct observation is that it shows what is happening but not why.

T   F   7.   Understanding can come from research as well as experience.

T   F   8.   Secondary research is information that has already been compiled for you.

T   F   9.   Primary research is information you find out for yourself.

T   F   10.   Message research may be the most difficult from which to draw generalizable conclusions.

T   F   11.   Concept testing helps creatives decide which ideas are worth pursuing and which are not.

T   F   12.   It is a gross misuse of focus group information to quantify it.

T   F   13.   The outcome of strategic research usually reaches agency creative departments in the form of a research analysis.

T   F   14.   Research contributes to advertising in a logical, systematic, and linear way.

T   F   15. Quantitative studies seek to understand how and why people think and behave as they do.

True/False Answers

1. T	6. T	11. T
2. T	7. T	12. T
3. T	8. T	13. F
4. F	9. T	14. T
5. F	10. T	15. F

Completion

Fill in the missing word or words in the blanks provided.

1. _____ is used to identify consumer needs, develop new products, evaluate pricing levels, assess distribution methods, and test the effectiveness of various promotional strategies.

2. _____ is a type of research used in the gathering of information about a specific market.

3. The major sources of information for advertising planning are _____ and _____.

4. _____ is gathered in interviewing, observing, and recording the behavior of those who purchase, or influence the purchase of, industrial consumer goods and services.

5. The two most important secondary research providers are _____ and _____.

6. Research that seeks to understand how and why people think and behave as they do is called _____.

7. Research that uses the statistics to describe consumers is called _____.

8. The major parts of the Strategy Document, also called the creative brief are: _____, _____, _____, _____, and _____.

9. Research used to identify the best advertising approach from among a set of alternatives is called _____.

10. The target audience's evaluation of alternative creative strategies is called _____.

11. Research that uses structured interview forms to ask large numbers of people the same questions is called _____.

12. All of the individuals included in a designated group for research are called _____.

13. A selection of people who are identified as representative of the larger population is called _____.

14. _____ is used to stimulate a group of people to talk candidly about a topic with one another. The interviewer sets up a general topic and then lets conversation develop as group interaction takes over.

15. Research that is used to decide whether or not an advertising campaign will run is called a _____.

Completion Answers

1. marketing research
2. market research
3. experience, formal research
4. primary research
5. FIND/SVP, Off-The-Shelf Publications, Inc.
6. qualitative research
7. quantitative research
8. marketing objective, product, target audience, promise, brand personality
9. diagnostic research
10. concept testing
11. survey research
12. population
13. sample
14. focus group
15. copy test

<u>Matching</u>

Match the terms and concepts with the appropriate statements. Each term or concept may be used only once; there are more terms and concepts than statements.

Terms and Concepts

a. account planner
b. brand personality
c. communication test
d. contact methods
e. content analysis
f. direct observation
g. experiments
h. exploratory research
i. in-depth interview

j. intercept survey
k. marketing objective
l. primary data
m. secondary research
n. the promise
o. verbatims
p. focus group
q. survey research
r. telephone survey

Statements

_____ 1. Reading everything that is available on the product, company, and industry: sales reports, annual reports, complaint letters, and trade articles about the industry are examples of this kind of informal intelligence gathering.

_____ 2. Information that was originally collected by some other organization (and usually for some other purpose).

_____ 3. The creation, implementation, and modification of the strategy on which creative work is based and the generation, selection, and interposition of the research evidence at each stage of the advertising process is the responsibility of this person.

_____ 4. The part of the Strategy Document that deals with the competitive situation, sales history and market share.

_____ 5. The part of the Strategy Document that would include facts about the product that are likely to make that product more acceptable to consumers.

_____ 6. These interviews are often conducted in malls or downtown areas to get a quick response on a strategy or creative idea.

_____ 7. Spontaneous comments.

_____ 8. A type of research that analyzes various dimensions of a message such as the length or the type of headline.

_____ 9. Research technique which is a one-on-one interview used to probe feelings, attitudes and behaviors such as decision making.

_____ 10. Part of the Strategy Document that would include consumer reactions to questions such as what would the product be like if it was a person.

_____ 11. Research technique designed to answer questions such as did the ad convey the intended message or how did consumers react to the message through the use of intensive interviewing and questioning about ads usually in research centers at shopping malls.

_____ 12. Information that is collected from original sources.

_____ 13. A research method that manipulates a set of variables to test hypotheses.

_____ 14. The method used to collect data from people, such as telephone or by mail are.

_____ 15. Type of field research in which the researchers are in a natural setting where they record the behavior of consumers.

Matching Answers

1.	h	9.	i
2.	m	10.	b
3.	a	11.	c
4.	k	12.	l
5.	n	13.	g
6.	j	14.	d
7.	o	15.	f
8.	e		

Multiple Choice

Place the letter of the correct answer in the blank provided.

_____ 1. What are the major sources of information for advertising planning?
   a. experience and formal research
   b. secondary and primary research
   c. survey and informal research
   d. records and survey research
   e. informal and formal research

_____ 2. Which of the following is a source of primary information?
   a. Simmons Market Research Bureau Report
   b. International Directory of Marketing Research Companies and Services
   c. A.C. Nielsen
   d. Mediamark Research Inc.
   e. all of the above

_____ 3. Which of the following is a provider of formal research information?
   a. advertisers' research departments
   b. government departments
   c. trade associations
   d. advertising agency research departments
   e. all of the above

_____ 4. All of the following are quantitative data **EXCEPT**:
   a. numerical data.
   b. research that uses statistics to describe consumers.
   c. research that seeks to understand how and why people think and behave the way they do.
   d. data reported as a percentage of the total.
   e. all of the above

_____ 5. Which of the following is **NOT** qualitative research?
   a. focus group
   b. direct observation
   c. experimental research
   d. in-depth interview
   e. communication test

_____ 6. Which of the following is **NOT** part of the Strategy Document?
   a. strategy statement
   b. promise and support
   c. brand personality
   d. situation analysis
   e. brand personality

_____ 7. The marketing objective section of the Strategy Document includes:
   a. consumers' perception of the brand.
   b. review of the competitive situation.
   c. profile of consumers who might be persuaded to accept the brand.
   d. facts about the product that are likely to make the product more acceptable to consumers
   e. all of the above

_____ 8. Which one of the following measurement methods is being used if it will result in a listing of the value a person places in an idea or product etc.?
   a. a level
   b. a rating
   c. a frequency
   d. the size
   e. the color

_____ 9. Diagnostic research is:
   a. research used to identify the best approach from among a set of alternatives.
   b. preliminary reactions to alternative creative strategies.
   c. research that seeks to understand how and why people think and behave as they do.
   d. research used to determine whether or not an advertising campaign will run.
   e. none of the above

_____ 10. What does concept testing primarily do for advertising creative people?
   a. how and why people think and behave as they do
   b. identify the best approach from among a set of alternatives
   c. helps decide which ideas are worth pursuing and which are not
   d. helps determine whether or not an advertising campaign will run
   e. all of the above

_____ 11. What is the purpose of the focus group?
      a. provide quantitative data for use in strategy development
      b. determine whether or not an advertising campaign will run
      c. identify the best approach from among a set of alternatives
      d. get people to talk candidly about a product
      e. all of the above

_____ 12. Which of the following is an advantage of communication tests?
      a. other tests don't use verbatims
      b. samples are generally larger and more representative
      c. more subjective analysis used
      d. provides quantitative data
      e. all of the above

_____ 13. Spontaneous comments by people who are being surveyed are called:
      a. verbatims.
      b. actual recall.
      c. intercepts.
      d. interviews.
      e. none of the above

_____ 14. Gathering information about a specific market is called:
      a. strategic research.
      b. marketing research.
      c. advertising research.
      d. sales research.
      e. market research.

_____ 15. Research that manipulates a set of variables to test hypotheses is called:
      a. survey research.
      b. experimental research.
      c. qualitative research.
      d. formal research.
      e. primary research.

Multiple Choice Answers

1.	a	9.	a
2.	e	10.	c
3.	e	11.	b
4.	c	12.	b
5.	c	13.	a
6.	d	14.	e
7.	b	15.	b
8.	b		

Career Exercise -- The Communication Plan

In the normal product/service planning situation, the next phase of the planning process would be developing the Advertising Plan. In the career plan, Communication Plan is more accurate. The individual must develop a reasoned approach to dealing with communication problems and opportunities. Only rarely will this involve advertising in career planning. Nonetheless, the model for the Advertising Plan provided in Chapter 7 will provide a sound model for the Career Communication Plan.

Situation Analysis

Communication Problem

What communication problem stands between you and successfully accomplishing your career objectives? No one knows me. I don't know what is expected. I don't know anyone in the field.

Communication Opportunities

What could be communicated to the target audience that would help in achieving your career objectives? Keep it simple at first. I am a student at a university. I am interested enough to ask questions. I am good at what I know how to do. I want to know more and to do better.

Key Strategy Decisions

Advertising Objectives

The key objectives derive well from the hierarchy of effects model discussed in the text in Chapter 7. The key steps are developing awareness, interest, desire, and ultimately purchase on the part of members of the target audience. Do employers know who you are? Do they know anything about your abilities? Do you compare favorably with your competition? Are there any employers who would be interested in hiring you now or in the future?

Target Audience

What special area of advertising do you want to work in? Can you identify professionals who work and hire in this area? What advertising professionals are likely to influence the employers in your chosen area of advertising? In other words, who would make useful references? Do you know what you need to know about the target audience? Can you find your target audience, for example, if you attended a professional meeting or convention?

Competitive product advantage

Is there an important skill, experience, or quality that separates you from the competition? Can you develop a significant advantage through experience, training, etc.? Could feature analysis as discussed in the text be used effectively in career planning?

Product position

What position do you occupy in the minds of the target audience? First, you will probably need to identify what position you and others like you occupy. A position that frequently comes up in career development can be described as "not professional" or perhaps pre-professional or student. Talk to professionals in the advertising business and try to identify what pre-professional or student means. Of course, the simplest position is simply to become a "professional" in the minds of the target audience. *Positioning: The Battle For Your Mind* by Al Ries and Jack Trout can provide some excellent insight into career planning, especially Chapter 20, "Positioning Yourself & Your Career."

Creative Plan

The creative plan will be discussed in detail in the Career Exercise for Chapter 7.

Media Plan

The media plan will be discussed in detail in the Career Exercise for Chapter 11.

7   Strategy and Planning

Chapter Objectives and Summary

- Identify the key elements of a marketing plan and an advertising plan.
- Understand how marketers allocate funds among advertising and other marketing functions.
- Explain the difference between product-centered and prospect-centered strategies.
- List the key elements of a creative platform.

Advertising is both an art and a science. The art comes from writing, designing, and producing exciting messages. The science comes from strategic thinking. Messages are developed to accomplish specific objectives, and then strategies are developed to achieve objectives. Planning is usually a three-tiered operation beginning with the business strategic plan, moving on to functional plans such the marketing plan, and ending with a specific plan such as the advertising plan. The plans used in the marketing/advertising process are the business plan, the marketing plan, the advertising plan, and the creative plan. The decisions involved in all theses plans are similar; the difference lies more in the time frame and scope of responsibility. The business plan consists of decisions about the business' mission, an examination of its strengths and weaknesses and any apparent opportunities, forming specific objectives and goals, and finally formulating a strategy of how to reach the objectives. The marketing plan consists of an analysis of the marketing situation, objectives, problems and opportunities, target markets, strategies, and implementation and evaluation. The heart of the strategic planning process is analysis -- the process of figuring out what all the information and data mean. The primary objective for most marketing efforts is sales or profit. Secondary objectives might focus on such areas as distribution levels and store traffic, or on actions that need to be taken to solve specific problems.

Advertising planning must dovetail with marketing planning. An advertising plan matches the right audience to the right message and presents it in the right medium to reach the audience. Three basic elements are at the heart of advertising strategy: targeting the audience, message strategy, and media strategy. Advertising planners are adept at spotting problems and turning them into opportunities. The crucial point is to use advertising to solve communication problems. The advertising plan consists of the situational analysis, key strategy decisions, the creative plan, the media plan, the promotion plan, implementation and evaluation, and the budget. At the center of advertising planning is the advertising objective. The objective identifies the effect that the message is intended to have on the audience. Hierarchy of effects model can be helpful in analyzing message impact and providing structure for advertising objectives. Advertising planners think in terms of target audiences instead of target markets. The target audience, the people who can be reached with a particular medium and a particular message, can be the same but often includes people other than prospects for purchase. To pinpoint messages advertisers develop profiles of typical users of the product. These profiles can be developed on the basis of product features and competitive advantage, brand personality, product positioning, or perceptual maps.

Decisions on the advertising budget are based on the emphasis given to marketing communication within the marketing mix and to advertising in particular. The methods for setting the advertising budget include the historical, the task-objective, the percent-of-sales, and competitive methods. In the final stage of the plan, the evaluation is based on how well the plan meets its objectives.

A copy strategy can also be developed for an individual advertisement. Such a plan, sometimes called the creative or copy platform, creative work plan, or creative blueprint, focuses directly on the message and the logic behind its development. The creative platform serves to guide others involved in developing the advertisement so that everyone is working with the same understanding of the message strategy. It usually combines the basic advertising decisions of objectives, target audience, competitive advantage, brand image, and positioning with the message strategies, selling premises, and execution details. The most common selling premises are categorized as either product-centered or prospect-centered. In the product-centered, the product feature can be transformed into a selling point by stating a claim, what the product can do or has done. Prospect-centered strategies focus on benefits, promises, reasons-why, or unique selling propositions. Regardless of the selling premise used, the copy strategy must develop support for the premise. The key to support is to make the selling premise believable.

Key Terms and Concepts

advertising objective	Statements of the effect of the advertising message on the audience.
advertising plan	Outlines a company's advertising program over a specified time, usually a year.
affective	One of the categories of message affects in the Lavidge and Steiner model that involves the emotional influence of messages.
awareness	When there has been an impact on your memory; in other words, you can either recognize having seen an ad or recall some of the information from it.
benefit	Statements about what the product can do for the user.
benefit segmentation	Segments identified by the appeal of the product to their personal interests.
brand development index	An index that identifies the demand for the brand within a region.
brand loyalty	Existing positive opinions about a product or service such that customers like the product well enough to buy it repeatedly.
business strategic plan	An overriding business plan that deals with the broadest decisions made by the organization.
claim	A statement about the product's performance.
cognitive	Mental or rational aspect of message effects.

competitive parity method	Budgeting that relates the amount invested in advertising to the product's share of market.
competitive product advantage	The identification of a feature that is important to the consumer where your product is strong and the competition is vulnerable.
comprehension	Means the audience understands the information in the ad.
conative	Decision or action aspect of message effects.
conviction	Means the audience believes the information in the ad.
copy strategy	The thinking behind the message strategy developed for a specific advertisement.
creative plan	Sustained advertising effort under a thematic umbrella that is carried across different media for a given time period.
creative platform	A document that outlines the message strategy decisions behind an individual ad.
direct competition	A product in the same category.
feature analysis	Comparison of your product's features against the features of competing products.
functional plan	Plan that relates to specific business functions such as marketing.
hierarchy of effects	A set of consumer responses that moves from the least serious, involved, or complex up through the most serious, involved, or complex.
indirect competition	A product that is in a different category but functions as an alternative purchase choice.
interest	Your curiosity is aroused and you are willing to hear more about the product.
marketing plan	Written document that proposes strategies for employing the marketing mix to achieve marketing objectives.
market segmentation	Process of identifying particular groups, singling out one, and developing a unique marketing program aimed only at the group.

market segments	Subgroup of the population that has characteristics that make it unique, and therefore, distinct from other groups who use the product.
percent-of-sales	Technique for computing the budget level that is based on the relationship between cost of advertising and total sales.
perceptual map	A map that shows where consumers locate various products in the category in terms of several important features.
positioning	The way in which a product is perceived in the marketplace by the consumers.
profile	A personality sketch of a typical prospect in the targeted audience.
promise	A benefit statement that looks to the future.
selling premise	The sales logic behind an advertising message.
share of market	The percentage of the total category sales owned by one brand.
share-of-mind	The share of advertising done by an advertiser--in other words, the advertiser's media presence--affects the share of attention the brand will receive, and that, in turn, will affect the share of market the brand can obtain.
situation analysis	The section of the marketing plan that analyzes the research findings.
strategic planning	Process of determining objectives (which state what you want to accomplish), deciding on strategies (which tell you how you will accomplish the objectives), and implementing the tactics (the execution details that make the plan come to life).
strategic thinking **strategy formulation**	Weighing the alternatives and identifying the best approach. States how the business expects to reach its goals.
target audience	People who can be reached with a certain advertising medium and a particular message.
task-objective budget method	Budgeting method that builds a budget by asking what it will cost to achieve the stated objectives.

True/False

Circle the appropriate letter.

T   F   1.   All the elements of the marketing mix--product, price, distribution, and marketing communication are coordinated in the advertising plan.

T   F   2.   The normal time frame for evaluating and developing the marketing plan is annually.

T   F   3.   The primary focus of most marketing objectives is increasing sales or market shares.

T   F   4.   The heart of strategic planning is analysis.

T   F   5.   A budgeting method that builds a budget by asking what it will cost to achieve the stated objectives is called the competitive parity method.

T   F   6.   In the "share of mind" concept used to determine the amount of the marketing communication budget to assign to advertising, share-of-media-voice (percent of total advertising for a particular brand represents) the advertising objective.

T   F   7.   Deciding whether or not to use a niche strategy or mass strategy is an example of a differentiation strategy.

T   F   8.   Market share of one brand cannot increase unless a competitor's market share decreases.

T   F   9.   Direct competition is always more important than indirect competition.

T   F   10.   The function of the creative platform is to provide a link between the creation of the ad and other elements of the advertising plan.

T   F   11.   The most effective message strategy is the product-centered strategy.

T   F   12.   Competitive advantage means you are strong in some area that matters to your target, and your competitors are weak in that area.

T   F   13.   The focus of advertising should be on benefits, not features. Advertising should explain what the product can do for the prospect

T   F   14.   The difference between a product benefit and a product feature is that a benefit is in the product, while a feature is in the mind of the consumer.

T   F   15.   Strategies are developed specifically to accomplish the objectives..

True/False Answers

1.	F	9.	F
2.	T	10.	T
3.	T	11.	F
4.	T	12.	T
5.	F	13.	T
6.	F	14.	F
7.	T	15.	T
8	T		

Completion

Fill in the missing word or words in the blanks provided.

1. In strategic planning, we call the execution that makes the plan come to life _____.

2. What is to be accomplished in a plan is called _____.

3. A sustained advertising effort under a thematic umbrella that is carried across different media for a given time period is called _____.

4. The percentage of the total category sales owned by one brand is called _____.

5. The process of identifying particular groups, singling out one, and developing a unique marketing program aimed only at that group is called _____.

6. A group of people who have been identified as prospects who might buy the product or service is called _____.

7. When advertisements focus on the product itself, this is called a _____.

8. When advertisements focus on the needs and wants of the consumer, this is called _____.

9. _____, _____, and _____ are factors that are analyzed in the implementation section of the marketing plan to determine how well the program is being executed.

10. The basic elements at the heart of advertising strategy are: _____, _____, and _____.

11. The three categories of message effects in the Lavidge and Steiner model are: _____, _____, and _____.

12. _____ and _____ are the dimensions on which analysis of competitive advantage are based.

13. The way in which a product is perceived in the marketplace by the consumers is called _____.

14. The process of determining objectives, deciding on strategies, and implementing the tactics within a specific time frame is called _____.

15. A document that outlines the message strategy decisions behind an individual ad is called _____.

Completion Answers

1. tactics
2. objective
3. campaign plan
4. share of market
5. market segment
6. target market
7. product-centered strategy
8. prospect-centered strategy
9. time, money, effectiveness
10. target audience, message strategy, media strategy
11. cognitive, affective, conative
12. importance to target, product performance
13. positioning
14. strategic planning
15. creative platform

Matching

Match the terms and concepts with the appropriate statements. Each term or concept may be used only once; there are more terms and concepts than statements.

Terms and Concepts

a. Brand Development Index (BDI)
b. brand loyal customers
c. brand objective
d. competitive parity method
e. competitive product advantage
f. copy strategy
g. affective
h. feature analysis
i. hierarchy of effects
j. indirect competition
k. interest
l. loss leader strategy
m. niche markets
n. profile
o. situation analysis
p. tactic
q. execution
r. brand share

Statements

_____ 1. The thinking behind the message strategy developed for a specific advertisement.

_____ 2. The section of the marketing plan that summarizes relevant information about the product, marketplace, competition, demand, consumer behavior, distribution channels, costs and environmental factors.

_____ 3. The percentage of the entire sales in a product category that are attributable to one particular product.

_____ 4. Narrowly focused markets that are defined by some special interest.

_____ 5. A product that is in a different category but functions as an alternative purchase choice.

_____ 6. The identification of a feature that is important to the consumer where your product is strong and the competition is vulnerable.

_____ 7. The most important market for a particular brand.

_____ 8. An index that identifies the demand for a brand within a region.

_____ 9. Products advertised at prices below cost in order to generate store traffic.

_____ 10. A set of consumer responses that moves from the least serious, involved, or complex up through the most serious, involved or complex.

_____ 11. When your curiosity is aroused and you are willing to hear more about the product.
_____ 12. In the Lavidge and Steiner model of analysis of message effects, the kind of effects that involve emotion.

_____ 13. Personality sketch of a typical prospect in the targeted audience used by advertising research planners to get a clear idea of the target audience.

_____ 14. A comparison of your product's features against the features of competing products.

_____ 15. A type of budgeting that relates the amount invested in advertising to the product's share of market.

Matching Answers

1. f
2. o
3. c
4. m
5. j
6. e
7. b
8. a

9. l
10. i
11. k
12. g
13. n
14. h
15. d

Multiple Choice

Place the letter of the correct answer in the blank provided.

_____ 1. What type of plan would include the mission statement?
    a. marketing plan.
    b. advertising plan.
    c. campaign plan.
    d. business plan.
    e. copy strategy.

_____ 2. Which of the following is **NOT** a part of the advertising plan?
    a. competitive advantage
    b. creative plan
    c. target audience
    d. media plan
    e. mission statement

_____ 3. The facts, proof, and explanations used to substantiate the claim, benefit, reason, or promise is called:
    a. support.
    b. proposition.
    c. strategy.
    d. tactic.
    e. none of the above.

_____ 4. Planning is:
    a. weighing alternatives when dealing with a problem and identifying the best approach to solving the problem.
    b. the process in which messages are developed to accomplish specific objectives and then strategies are developed specifically to achieve those objectives.
    c. the process of identifying particular groups, singling out one, and developing a unique marketing program aimed at only at that one group.
    d. deciding to divide the market into several parts, each of which tends to have very similar customers in all significant aspects.
    e. none of the above

_____ 5. The marketing plan begins with which of the following?
    a. objectives
    b. strategy
    c. problems and opportunities
    d. situation analysis
    e. market review

_____ 6. An objective is:
   a. how the plan will accomplish what is to be accomplished.
   b. the execution that makes the plan come to life.
   c. an area in which a business has a competitive advantage.
   d. what is to be accomplished in a plan.
   e. all of the above

_____ 7. Which of the following is one of the tiers of planning?
   a. business strategic plan
   b. specific plan
   c. functional plan
   d. all of the above
   e. none of the above

_____ 8. Market segmentation is:
   a. weighing alternatives when dealing with a problem and identifying the best approach to solving the problem.
   b. the process in which messages are developed to accomplish specific objectives and then strategies are developed specifically to achieve those objectives.
   c. the process of identifying particular groups, singling out one, and developing a unique marketing program aimed at only at that one group.
   d. deciding to create a single product supported by a single marketing program designed to reach as many customers as possible.
   e. none of the above

_____ 9. Which of the following is a stage in the AIDA hierarchy of effects model?
   a. attitude
   b. decision
   c. interest
   d. analysis
   e. all of the above

_____ 10. In the hierarchy of effects model, awareness is:
   a. when your curiosity is aroused by an ad.
   b. when you understand the information in an ad.
   c. when you believe the information in an ad.
   d. when there has been some impact on your memory by an ad.
   e. none of the above

_____ 11. Which of the following is a think-feel-do model of effects?
   a. rationalization model of effects
   b. high-involvement model of effects
   c. low-involvement model of effects
   d. all of the above
   e. none of the above

12. Competitive advantage is:
   a. comparison of a product's features against features of competing products.
   b. when a product is strong in one area and competition is weak in that area.
   c. the way in which the product is perceived in the marketplace by consumers.
   d. a feature that will benefit the consumer.
   e. all of the above

13. The task-objective budgeting method:
   a. compares total sales during the previous year with the advertising budget to compute the current year's budget.
   b. uses previous advertising expenditures as a basis for establishing a budget.
   c. relates the amount invested in advertising to the product's share of market.
   d. builds a budget by asking what it will cost to achieve the stated objectives.
   e. none of the above

14. What is at the heart of product-centered message strategies?
   a. features
   b. benefits
   c. claims
   d. positions
   e. all of the above

15. What is the function of the creative platform?
   a. provide systematic analysis of problem to be solved
   b. guide for copywriters
   c. provide for uniform understanding of message strategy
   d. link creation of ad with other elements of advertising plan
   e. all of the above

Multiple Choice Answers

1.	d	9.	c
2.	e	10.	d
3.	a	11.	c
4.	b	12.	b
5.	d	13.	d
6.	d	14.	a
7.	d	15.	e
8.	c		

Career Exercise -- The Creative Platform

At the core of the creative platform for your career planning should be the central theme that you are an emerging professional. You position yourself as a pre-professional, not a student. While you are in school, you should be working along a continuum between pre-professional status and beginning professional. The closer you get to graduation, the more you should take on the characteristics of the professional in your field. To the extent that you succeed in achieving professional status prior to graduation, you will be more able to launch your career with greater confidence. The people who are in school and yet are barely distinguishable from professionals in their field consistently have less trouble finding jobs.

Another important theme is specialization. As soon as possible, you need to identify the niche in your career field in which you fit the best. What part of your chosen field do your attributes and abilities fit the best? You will not be as successful in your campaign as you deserve if you insist on remaining a generalist. The sooner that you commit to a special area such as account management, media buying, copywriting, etc., the better. Frequently, you need to go even further in specializing -- targeting large agencies as opposed to small ones, Fortune 500 companies as opposed to small local firms. Specialization simplifies everything about the campaign from target audience identification to skill development. The expectations of the target audience become much more focused and greatly simplifies the problem of message development.

Your presentation needs to emphasize the idea that you are an achiever. It is not enough to suggest that you have done the job -- that you have experience. When comparing you to your competitors, the question will be: how well did you do the job? What means can you offer that can demonstrate that you are able to do the job better than someone else who could be hired? As much as possible, you need to find specific indicators of your work accomplishments -- something concrete and measurable is normally preferable. When looking for this information, you look for work standards and objectives. Did you exceed the standards or objectives? Did you just do your job, or did you look for ways to improve and add to it? Did you create anything new? Of course, the easiest way of documenting these accomplishments is through rewards, recognition, and promotions. Learn to be very specific in your explanation and description of what you have done. Also, learn to look beyond job experience for opportunities to prove you are an achiever. If you excel at church, in a professional association, in a fraternity, wherever, that should become a part of your message to prospective employers and references.

Finally, you should view the development of the creative platform as an additional source of information for your career planning. If you find, for example, that your previous work background does not include much in the way of achievement, plan to change it. Look for ways that you can begin to work more effectively. Make yourself more aware of standards and objectives. Set goals for yourself to exceed them. Talk to your supervisors to determine what would be needed to get recognition. Find out what they consider to be merely acceptable as opposed to outstanding performance and work to be outstanding. Plan to create the information that you will need to be able to deliver the messages that will have to be communicated to your target audience in order to persuade them. For example, if you are not satisfied with the resume that you can develop on what you have done until now, set about to develop the experience, achievements, the skills, and personal qualities that would lead to the creation of an effective resume.

The creative platform becomes the strategic guide for every communication decision that will be made in your career planning from resume job descriptions to interview discussions. Refer to the material in the text along with the suggestions for your career planning and write a creative platform for yourself. After you have written the creative platform based on who your are now, write a creative platform for what you want to be when you graduate and are looking for your beginning professional job.

8   How Advertising Works

<u>Chapter Objectives and Summary</u>

- **Understand the barriers that an effective advertisement must overcome.**
- **Be familiar with the different levels on which a viewer or reader will react to an ad.**
- **Explain the different functions of an ad.**
- **Explain what "breakthrough advertising" is and how it works.**

Most advertisements just wash over their audiences without any effect. Effective advertisements have impact -- they overcome audience indifference and focus attention on the message. Today, audiences for advertising messages have a variety of technological mechanisms for expressing and executing their dislike or disinterest in advertising. The remote control, for example, allows television audiences to zap ads or zip by ads to avoid messages. To avoid the zapping and zipping and other means of avoidance, advertising must keep the viewers' attention and address needs that are relevant to them. Relevance, originality, and impact are the three keys to effective advertising. Advertising that is relevant speaks about things you care about; advertising that is original catches your attention; and advertising that has impact accomplished the ultimate objective -- it makes an impression.

In the modern cluttered, advertising environment most people only give advertising their divided attention. It is rare for an ad to break through and receive even some kind of attention. In addition, advertisers are up against the human limitation that concentration happens in bursts. Media messages get caught up in our information processing. Every time you watch a commercial, you have to make a decision whether to attend to it or not. Most people avoid most ads in one way or another. Maybe only half the ads get noticed on a "thinking" level. Perhaps only 20 percent get read a little, and very few are read thoroughly.

Advertising must have stopping power, i.e., it must be noticed -- get attention. The first step is simple exposure. The message must appear in a medium that your target sees. In addition, the message must survive the initial scan-and-avoid decision. Then, the ad can gain the attention of the target -- get the target to focus on the product. Ads that stop the scanning and get attention are usually high in intrusiveness, originality, and personal interest. Once the message has caught the target's attention, then the perceptual process can move on to awareness. Awareness implies that the message has made an impression. Attention and awareness are message design problems. In order to achieve awareness, there must be something in the ad that interests the target. Most people attend to things that speak to their wants and needs -- that are worth their time.

Getting attention is stopping power; keeping attention is pulling power. Pulling power keeps the reader or viewer moving through to the end of the message. Maintaining interest is more difficult than initially getting attention. Suspense, drama, and narrative are good literary tools for maintaining interest. Teaching is a very important element of advertising because most advertising wants people to know something after they've been exposed to the ad. Understanding is key to the effectiveness of the ad. Literary tools for developing understanding include definition, explanation, demonstration, comparison, and contrast. Another way of knowing something is to make an association. Ads that use association try to link the product with something you aspire to, respect, value, or appreciate.

In addition to stopping and pulling power, an advertisement should have locking power -- cause the target to remember the message. A key to memorability is repetition. Psychologists maintain that you need to hear or see something a minimum of three times before it crosses the threshold of perception and enters memory. Devices for achieving repetition include jingles, slogans, taglines, key visuals, logos, and signatures. Advertising focuses on two types of memory: recognition and recall. One of the greatest challenges in advertising is to create memorability.

However, advertisers must also avoid vampire creativity in which the creativity is too original, too entertaining; so much so that the story gets in the way of the product. The ultimate test of memorability in advertising comes in the area of brand images. Brand personalities and images are developed to create a feeling of familiarity with a known product. Branding is a way to assist the consumer's memory process. It identifies a product and also makes it possible to position the product relative to other brands.

In addition to providing information, advertisements must persuade people to believe or do something. A persuasive message will shape attitudes, build a logical argument, touch emotions, and make the prospect believe something about the product. Persuasion in advertising rests on the psychological appeal to the consumer. Appeals will center on attitudes and opinions, likability, arguments, emotions, and convictions.

Ultimately, advertising must do more than provide information. Advertising should transform the experience of buying and using the product. Transformation advertising is expensive because it requires consistent, frequent exposure of a positive, upbeat message that has the ring of truth. Advertising must overcome audience indifference without being irritating and keep attention while penetrating the mind. Advertisements that deliver impact have stopping power, pulling power, and lock the message into the mind of the target audience.

Key Terms and Concepts

appeal	Something that moves people by making the product attractive or interesting.
argument	A line of reasoning where one point follows from another, leading up to a conclusion.
association	Another way to "know" something by making a connection in your mind.
attention	Means the mind is engaged, that it is focusing on something.
awareness	Implies that the message has made an impression on the viewer or reader who can subsequently identify the advertiser or product.
brand equity	The idea of accumulating a reservoir of goodwill and good impressions.
brand image	Mental image that reflects the way a brand is perceived including all the identification elements, the product personality, and the emotions and associations evoked in the mind of the consumer.

brand loyalty	An existing positive opinion held by customers about the product or service.
breakthrough advertising	Developing ads that have stopping power to prevent zapping, that keep viewers' attention, and address needs that are relevant to them.
built-in-interest	The inherent interest of some products to appeal to some individuals and groups rather than others.
conviction	A particularly strong belief that has been anchored firmly in the attitude structure.
exposure	First the message has to be in a medium that your target sees, reads, watches, or listens to. In addition, the message must survive the initial scan-and-avoid decision.
grazing	When a viewer flips around the channels, stopping now and then to look briefly at something and then moving on.
human interest	Topics that strikes some universal chord in all of us, such as babies, kittens, and puppies, as well as tragedies and success stories.
interest	When someone is tuned in to the ad because it speaks to his/her wants and needs.
jingle	Commercials with a message that is presented musically.
key visual	Dominant image around which the commercial's message is planned.
locking power	The ability of the ad to make the audience remember it.
logo	Distinctive mark that identifies the product, company, or brand.
pulling power	Keeping the attention in an ad.
recall	Ability to remember specific information content of the message.
recognition	When you can remember having seen something before.
signature	Name of the company or product written in a distinctive type style.
slogan	The "umbrella" theme that connects a series of ads in a campaign for a brand.

stopping power	Getting attention in an ad.
support	Everything in the message that lends credibility to the promise.
tagline	Clever phrases used at the end of an advertisement to summarize the point of the ad's message in a highly memorable way.
transformation advertising	Image advertising that changes the experience of buying and using a product.
trigger	Something that "catches" attention.
understanding	Conscious mental effort to make sense of the information being presented.
vampire creativity	When the advertisement is more memorable than the product.
zapping	When the viewers bypass ads by changing the channel using the remote control.
zipping	Fast forwarding past the commercials on pre-recorded videotapes.

True/False

Circle the appropriate letter.

T   F   1.   An appeal is something that moves people by making the product attractive or interesting.

T   F   2.   Most people give a great deal of attention to advertising.

T   F   3.   Advertisers must deal with an audience that has a short attention span.

T   F   4.   Media messages become entangled in what psychologists call our fragmented mind set.

T   F   5.   When we see both editorial and advertisements, we tune in the editorial first.

T   F   6.   Psychologists maintain that you need to hear something three times before it crosses the threshold of perception and enters into understanding.

T   F   7.   Emotional information is needed if an advertising message is to achieve understanding.

T	F	8. Involvement is the intensity of the consumer's interest in a product.
T	F	9. A persuasive message will make the prospect believe something about the product.
T	F	10. It is not usually possible through advertising alone to completely change a negative attitude to a positive one.
T	F	11. People buy products because they find the advertising convincing, not because they find it amusing.
T	F	12. An advertisement should make the ad memorable.
T	F	13. Brand equity is entirely due to information, reason, and logic.
T	F	14. The first step in attracting and holding attention is to amuse the viewer or reader.
T	F	15. Effective advertisements focus attention on the advertiser's message.

True/False Answers

1.	T	9.	T
2.	F	10.	T
3.	T	11.	T
4.	F	12.	F
5.	F	13.	F
6.	F	14.	T
7.	F	15.	T
8.	T		

Completion

Fill in the missing word or words in the blanks provided.

1. When viewers bypass ads by changing channels with a remote control, it is called _____.

2. Fast forwarding past the commercials on pre-recorded videotapes is called _____.

3. The keys to effective advertising according to Keith Reinhard, President of DDB Needham, are: _____, _____, and _____.

4. People look for _____ when they watch television, scan a magazine or read a paper.

5. _____ of an ad is getting the attention of the target audience.

6. _____ is to make a connection in your mind. Advertisers use it to get you to know something by linking the product with something like an envied lifestyle or person-- something you aspire to, respect, value, or appreciate.

7. _____ , _____ , and _____ are the kinds of power an ad has.

8. The "umbrella" theme that connects a series of ads in a campaign for a brand is called _____.

9. Clever phrases that are used at the end of an ad to summarize the point of the ad's message in a highly memorable way are called _____.

10. The ability to remember specific information content of the message is called _____.

11. Mental image reflecting how brand is perceived including identification elements, product personality, and emotions and associations evoked in consumers is called _____.

12. The idea of accumulating a reservoir of goodwill and good impressions is called _____.

13. An advertisement's ability to overcome audience indifference and focus sharp attention on the message is called _____.

14. Literary tools such as definition, explanation, demonstration, comparison and contrast are designed to stimulate _____.

15. When the advertising is more memorable than the product, this is called _____.

Completion Answers

1. zapping
2. zipping
3. impact, originality, relevance
4. useful information
5. stopping power
6. association
7. locking, pulling, stopping
8. slogans
9. taglines
10. recall
11. brand image
12. brand equity
13. impact
14. understanding
15. vampire creativity

Matching

Match the terms and concepts with the appropriate statements. Each term or concept may be used only once; there are more terms and concepts than statements.

Terms and Concepts

a. breakthrough advertising
b. built-in interest
c. conviction
d. exposure
e. grazing
f. human interest

g. interest
h. intrusiveness
i. key visual
j. logo
k. mnemonic
l. personal interest

m. signature
n. transformation advertising
o. trigger
p. tactic
q. avoidance
r. zapping

Statements

_____ 1. When a viewer flips around the channels, stopping now and then to look briefly at something and then moving on.

_____ 2. Developing ads that have stopping power to prevent zapping, that keep viewers' attention, and that address needs that are relevant to them.

_____ 3. When the message is in a medium that your target sees, reads, watches, or listens to, and the message survives the initial scan-and-avoid decision.

_____ 4. Something in the message that "catches" attention in the message or something within the reader or viewer that makes him or her "lock onto" a particular message.

_____ 5. The quality of a message that is designed to be attention getting and forces attention.

_____ 6. When someone is tuned in to the ad because it speaks to wants and needs.

_____ 7. Devices such as rhyme, rhythmic beats, and repeating sounds.

_____ 8. A dominant image around which the commercial's message is planned.

_____ 9. A distinctive mark that identifies the product, company, or brand.

_____ 10. The name of the company or product written in a distinctive type style.

_____ 11. Image advertising that changes the experience of buying and using a product.

_____ 12. Topic that strikes a universal chord in all of us, such as babies, kittens, and puppies.

_____ 13. When a product is just inherently more interesting than others.

_____ 14. When people want to read about themselves and things they care about, it is called:

_____ 15. A particularly strong belief has been anchored firmly in the attitude structure. Which one of the following is built on strong rational arguments that use such techniques as test results, before and after visuals, and demonstrations to prove something?

Matching Answers

1.	e	9.	j
2.	a	10.	m
3.	d	11.	n
4.	o	12.	f
5.	h	13.	b
6.	g	14.	l
7.	k	15.	c
8.	i		

Multiple Choice

Place the letter of the correct answer in the blank provided.

_____ 1. When viewers use remote controls to avoid television ads, this is called:
   a. zapping.
   b. grazing.
   c. zipping.
   d. screening.
   e. avoidance.

_____ 2. Which of the following is a key to effective advertising?
   a. originality
   b. impact
   c. relevance
   d. all of the above
   e. none of the above

_____ 3. Developing ads that have stopping power to prevent zapping, keep viewers' attention, and address needs that are relevant to them is called:
   a. impact advertising.
   b. transformational advertising.
   c. transactional advertising.
   d. breakthrough advertising.
   e. vampire advertising.

_____ 4. Exposure is:
   a. when the mind is engaged and focusing on an ad.
   b. when an ad makes an impact.
   c. when something in the message catches the attention of the reader, viewer, or listener.
   d. the message being in the medium which the target audience reads, watches, or listens to, and the message surviving the initial scan-and-avoid decision.
   e. none of the above

_____ 5. Association is:
   a. a conscious mental effort to make sense of information.
   b. to make a connection in your mind.
   c. getting messages locked into people's minds.
   d. hearing what you want to hear.
   e. all of the above

_____ 6. Maintaining the attention of the target audience is:
   a. stopping power.
   b. persuasive power.
   c. pulling power.
   d. locking power.
   e. none of the above

_____ 7. When we see editorial information and advertisements we:
   a. do not see much difference.
   b. tune in the editorial first.
   c. tune in the advertisement first.
   d. develop a cognitive discourse.
   e. process our fragmented mind set.

_____ 8. Which of the following is one of the kinds of power an ad can have?
   a. locking power
   b. pulling power
   c. stopping power
   d. all of the above
   e. none of the above

_____ 9. Recognition is:
   a. to make a connection in your mind.
   b. when you can remember something specific about the content of a message.
   c. a conscious mental effort to make sense of information.
   d. when you can remember having seen something before.
   e. all of the above

10. Recall is:
   a. to make a connection in your mind.
   b. when you can remember something specific about the content of a message.
   c. a conscious mental effort to make sense of information.
   d. when you can remember having seen something before.
   e. all of the above

11. A slogan is:
   a. the umbrella theme that connects a series of ads in a campaign together.
   b. a dominant visual image around which the ad's message is planned.
   c. clever phrases that are used at the end of an ad to summarize the point of the ad's message in a highly memorable way.
   d. the name of the company or product written in distinctive type.
   e. all of the above

12. Advertising that is so entertaining that it overwhelms the product is called:
   a. breakthrough advertising.
   b. transformational advertising.
   c. transactional advertising.
   d. effective advertising.
   e. vampire advertising.

13. Brand image is:
   a. the reservoir of goodwill and good impressions developed for a brand.
   b. the idea that the product takes on familiar human characteristics.
   c. a mental image that reflects the way a brand is perceived.
   d. a dominant image around which the ad's message is planned.
   e. none of the above

14. Transformational advertising is:
   a. advertising that is so entertaining that it overwhelms the product.
   b. advertising that has stopping power to prevent zapping, keep viewers' attention, and address needs that are relevant to them.
   c. image advertising that changes the experience of buying or using a product.
   d. advertising that makes an impact and breaks through the inattention and the mindless scanning.
   e. all of the above

15. If understanding is a key objective in the design of an advertising message, with what kind of information will you probably be dealing?
   a. emotional
   b. human interest
   c. outrageous effects
   d. factual
   e. all of the above

Multiple Choice Answers

1.	a	9.	d
2.	d	10.	b
3.	d	11.	a
4.	d	12.	e
5.	b	13.	c
6.	c	14.	c
7.	a	15.	d
8.	d		

Career Exercise -- Planning a Career Questionnaire

You must get a sharp focus on what you are trying to accomplish with your research. You must collect as much information as you can about your target audience while ensuring that you leave your target audience with a good impression. The target audience will learn a great deal about you as you collect information from them.

The key to developing a questionnaire to collect information for the Situation Analysis of your Career Marketing Plan is to get as much good information as possible with the minimum effort and time expended by the professionals who complete the questionnaire. The time to complete the questionnaire should be around 10 minutes. That means the questionnaire needs to include a high percentage of closed-ended types of questionnaire items and be limited to about two pages.

A major consideration in developing a career questionnaire is the mixture of the two basic categories of questionnaire items. While there are several different types of items, there are essentially two major categories: the open-ended item and the closed-ended item. The open-ended item is a question or statement that allows the respondent to determine the exact nature of the response. There may be greater or less freedom in the nature of the response, but the respondent creates the response whatever it is. The open-ended item is the typical essay question or fill-in-the-blank item on a college exam. On the other hand, the closed-ended item offers only a specific set of responses. The closed-ended item allows the respondent only certain answers and no others. The respondent must choose one and does not create anything. Four major decisions dominate the choice between open-ended and closed-ended items: the nature of the information sought, the sharing of the effort of collecting the information between the researcher and the respondent, analyzing the information, and the impression made on the respondent.

First, you should choose a type of item that is appropriate to the information. If you can anticipate the range of responses and the range is reasonably small, the closed-ended item is best. For example, you want to identify the level of education of the respondent. The range of education of the target audience can be readily established through secondary research. Use a closed-ended item such as a multiple choice item. On the other hand, if you want to know why an employer hired the last person they hired, the range of possible answers could be as wide as the number of respondents. Let the respondent define the response entirely with an open-ended item such as why did you hire the last advertising professional that you hired?

Second, you must consider the effort involved in providing the information. You need to keep in mind that most respondents are going to limit the amount of time that they will give you. The open-ended item is going to take more of the respondents' time because they must not only decide on a response but must also create form and substance of the response. However, the closed-ended item limits the time required to respond entirely to a choice among the offered alternatives.

The third factor in choosing between open-ended and closed-ended items is the time spent analyzing the information. While the personal and dynamic nature of the information collected from the open-ended item may be exciting and useful, a great deal of time and effort must go into making sense of the information, especially across a series of respondents. For one thing, you cannot even be certain what direction the respondent will take in replying to any particular question. The time-consuming analysis of open-ended items is a matter of identifying after the fact a range of responses into which the various open-ended responses can be categorized. The results of the closed-ended items take much less time to tabulate and appreciate because it is largely a matter of counting.

Finally, the type of questionnaire items chosen and developed for the questionnaire influence the impression formed by the respondent. The response alternatives of the closed-ended items offer an opportunity to display your fundamental knowledge of the advertising field and your ability and willingness to do your homework.

Begin preparation of your career questionnaire by identifying 20-25 kinds of information you would like to know if you could talk to a professional. Focus on three kinds of information: descriptive characteristics of the professionals who respond to your questionnaire (position, years of experience, educational background, etc.), job expectations of the professionals (desired skills, personality traits, etc.), and attitudes of the professionals (toward students, the career field, the job, etc.). The descriptive characteristics help you identify the best sources of information and also help you find the target audience later. Job expectations help in your preparation for the field as well as providing a means to infer how professionals are likely to respond to you given your skills, experience, etc.

9   Media Strategy and Planning

Chapter Objectives and Summary

- Understand the central position of media planning in campaign development and how this function utilizes information from numerous sources, including product sales performance, competitor surveillance, and message creative strategy, to form the campaign design.
- Understand the organization and purpose of the media plan, and see how each decision on selection and scheduling is coordinated with the client's sales objectives.
- Explain how planners use communication aperture to give direction to media planning strategy.
- Explain how the media's qualitative features (atmosphere and environment) are blended with their quantitative dimensions (reach, frequency, and efficiency) to provide the needed profile for selection.

Media planning uses marketing information to create an advertising schedule for an ad campaign. The goal is to place the advertising message before the target audience. Media planning is crucial because it deals with the most significant portion of the advertiser's budget. Each prospect for a product has an ideal point in time and place at which he or she can be reached with an advertising message. The goal of the media planner is to expose consumer prospects to the advertiser's message at this crucial point -- called aperture. Success depends on accurate marketing research, appreciation of the message concept, and a sensitive understanding of the channels of mass communication. Media planning information comes from marketing sources, creative sources, and media sources. Marketing information includes area sales patterns, month-by-month sales patterns, distribution patterns, and competitor's advertising patterns. Creative information includes theme characteristics, message characteristics, and creative performance research. Media information includes media popularity, media audience characteristics, and media cost forecasting.

Each media plan must determine who to advertise to, which geographic areas to cover, when to advertise, what the duration of the campaign should be, and what media environments are best for the advertiser's message. The media planner's job is to translate the target descriptions into information that will fit the audience profiles provided by media research. Media planners have several categories of information they can use in planning including demographic profiles, psychographics and lifestyles, and product-use segmentations. For the media planner, geographic specification means identifying each market and allocating a sum of dollars to each. Also, advertising is most effective when people are exposed at a time when they are more receptive to the information. The strategy used to deal with duration is known as continuity. The selection of the best continuity pattern depends on the budget, consumer-use cycles, brand loyalty, and competitive continuity strategies. Three continuity scheduling strategies are used: continuous, pulsing, and flighting. Success in media planning is also influenced by media environments.

Selecting the media and the specific vehicles that will carry the message is based on three yardsticks that measure the number of people exposed to the message (reach), the degree of exposure repetition (frequency), and the efficiency (cost per thousand or CPM) of the selected vehicles. Impressions measure the total audience exposure but do not take duplication into account. Gross impressions and gross rating points (GRPs) give a clearer picture of the intensity of schedules. Reach is more specific than impressions in that it measures the ability to attract different members of the target audience. Frequency refers to the potential of the media schedule to generate repeat exposure to the advertising message. Average frequency, frequency distribution, and effective distribution are alternate measures of frequency. The media plan is not only evaluated in terms of audience. The cost of time and space determines the number of message units that can be placed. The process of measuring the target audience size against the cost of that audience is called efficiency. Efficiency is usually analyzed on a cost-per-thousand basis. These costs can be compared within the same medium, but comparisons between different media are usually not valid.

Media plans do not have a universal form, but there is a logical pattern to the decision stages. The plan would begin with the general elements and work down to the more specific questions. The stages include a situation/background analysis, media objectives/aperture opportunities, strategy, and the flow sheet (scheduling and budget).

Key Terms and Concepts

aperture	Ideal moment for exposing consumers to an advertising message.
average frequency	A "shorthand" summary of repeat exposure to an ad message.
carry-over effect	A measure of residual effect (awareness or recall) of the advertising message some time after the advertising period has ended.
commercial pod	Continuous string of broadcast messages run during program interruptions.
continuity	Strategy and tactics used to schedule advertising over the time span of the advertising campaign.
continuous pattern	Advertising spending that remains relatively constant during the campaign period.
cost per rating point (CPRP)	A method of comparing media vehicles by relating the cost of the message unit to the audience rating.
cost per thousand (CPM)	The cost of exposing each 1,000 members of the target audience to the advertising message.
effective frequency	A recent concept in planning that determines a range (minimum and maximum) of repeat exposure for a message.
flighting	Advertising pattern characterized by a period of intensified activity, followed by periods of no advertising, called a hiatus.

frequency	The number of times an audience has an opportunity to be exposed to a media vehicle or vehicles in a specified time span.
frequency distribution	Shows the pattern of exposures for each of the target audience members. The frequency distribution method is more revealing and thus more valuable than the average frequency method of reporting repetition.
gross impressions	The sum of the audiences of all media vehicles used within a designated time span.
gross rating points (GRPs)	The sum of the total exposure potential of a series of media vehicles expressed as a percentage of the audience population.
impact	A value of media influence on the audience that is expected to produce higher-than-normal awareness of the advertiser's message.
media objective	A goal or task to be accomplished by the media plan.
media planning	Decision process leading to the use of advertising time and space to assist in the achievement of marketing objectives.
pulsing	Advertising pattern in which time and space are scheduled on a continuous but uneven pattern, and lower levels are followed by burst or peak periods of intensified activity.
reach	The percentage of different homes or people exposed to a media vehicle or vehicles at least once during a specific period of time. It is the percentage of unduplicated audience.
share of voice	Percentage of advertising messages in a medium or vehicles owned by one brand among all messages for that product or service.

True/False

Circle the appropriate letter.

T   F   1.   The ideal moment for exposing consumers to an advertising message is called the search corridor.

T   F   2.   The lifestyle profile provides a perspective on the social and cultural environment chosen by the target audience.

T   F   3.   Media plans are interwoven with all other areas of advertising.

T	**F**	4.	Flighting strategy is a popular alternative to continuous advertising.
T	**F**	5.	Reach for newspapers in a city can be found by adding together the circulations of the newspapers.
T	**F**	6.	CPM and CPRP are more valid when used to compare alternatives within a medium.
T	**F**	7.	Media strategy is considered the "blueprint" of the recommended media plan.
T	**F**	8.	Continuity measures the degree of exposure repetitions.
T	**F**	9.	Due to the compartmentalization of the various functions within an advertising agency, it is important to emphasize that creative and media have to be tightly coordinated.
T	**F**	10.	In the ideal situation the media planner knows both brand and competitor patterns before deciding on month-by-month media budget allocations.
T	**F**	11.	The target market and the target audience are always identical.
T	**F**	12.	People with special interests often buy or subscribe to special interest magazines for the advertising.
T	**F**	13.	A gross rating point is the equivalent of 10% of the target audience.
T	**F**	14.	Gross ratings points refers to the number of potential audience members exposed to a message or plan.
T	**F**	15.	Media are compared on the basis of their relative efficiency.

True/False Answers

1.	F	9.	T
2.	T	10.	T
3.	T	11.	F
4.	F	12.	T
5.	F	13.	F
6.	T	14.	F
7.	F	15.	T
8	F		

Completion

Fill in the missing word or words in the blanks provided.

1. A problem-solving process leading to the use of advertising time and space to assist in the achievement of marketing objectives is called _____.

2. The planning decisions that are involved in media planning are: _____, geographic emphasis, _____, campaign length, and _____.

3. The ideal moment for exposing consumers to an advertising message when their interest and attention are high is called _____.

4. The key factors on which successful message placement depends are: _____ research, appreciation of _____ concept, and understanding of _____ channels.

5. The critical decision factors on which the selection of a medium and specific media vehicles depend are: _____, _____, and _____.

6. The fundamental issues that direct media strategy are: _____, geographic coverage, timing, campaign duration, and _____.

7. The kinds of information on target audiences that media planners use to assist them in planning are: _____, _____, and _____.

8. If an advertiser runs five ads in a medium with an audience of 10,000, the gross impressions would be _____.

9. If a medium has an audience of 200,000 and the target audience is 800,000, the gross rating point total for four messages delivered in that medium would be _____.

10. What is the reach in the following situation? There are two newspapers in a city with a population of 600,000. The circulations of the papers are 200,000 and 160,000. Research has revealed that 60,000 households subscribe to both papers. If a media plan calls for using both papers, the reach would be _____%.

11. Calculate the average frequency. You know that the city in question has a population of 100,000. There are two newspapers. Paper one has a circulation of 50,000 and paper two has has a circulation of 40,000. There are 5,000 people among the subscribers of each paper who subscribe to the other paper. The media plan calls for running 10 ads in paper one and 6 ads in paper two. The average frequency would be _____.

12. _____ is the typical means of comparing the efficiency of different media.

13. Suppose a newspaper has 10,000 readers who could be considered a target audience. The cost for a one-page ad is $2,000. The paper's cost per thousand would be _____.

14. Suppose a magazine has a circulation of 200,000 who could be considered a target audience. The total of the target audience is 1,000,000. The cost of a 4-color, one-page ad is $10,000. The cost per rating point would be _____.

15. What are the gross rating points in the following situation? There are two newspapers in a city with a population of 600,000. The circulation of the papers are 200,000 and 160,000. Research has revealed that 60,000 households subscribe to both papers. If a media plan calls for using five ads each in both papers, the gross rating points would be _____.

Completion Answers

1. media planning
2. audience, timing, intensity of exposure
3. aperture
4. marketing, message, media
5. popularity, cost forecast, audience characteristics
6. who to advise, best media for the message
7. product use, demographics, psychographics/lifestyles
8. 50,000
9. 100
10. 50
11. 8.5
12. cost per thousand
13. $200
14. $500
15. 2501

Matching

Match the terms and concepts with the appropriate statements. Each term or concept may be used only once; there are more terms and concepts than statements.

Terms and Concepts

a. carry-over effect
b. commercial pod
c. continuity
d. continuous pattern
e. cost per rating point
f. efficiency
g. flighting
h. flow sheet
i. frequency distribution
j. frequency
k. gross impressions
l. hiatus
m. impact
n. pulsing
o. reach
p. zapping
q. distribution pattern
r. cost forecasting

Statements

_____ 1. The strategy and tactics used to schedule advertising messages over the time span of the advertising campaign.

_____ 2. Advertising spending that remains relatively constant during the campaign period.

_____ 3. An advertising pattern in which time and space are scheduled on a continuous but uneven pattern, and lower levels are followed by burst or peak periods of intensified activity.

_____ 4. An advertising pattern characterized by a period of intensified activity, followed by periods of no advertising.

_____ 5. A measure of residual effect (awareness or recall) of the advertising message some time after the advertising period has ended.

_____ 6. A value of media influence on the audience that is expected to produce higher-than-normal awareness of the advertiser's message.

_____ 7. A string of continuous broadcast messages run during program interruptions.

_____ 8. The sum of the audiences of all media vehicles used within a designated time span.

_____ 9. The percentage of different homes or people exposed to a media vehicle or vehicles at least once during a specific period of time.

_____ 10. The number of times an audience has an opportunity to be exposed to a media vehicle or vehicles in a specified time span.

_____ 11. Shows the pattern of exposures for each of the target audience members.

_____ 12. A method of comparing media vehicles by relating the cost of the message unit to the audience rating.

_____ 13. The process of measuring the target audience size against the cost of that audience.

_____ 14. The period following a flighting schedule.

_____ 15. Shows the month-by-month placement of messages, details the anticipated impact through forecasted levels of GRP, and illustrates how the campaign budget is allocated by medium and by month.

Matching Answers

1.	c	9.	o
2.	d	10.	j
3.	n	11.	i
4.	g	12.	e
5.	a	13.	f
6.	m	14.	l
7.	b	15.	h
8.	k		

Multiple Choice

Place the letter of the correct answer in the blank provided.

_____ 1.   Which of the following is one of the planning decisions involved in media planning?
a.   campaign length
b.   intensity of exposure
c.   timing
d.   geographic emphasis
e.   all of the above

_____ 2.   Aperture is:
a.   the ideal moment for exposing consumers to an advertising message.
b.   a problem-solving process leading to the use of advertising time and space to achieve marketing objectives.
c.   the strategy used to schedule advertising over the span of the advertising campaign.
d.   a competitive advantage that creates an opening to persuade consumers.
e.   all of the above

_____ 3.   In media planning, media planners use the information from creative performance research to make which of the following decisions?
a.   intensity of exposure
b.   the number of messages
c.   campaign length
d.   the target audience
e.   all of the above

_____ 4.   All of the following are critical decision factors in the selection of a medium and specific media vehicles **EXCEPT**:
a.   audience characteristics
b.   popularity
c.   availability
d.   cost forecast
e.   all of the above

_____ 5.   Psychographics involves:
a.   attempts to classify people according to how they feel and act.
b.   a lifestyle profile describing people by the way they view their careers.
c.   perspective on social and cultural environment chosen by target audience.
d.   a description of people by how they view their leisure/recreation pursuits.
e.   all of the above

_____ 6. Which of the following is **NOT** an important issue that directs media strategy?
   a. whom to advertise to
   b. timing
   c. campaign duration
   d. cost
   e. geographic coverage

_____ 7. Share-of-voice is:
   a. the percentage of sales of a product among all products in a category.
   b. the percentage of the advertising budget among all factors in marketing communication.
   c. the percentage of advertising messages in a medium or vehicles owned by one brand among all messages for that product or service.
   d. the percentage of different homes exposed to a message during a specific period of time.
   e. none of the above

_____ 8. Continuity is:
   a. the percentage of different homes exposed to a message during a specific period of time.
   b. the strategy and tactics used to schedule advertising messages over the time span of the advertising campaign.
   c. the sum of of the total exposure potential of a series of media vehicles.
   d. a measure of residual effect of the advertising message some time after the advertising period has ended.
   e. none of the above

_____ 9. A continuous pattern media strategy is:
   a. an advertising scheduling pattern characterized by a period of intensified activity followed by periods of no advertising.
   b. an advertising scheduling pattern in which time and space are scheduled on a continuous but uneven basis; lower levels are followed by bursts or peak periods of intensified activity.
   c. an advertising scheduling pattern characterized by advertising spending that remains relatively constant during the campaign period.
   d. an advertising scheduling pattern characterized by spreading the advertising message to as many different media and media vehicles as possible.
   e. none of the above

_____ 10. In media planning, an impression is:
   a. an exposure of a member of the audience.
   b. the contribution of one message to the brand image.
   c. creating top-of-mind awareness in the mind of a member of the audience.
   d. an opportunity for a member of the audience to be exposed to the advertising message.
   e. none of the above

11. If an advertiser needs to achieve, a total of 30,000 gross impressions with 10 ads run in a selected medium, what would the audience of the medium need to be?
    a. 1,000
    b. 3,000
    c. 10,000
    d. 30,000
    e. 3,333

12. Reach is:
    a. the percentage of different homes exposed to a media vehicle or vehicles at least once during a specific period of time.
    b. the sum of the audiences of all the vehicles used within a designated time span.
    c. the sum of of the total exposure potential of a series of media vehicles.
    d. a measure of residual effect of the advertising message some time after the advertising period has ended.
    e. the degree of exposure repetitions.

13. In media planning, gross ratings points are equal to:
    a. frequency times reach.
    b. gross impressions times frequency.
    c. reach divided by frequency.
    d. frequency divided by reach.
    e. reach times gross impressions.

14. How many gross rating points have been achieved if an advertising campaign exposes 10 % or 10,000 people an average of 10 times?
    a. 1,000
    b. 100,000
    c. 100
    d. 10,000
    e. 1,000,000

15. In a city which has 1,000,000 total population, the local newspaper is purchased by 100,000. If this paper is used in a media plan, what is the reach?
    a. 10
    b. 1%
    c. 100
    d. 10%
    e. 1,000

Multiple Choice Answers

1.	e	9.	c
2.	a	10.	d
3.	b	11.	b
4.	c	12.	a
5.	e	13.	a
6.	d	14.	c
7.	c	15.	d
8.	b		

Career Exercise -- Types of Questionnaire Items

The range of different open-ended items is almost infinite, but there are two predominant types that are simply characterized by the length of the open-ended response that is sought. These types are loosely thought of as short answer and essay type items.

The major concerns in developing open-ended items are being clear and asking one question at a time. Keep the questions or statements as simple and straightforward as possible. Use only the words that are absolutely necessary and no more. As much as possible, phrase the items in the terminology and style of target audience. The best items come straight from conversations with members of the target audience. In addition, avoid the trap of trying to squeeze too much into each question. This often results in an item of the following form: What do you think of the advertising and public relations students whom you have met? There are two questions being asked. Only ask one at a time.

The following are examples of short answer open-ended items:

Please indicate the percentage of time that you spend each week performing the following activities in your job.

copy writing	_____	ad layout	_____
primary research	_____	secondary research	_____
writing plans	_____	creating ad concepts	_____
budgeting	_____	meetings	_____

How long have you worked in the advertising agency business?

The following are examples of essay-type open-ended items:

What qualities would lead you to hire one applicant over another? Why are these qualities so important to you?

What skill do you feel will be the key to success in advertising 10 years from now?

The most common types of closed-ended questionnaire items are the dichotomous, multiple choice, ranking, the Likert scale, and the semantic differential. The dichotomous item has two possible answers, yes/no, true/false, etc. The dichotomous item should be used only rarely because of the limited nature of the information it provides. It gives no indication of the strength of the answer, so it is useful only for screening. **Are you a registered voter? Do you work in advertising? Do you hire ad people?** Each requires only a yes or no response. In the preceding items, the only concern is with screening out people who do not meet the criteria. The respondent is either a registered voter or not, working in advertising or not, hires advertising people or not. Do not use the dichotomous item to measure knowledge or attitudes. You only get an indication of direction, positive or negative. We almost always need some idea of strength as well as direction.

The most common type of closed-ended item is the multiple choice item. The key to the success of the multiple choice item is to be able to limit the range of responses to five or less. The second major concern is to create multiple choice answers that are mutually exclusive If the range of alternatives is too large, you may be asking respondents to make discriminations of which they are not capable. They will give you an answer, but it may not be meaningful. Second, the answers cannot overlap. For example, a typical multiple choice item would involve salary ranges.

The salary range most often paid entry-level advertising professionals is:

(Ranges **ARE NOT** mutually exclusive.)   (Ranges **ARE** mutually exclusive.)

a.	less than $15,000		a.	less than $15,000
b.	$15,000 - $18,000		b.	$15,000 - $18,000
c.	**$18,000 - $21,000**		c.	$18,001 - $21,000
d.	**$21,000 - $24,000**		d.	$21,001 - $24,000
e.	more than $24,000		e.	more than $24,000

A respondent who thought the answer was $18,000 would not be able to determine whether to use answer "b" or answer "c" because the ranges overlap. They are not mutually exclusive; that is, there is more than one correct answer for a given response.

Ranking items provide an additional level of information that the multiple choice item does not. While we find out which answer would be selected given a choice, we also discover the respondents' order of importance for all alternatives. Ranking gives the respondent the opportunity to tell you the pecking order of the alternatives; that is, which alternative has priority over another. For example, a common ranking item would involve a skills inventory.

Which of the following is the most important skill for entry-level professionals in advertising? Please rank the skills in descending order of importance. Place a 1 next to the most important; place a 2 by the next most important; etc. If you consider a skill unimportant, do not rank it.

_____ ad layout   _____ computer

_____ copywriting   _____ creating ad concepts

_____ research   _____ strategic planning

If we used a multiple choice item for this question, we would only know which skill was the most important. We would know nothing about the five that were not selected. In the same space and effort, we can greatly increase the amount of information collected.

The most difficult of the closed-ended items to create are the scale items. However, scales represent the only meaningful method to tap the attitudes of respondents. The scale measures the attitude toward an idea or thing by measuring the direction and strength of the attitude. Direction is the positive or negative evaluation. The scale is best represented by a number line with positive on one end and negative on the other and with a zero point in the middle -- hence, a scale. The major concern in developing scales is to avoid bias. Balance, equal numbers of positive and negative alternatives, is the key to avoiding bias in a scale.

The most common and simplest scale is the Likert scale. The Likert scale is a five-point scale.

-2	-1	0	+1	+2
Strongly Agree	Agree	No Opinion	Disagree	Strongly Disagree

The Likert uses verbal statements rather than positive and negative numbers to indicate the alternative responses. It asks the respondent to place himself/herself on the scale depending on the attitude toward a statement.

Advertising students that I have met are professional.

_____	_____	_____	_____	_____
Strongly Agree	Agree	No Opinion	Disagree	Strongly Disagree

The semantic differential is a seven-point scale and uses only bi-polar adjectives on each end of the scale to indicate the range of response.

-3	-2	-1	0	+1	+2	+3
bad						good

The typical semantic differential would associate a series of bi-polar adjectives with a person, idea, product, etc.

Evaluate advertising students by indicating your attitude toward them on each of the following scales. Advertising students are:

good	____	____	____	____	____	____	____	bad
professional	____	____	____	____	____	____	____	not professional
passive	____	____	____	____	____	____	____	active
not informed	____	____	____	____	____	____	____	informed

Continue preparation of your questionnaire by constructing 15-20 items from the information assembled in the previous exercise. Determine the appropriate type of item for each. Begin considering the order of the items. Start with the background items to identify the respondent. Seek out job expectation information next. Finally, consider attitude items, especially information that might be sensitive such as personal salary range.

10 Print Media

Chapter Objectives and Summary

- **Understand the similarities and differences between newspapers and magazines.**
- **Explain the advantages and disadvantages of newspaper, magazine, and other forms of media advertising.**
- **Explain the major trends in print advertisements.**

What was once the only source of information, and recently the dominant source, newspapers are now just another alternative. The immediate problem is the rapid drop in household penetration from a time three decades ago when many homes were receiving more than one paper to today's more vulnerable 70 percent. Cold type, text editing, offset printing, on-line circulation information systems, electronic libraries, database publishing, and most recently, satellite transmission and computerization are technological responses of the newspaper industry to try to combat the steady decline of the industry.

Newspapers can be classified by three factors: frequency of publication, size, and circulation. Newspapers are published either daily or weekly. The circulation of Sunday papers is usually greater than that of dailies because they contain more information and because the reader is able to spend more time with the paper. Weekly papers appear in towns, suburbs, and smaller cities where the volume of hard news and advertising is not sufficient to support a daily newspaper. Weeklies are often shunned by national advertisers because they are relatively high in cost, duplicate the circulation of daily or Sunday papers, and generate an administrative headache because ads must be placed separately for each newspaper. Statements regarding newspaper circulation are verified by the Audit Bureau of Circulation (ABC), and independent auditing group that represents the advertiser, the agency, and the publisher.

There are three general types of newspaper advertising: classified, display, and supplements. Display advertising is the dominant form of newspaper advertising. Syndicated supplements are published by independent publishers and distributed to newspapers throughout the country. Best known syndicated supplements are Parade and USA Weekend. Local supplements are produced by either one newspaper or a group of newspapers in the same area. The difference between what is charged for local display advertising and national display advertising is referred to as the rate differential. Co-op advertising refers to an arrangement between the advertiser and the retailer whereby both parties share the cost of placing the ad. The lack of standardization of advertisement format have made it nearly impossible to prepare one ad that would fit every newspaper. The Standard Advertising Unit (SAU) is the newspaper industry's attempt to provide a uniform format for national advertisers.

The most obvious asset of newspapers is extensive market coverage. Other advantages of newspapers include comparison shopping, positive consumer attitudes, flexibility, and interaction of national advertising and local retailers. The disadvantages of newspapers include short life span, clutter, limited coverage of certain groups, product limitations, and poor reproduction, especially for photographs and color.

Individual magazines have become bigger and brighter. Upscale magazines seem to have an edge over mass consumer magazines in attracting advertisers. The magazine industry has entered the "age of skimming," where 80 percent of the information is acquired from the story titles, subheadings, captions, and pictures rather than the editorial content.

Magazines are classified by frequency of publication, audience, geographic coverage, demographics, and editorial diversity. Three types of magazines are categorized by the audiences they serve: consumer magazines; business magazines, which include trade papers and industrial magazines; and professional magazines. Vertical publications present stories and information about an entire industry. A horizontal publication deals with a business function that cuts across industries. Current research indicates that 92 percent of all adults (male and female) read at least one magazine per month. On average, adults read nine different issues of magazines per month. They spend an average of 54 minutes in total reading time. As with newspapers, the ABC audits magazine circulation. It monitors subscriptions and newsstand sales.

Magazines must fill a niche with their unique editorial content in order to satisfy specific groups of readers. As a result, magazines are extremely diverse in terms of their characteristics, readers, and reader interaction. The ability of magazines to target and deliver specialized audiences has become a primary advantage. The greatest areas of growth are expected to be in special interest magazines and special editions of existing publications. Another advantage of magazines is strong audience receptivity. The editorial environment of a magazine lends authority and credibility to the advertising. Magazines also have the longest life span of all media. Other advantages include high visual quality and the capability of involvement in sales promotions. The disadvantages of magazines are limited flexibility, high cost, and difficulty of distribution. techniques.

Key Terms and Concepts

bleed page	A page without outside margins in which the color extends to the edge of the page.
broadsheet	Newspaper with a size of eight columns wide and 22 inches deep.
circulation	A measure of the number of copies sold.
classified advertising	Commercial messages arranged in the newspaper according to the interests of readers.
controlled circulation	Magazines distributed through nontraditional delivery systems for free.
co-op advertising	An arrangement between the advertiser and the retailer whereby both parties share the cost of placing the ad.
display advertising	Sponsored messages that can be of any size and location within the newspaper with the exception of the editorial page.
first cover page	The front cover of a magazine.
fourth cover page	The back cover of a magazine.
fractional page space	A single or double page broken into a variety of units.

free-standing insert advertising	Preprinted advertisements that are placed loosely within the newspaper.
gatefold	More than two connected pages (four is the most common number) offered by a magazine.
guaranteed circulation	Circulation that a publisher promises to provide.
gutter	The white space between the pages running along the outside edge of the page.
horizontal publication	Deals with a business function that cuts across industries, such as Direct Marketing.
local supplements	Produced by either one newspaper or a group of newspapers in the same area.
rate differential	The difference between what is charged for local display advertising and national display advertising.
second cover page	The inside of the front cover of a magazine.
selective binding	A new technology that allows magazines to combine information on subscribers kept in a database with a computer program so that the end result is a magazine that includes special sections for subscribers based on their demographic profiles.
supplements	Syndicated or local full-color advertising inserts that appear in newspapers throughout the week.
syndicated supplements	Published by independent publishers and distributed to newspapers throughout the country.
tabloid	Newspaper with a page size of five to six columns wide and 14 inches deep.
third cover page	The inside of the back cover of a magazine.
vertical publication	Presents stories and information about an entire industry.

True/False

Circle the appropriate letter.

T   F   1.   Daily newspapers implemented the Standard Advertising Unit to encourage national advertisers to use newspapers more.

T   F   2.   National advertisers pay more than 50 percent more for newspaper display advertising than do local advertisers.

T   F   3.   Cooperative advertising helps national advertisers avoid the rate differential charged to national advertisers by newspapers.

T   F   4.   The National Advertising Bureau is responsible for establishing the official circulation of magazines.

T   F   5.   Normally, the largest unit of space sold by magazines is a gatefold.

T   F   6.   Newspaper advertising is viewed positively by consumers who use it for a shopping reference.

T   F   7.   Newspapers in medium-size and large markets typically offer "zoned editions," which allow an advertiser with one location on one side of the city to run an ad for only the area served by the advertiser.

T   F   8.   The long lead time of most newspapers prevents them from being viable for price-oriented advertising.

T   F   9.   Most magazines provide highly specialized forms of information to highly specialized audiences.

T   F   10. Magazines are increasingly relying only on postal delivery in larger markets.

T   F   11. Newspapers offer excellent reproduction of quality visual images such as color photographs.

T   F   12. Magazine production schedules provide for a great deal of flexibility in terms of placing and changing ads right up to the time of distribution.

T   F   13. Print media are superior to broadcast media in credibility.

T   F   14. Newspapers are the leading local medium.

T   F   15. Magazines have the greatest ability to reach preselected or tightly targeted audiences.

True/False Answers

1.	T	9.	T
2.	T	10.	F
3.	T	11.	F
4.	F	12.	F
5.	F	13.	T
6.	T	14.	T
7.	T	15.	T
8.	F		

Completion

Fill in the missing word or words in the blanks provided.

1. _____ are the leading local medium.

2. The structure of newspapers is determined by frequency of _____, _____, and _____.

3. A measure of the number of copies sold is called _____.

4. The organization responsible for verifying newspaper circulation is the _____.

5. Sponsored messages that can be of any size and location within the newspaper, with the exception of the editorial page are called _____.

6. Syndicated or local full-color advertising inserts that appear in newspapers throughout the week are called _____.

7. The three general types of newspaper advertising are: _____, _____, and _____.

8. _____ and _____ are the two types of display advertising.

9. The characteristics used to classify magazines are: frequency of publication, audience _____ diversity, _____, and _____ coverage.

10. The types of magazines categorized by audience are: _____, _____, and _____.

11. Magazines which are directed to retailers, wholesalers, and other distributors are called _____.

12. _____ is spent reading the average magazine.

13. The distribution of magazines through nontraditional delivery systems for free is called _____.

14. Magazine advertising rates are based on _____ .

15. The primary advantage of magazines today is the ability to reach _____ audiences.

Completion Answers

1. newspapers
2. publication, size, circulation
3. circulation
4. Audit Bureau of Circulation
5. display advertising
6. supplements
7. classified, display, supplements
8. local, national
9. editorial, demographics, geographic
10. farm, consumer, business
11. trade papers
12. almost one hour
13. controlled circulation
14. circulation
15. specialized

Matching

Match the terms and concepts with the appropriate statements. Each term or concept may be used only once; there are more terms and concepts than statements.

Terms and Concepts

a. bleed page
b. classified advertising
c. desktop publishing
d. fractional page space

e. free-standing insert advertising
f. gatefold
g. gutter
h. horizontal
i. ink-jet printing
j. rate differential
k. second cover
l. selective binding
m. Simmons-Scarborough Syndicated Research Association
n. syndicated supplement
o. vertical
p. lead space
q. third cover
r. offset printing

Statements

_____ 1. A research firm that provides an analysis of newspaper readership for approximately 70 of the nation's largest cities.

_____ 2. Commercial messages arranged in the newspaper according to the interests of readers.

_____ 3. Preprinted advertisements that are placed loosely within the newspaper.

_____ 4. A full-color advertisement insert that is published by independent publishers and distributed to newspapers throughout the country such as Parade and USA Weekend.

_____ 5. Difference between what is charged for local display and national display advertising.

_____ 6. Type of publication that presents stories and information about an entire industry.

_____ 7. Type of publication that deals with a business function that cuts across industries, such as Direct Marketing.

_____ 8. A new technology that allows magazines to combine information on subscribers kept in a database with a computer program so that the end result is a magazine that includes special sections for subscribers based on their demographic profiles.

_____ 9. A new technology that allows a magazine such as *U.S. News & World Report* to personalize its renewal form so that each issue contains a renewal card already filled out with the subscriber's name, address, and so on.

_____ 10. A new technology that allows magazines to close pages just hours before press time and thus eliminating a long lead-time, a serious drawback long associated with magazine advertising.

_____ 11. The inside of the front cover of a magazine.

_____ 12. The white space between the pages running along the outside edge of the page.

_____ 13. A page without outside margins in which the color extends to the edge of the page.

_____ 14. More than two connected pages (four is the most common number) offered by a magazine.

_____ 15. A single or double page broken into a variety of units.

Matching Answers

1. m	6. o	11. k
2. b	7. h	12. g
3. e	8. l	13. a
4. n	9. i	14. f
5. j	10. c	15. d

Multiple Choice

Place the letter of the correct answer in the blank provided.

_____ 1. A serious problem facing the newspaper industry is:
   a. newspapers contain mostly local news.
   b. the rapid drop in household penetration.
   c. newspapers are relatively expensive.
   d. newspapers must allow a commission to ad agencies normally used by advertisers.
   e. all of the above

116

_____ 2. Which of the following is one of the factors by which the structure of the newspaper industry is determined?
   a. audience
   b. geography
   c. frequency of publication
   d. demographics
   e. all of the above

_____ 3. In what ways are print media considered to be superior to broadcast media?
   a. impact
   b. respectability
   c. relative cost
   d. prestige
   e. all of the above

_____ 4. Which of the following are the two independent agencies who measure newspaper audiences?
   a. Simmons-Scarborough and Audit Bureau of Circulation
   b. Marketing Research Inc. and National Advertising Bureau
   c. A. C. Nielsen and Simmons-Scarborough
   d. MediaMark and Advertising Bureau of Circulation
   e. A. C. Nielsen and the Audit Bureau of Circulation

_____ 5. Which of the following measures magazine readership?
   a. Simmons Market Research Bureau
   b. Audit Bureau of Circulation
   c. MediaMark
   d. all of the above
   e. none of the above

_____ 6. To what has the decline of afternoon newspapers been attributed?
   a. changes in readers tastes
   b. strong influence of television
   c. rapidly increasing production costs
   d. competition from radio
   e. all of the above

_____ 7. Which of the following statements about newspaper readership is **TRUE**:
   a. it increases with educational attainment.
   b. average weekday readership increased from 1991 to 1992.
   c. an average reader spends 45 minutes reading the weekday paper.
   d. it increases with age.
   e. all of the above

_____ 8. Which of the following represent the two newspaper advertising departments?
   a. local and national
   b. retail and brand
   c. display and classified
   d   classified and retail
   e. display and retail

_____ 9. What factor has motivated magazines to look to alternative forms of delivery?
  a. rapidly increasing production costs
  b. changing demographics of magazine audiences
  c. decreases in the cost of specialized delivery systems
  d. inefficiency of current delivery systems
  e. postal rate increases

_____ 10. What are the two categories of magazine readership?
  a. primary and secondary
  b. local and national
  c. consumer and trade
  d. primary and local
  e. none of the above

_____ 11. All of the following are disadvantages of newspapers EXCEPT:
  a. production flexibility.
  b. poor reproduction.
  c. clutter.
  d. short life span.
  e. limited coverage of the elderly.

_____ 12. All of the following are disadvantages of magazines EXCEPT:
  a. flexibility
  b. cost
  c. mass audience
  d. visual quality
  e. distribution

_____ 13. Which of the following is one of the factors by which the magazine industry is categorized?
  a. circulation
  b. frequency of publication
  c. demographics
  d. size
  e. all of the above

_____ 14. Which of the following is an advantage of print media?
  a. deliver one thought at a time
  b. credibility
  c. selectivity
  d. deliver one message at a time
  e. all of the above

_____ 15. What major problem has discouraged national advertisers from using newspapers?
  a. lack of selectivity
  b. lack of standardization of advertising format
  c. inability to deliver mass audiences
  d. poor quality of newsprint
  e. inadequate buying power of newspaper audiences

Multiple Choice Answers

1.	b	6.	b	11.	a
2.	c	7.	e	12.	d
3.	b	8.	c	13.	c
4.	a	9.	e	14.	e
5.	d	10.	a	15.	b

Career Exercise -- Career Questionnaire Content

Two kinds of information are crucial to career planning: descriptive and attitudinal. Descriptive information provides the demographic and psychographic characteristics that allow you to identify the target audience and to judge the relevance of the information you receive. Descriptive identification information allows you to pick your target audience out of a crowd. Age, job title, etc., are characteristics that let you find the target audience. But descriptive information also tips you off to the value of your information. For example, you are more interested in someone who has been in the field for 10 years than someone who has only been in the business for six months. A director or vice president is more likely to make hiring and firing decisions and therefore may be more useful.

Attitudinal information is at the core of your research. Ultimately, you are trying to get a line on how those people who will respond to you. While you may have difficulty asking an employer if she likes you and getting a reliable answer, you can infer the underlying attitudes from her attitude toward the skills, knowledge, training, experience, etc., needed to be successful in the field. For example, if you find that 90 percent of the people whom you interview through your career questionnaire tell you that creativity is the number one trait needed to be successful, and these employers already know that you are creative, you can reasonably infer that their attitude toward you will be very favorable. If your research has also indicated that you have a significant advantage compared to your competition, you can infer that the employers would prefer you over other job candidates. You do not have to ask them directly.

The following are some of the types of descriptive information that you may want to consider for your questionnaire: title, age, education, type of education, where educated, coursework in college, professional training outside of college, hiring/firing responsibilities, years in advertising, years in current position, years with current firm, number of people in firm, number of people in advertising program, sales of firm, and location of firm.

Attitudinal information might include impression of students, impression of advertising students, impression of recent graduates, impression of most recently hired pre-professionals, most important skills, most important personal qualities, most important college courses, most important technical training, value of internships, value of professional organization involvement, value of social organization involvement, hiring decision factors, and appropriate style of dress and appearance.

Other general information that you may want to seek out through the questionnaire might include salary ranges for both beginning professional and other positions, attitudes toward specific resume elements such as the career objective, personal information, salary history, skills listing, number of pages, unusual designs, colored paper, and approach to organizing the resume.

11   Broadcast Media

Chapter Objectives and Summary

- **Understand the basic nature of both radio and television.**
- **Describe the audience for each medium and explain how that audience is measured.**
- **List the advantages and disadvantages of using radio and television.**

Broadcast media, the process of sending sounds and images, includes television and radio. Whereas print media are bound by space, broadcast media convey transient messages and are bound by time. Among the different television systems that advertisers can use are network, public, cable, subscription, local, specialty, and interactive television. Network is still the dominant form but is in apparent decline. Television advertisers can run their commercials through over-the-air network scheduling, local scheduling, cable scheduling, or unwired networks. Network television advertising is dominated by large national advertisers. Television commercials can take the form of sponsorships, participations, or spot announcements.

A great number of advertisers consider television their primary medium because the medium is so pervasive. While large numbers of people spend a great number of hours viewing television, many of those viewers do other things as they watch and don't pay all that much attention when they do watch. A study of television viewing concluded that most people are not television addicts. Instead, most people seldom give their full attention to television. The television audience is measured using audimeters, diaries, and people meters. Two ratings companies dominate: A.C. Nielsen and Arbitron. Nielsen has recently begun to offer a new audience analysis called ClusterPLUS, which divides the country into 47 cluster groups based on demographic characteristics and geographic location.

Television offers advertisers cost efficiency, impact, and influence. The major advantage of television is its wide reach. It reaches mass audiences and is very cost efficient. Despite the effectiveness of television, problems do exist. They include expense, clutter, nonselective targeting, and inflexibility. The most serious limitation of television is the extremely high absolute cost of producing and running commercials.

Radio is a highly segmented medium. While virtually every household in the United States has a radio set, most of these sets are tuned into a vast array of different programs. Radio is classified as either AM, FM, cable, or digital audio broadcast (DAB), according to transmission and power. FM stations are out-performing AM stations in both listeners and revenues because of a perception that FM offers better sound quality. There are three types of radio advertising: network, spot, and local. Spot advertising dominates radio advertising.

Advertisers considering radio are most concerned with the number of people listening to a particular station at a given time. The radio audience can be measured in terms of coverage or circulation. Arbitron, RADAR (Radio's All-Dimension Audience Research), and Birch/Scarborough-VNU are the major rating services for radio. The advantages of radio include specialized target audiences, speed and flexibility, cost, mental imagery, and high levels of acceptance. The most important advantage offered by radio is that it reaches specific types of audiences by offering specialized programming. Also, radio has the shortest closing period of all media, in that copy can be submitted up to air time. Radio may be the least expensive of all media. Because costs are so low, extensive repetition is possible. This makes radio an excellent support medium. The most appropriate role for radio advertising is a support role. The disadvantages of radio are inattentiveness, lack of visuals, clutter, and scheduling and buying difficulties.

Key Terms and Concepts

affiliate
A station that is under contract with a national network to carry network-originated programming during part of its schedule.

audimeter
Also known as the Nielsen Storage Instantaneous Audimeter, can record when the television is being used and which station it is tuned to, but cannot identify who is watching the program.

barter syndication
Programs that are offered to a station at a reduced price or free of charge with presold national spots.

cable television
A form of subscription television in which the signals are carried to households by a cable.

circulation
Measures the number of homes that are actually tuned in to the particular station.

clear channel station
The most powerful stations, which may use up to 50,000 watts.

coverage
The geographical area (which includes a given number of homes) that can pick up the station clearly, whether or not they are actually tuned in.

digital audio broadcast (DAB)
Essentially perfect quality audio delivery which is available in Europe and is expected to be introduced to the United States by 1995.

first-run syndication
Network shows that did not meet the minimal number of episodes are purchased from the networks and moved into syndication even as they continue to produce new episodes.

interactive television
Viewer controlled television such as video-on-demand, pay=per=view, or the simulcast.

interconnects
Special cable technology that allows local advertisers to run their commercials in small geographical areas through the interconnection of a number of cable systems.

network
Two or more stations able to broadcast the same program which originates from a single source.

off-network syndication
Syndication which includes reruns of network shows.

participation	An arrangement in which a television advertiser buys commercial time from a network.
people meters	Provides information on what television shows are being watched, number of households that are watching, and which family members are viewing. The type of activity is recorded automatically; household members merely have to indicate their presence by pressing a button.
simulcast	Form of viewer controlled, interactive television in which digital information is transmitted along with an actual broadcast and which allows the viewer to have some control over content.
sponsorship	An arrangement in which the advertiser produces both a television program and the accompanying commercials.
spot radio advertising	A form of advertising in which an ad is placed with an individual station rather than through a network.
spot television announcement	The breaks between programs with local affiliates sell to advertisers who want to show their ads locally. Commercials of 10, 20, 30, and 60 seconds are sold on a station-by-station basis to local, regional, and national advertisers.
sweeps	Rating periods when all 214 markets are surveyed.
syndication	Television or radio shows that are reruns or original programs purchased by local stations to fill in during open hours.
television market	An unduplicated geographical area to which a county is assigned on the basis of the highest share of the viewing of television stations.
television market report	Both Nielsen and Arbitron publish their findings between four and seven times per year in this descriptive format.
waste coverage	Communication directed at an unresponsive, often uninterested audience.

True/False

Circle the appropriate letter.

T   F   1.   People meters can record when the television set is used and which station it is turned to but cannot identify who is watching the program.

T   F   2. An unduplicated geographical area to which a county is assigned on the basis of the highest share of the viewing of television stations is called a television coverage area.

T   F   3. Television's problem of too many ads in too little time leading to too much competition for viewer attention is called clutter.

T   F   4. The share ratings of the three major networks have been steadily increasing since 1987.

T   F   5. When we say, "radio is a highly segmented medium," we mean that the content and audience of a particular station reflect distinct differences in audience tastes.

T   F   6. The government assigns broadcast frequencies to ensure that station signals do not interfere with one another.

T   F   7. FM stations perform better than AM stations both in terms of revenues and audience because they have more powerful broadcast capabilities.

T   F   8. In radio advertising, extensive repetition is possible because of the extensive availability of time slots.

T   F   9. The primary method of television audience measurement used by Arbitron is the audimeter.

T   F   10. The Audimeter and diary system were replaced by Nielsen with the people meter.

T   F   11. Spot advertising dominates television scheduling.

T   F   12. Only three national over-the-air television networks are currently serving the United States.

T   F   13. Most advertisers on local television are local retailers.

T   F   14. Radio should be used as a support medium when the target audience is clearly defined and visualization of the product is not critical.

T   F   15. The growth in television syndication has been fueled by growth of independent television stations.

True/False Answers

1.	F	6.	T	11.	T
2.	F	7.	T	12.	T
3.	T	8.	T	13.	F
4.	T	9.	T	14.	T
5.	F	10.	F	15.	T

Completion

Fill in the missing word or words in the blanks provided.

1. _____ and _____ are the two primary types of syndicated programming.

2. Network advertising schedules are dominated by _____ advertisers.

3. An arrangement in which the advertiser produces both a television program and the accompanying commercials is called _____.

4. Spot buys are dominated by _____ advertising.

5. _____ and _____ are the two dominant ratings companies for television.

6. _____ is the primary method for measuring national TV audiences.

7. The quarterly measurement of TV audiences by Arbitron, during which all 214 markets are surveyed, is called _____.

8. The major advantage of television is _____.

9. The most serious limitation of TV ads is high _____.

10. _____ is the average cost for a 30-second spot in television's prime-time viewing periods.

11. _____ is the household CPM for a 30-second spot on one of the three major network evening news programs.

12. How much time per hour are television broadcasters allowed to use for advertising?

13. The three types of radio advertising are: _____, _____, and _____.

14. Of all the media, _____ has the shortest closing period.

15. _____ is sometimes referred to as the "theater of the mind."

Completion Answers

1. off-network, first run
2. national
3. sponsorship
4. local
5. A.C. Nielsen, Arbitron
6. people meters
7. sweeps
8. wide reach
9. absolute cost
10. $185,000
11. $5
12. no limit
13. spot, network, syndication
14. radio
15. radio

Matching

Match the terms and concepts with the appropriate statements. Each term or concept may be used only once; there are more terms and concepts than statements.

Terms and Concepts

a. barter
b. circulation
c. coverage
d. first-run syndication
e. inflexibility
f. influence
g. mental imagery
h. multipoint distribution system
i. off-network

j. participation
k. spot announcements
l. spot radio advertising
m. subscription television
n. vertical program
o. waste coverage
p. wide reach
q. clutter
r. mass coverage

Statements

_____ 1. Delivers limited programming without incurring the cost of cable installation. It is used by hotels and restaurants to give guests access to special movies and other entertainment.

_____ 2. Delivers limited one-channel capabilities of pay-cable-type programming transmitted to individual homes through a signal decoder.

_____ 3. Type of syndication which includes reruns of network shows such as Star Trek, The Bob Newhart Show and Remington Steele. The FCC imposes several restrictions on such shows. Most important, a network show must produce 65 episodes before it can be syndicated.

_____ 4. Type of syndication which involves network shows that did not meet the minimal number of episodes such as Too Close for Comfort, It's a Living and What's Happening! are purchased from the networks and moved into syndication even as they continue to produce new episodes.

_____ 5. When a show is offered to a station at a reduced price or free of charge with pre-sold national spots.

_____ 6. An arrangement in which a television advertiser buys commercial time from a network.

_____ 7. Breaks between programs, which local affiliates sell to advertisers who want to show their ads locally.

_____ 8. The advantage of television in which it has become a primary facet of our culture.

_____ 9. Term used to describe the problem of television in which advertisers have little assurance that targeted people are viewing the message.

_____ 10. One of the drawbacks to television involving the difficulty in making last-minute adjustments in terms of scheduling, copy, or visuals.

_____ 11. A form of advertising in which an ad is placed with an individual station rather than through a network.

_____ 12. Means that a variety of programs are offered, each appealing to a different radio audience.

_____ 13. The geographical area (which includes a given number of homes) that can pick up the station clearly, whether or not they are actually tuned.

_____ 14. The measure of the number of homes that are actually tuned in to the particular radio station.

_____ 15. The advantage of radio in which words, sound effects, music and tonality enable listeners to create their own picture of what is happening.

Matching Answers

1.	h	9.	o
2.	m	10.	e
3.	i	11.	l
4.	d	12.	n
5.	a	13.	c
6.	j	14.	b
7.	k	15.	g
8.	f		

Multiple Choice

Place the letter of the correct answer in the blank provided.

_____ 1. From 1992 to 1993, the share ratings of the three major networks:
   a. did not change.
   b. decreased.
   c. increased.

_____ 2. Which of the following is an advantage of television?
   a. wide reach
   b. cost efficiency
   c. influence
   d. impact
   e. all of the above

_____ 3. All of the following are disadvantages of television **EXCEPT**:
   a. relative cost.
   b. clutter.
   c. absolute cost.
   d. inflexibility.
   e. nonselective targeting.

_____ 4. What is the risk of having cable or telephone companies involved in the "Information Superhighway?"
   a. restrictions on the type of information available
   b. poor quality of information transmission
   c. risk of having them control the only wire coming into each home
   d. having low-income people cut off from the "Information Superhighway"
   e. all of the above

_____ 5. What determines how much money each affiliate station receives from the network for carrying network programming?
   a. the affiliate's contribution to the network's total audience
   b. a negotiated contract between the affiliate and the network
   c. the national rank of the market served by the affiliate
   d. the population of the metropolitan area served by the affiliate
   e. all of the above

_____ 6. Since the 1970s, the number of independent television stations has:
   a. not changed.
   b. decreased.
   c. increased.
   d. fluctuated up and down.
   e. none of the above

_____ 7. Network television advertising schedules are dominated by:
   a. local retail advertisers.
   b. syndicated advertisers.
   c. cooperative advertising.
   d. large national advertisers.
   e. all of the above

_____ 8. What is the biggest distinction between program sponsorship and program participation?
   a. participation is buying the program while a sponsor buys an audience
   b. program content is more important to the participant
   c. a sponsor buys the program while participation is buying an audience
   d. how the advertising is paid for
   e. none of the above

_____ 9. What type of television advertising is dominated by local advertising?
   a. network
   b. spot
   c. sponsorship
   d. participation
   e. all of the above

_____ 10. What TV audience research firm will no longer be doing television ratings?
   a. A.C. Nielsen
   b. RADAR
   c. MediaMark
   d. Arbitron
   e. none of the above

_____ 11. Advertisers use radio to:
   a. increase reach.
   b. increase frequency.
   c. improve continuity.
   d. all of the above
   e. none of the above

_____ 12. What is the primary method of radio audience measurement used by Arbitron?
   a. audimeter
   b. people meter
   c. personal interviews
   d. diaries
   e. surveys

_____ 13. What type of advertising dominates radio advertising?
   a. network
   b. spot
   c. sponsorship
   d. participation
   e. syndication

_____ 14. What research firm dominates the rating services for measuring audiences of local radio stations?
   a. A.C. Nielsen
   b. RADAR
   c. MediaMark
   d. Arbitron
   e. Birch/Scarborough-VNU

_____ 15. Which of the following is an advantage of radio as an advertising medium?
   a. low cost
   b. mental imagery
   c. flexibility
   d. high levels of acceptance
   e. all of the above

Multiple Choice Answers

1.	c	9.	b
2.	e	10.	d
3.	a	11.	b
4.	c	12.	d
5.	a	13.	b
6.	c	14.	d
7.	d	15	e
8.	c		

Career Exercise -- Career Questionnaire

Below is a sample questionnaire that you can use as a guide for preparing your own. It's not necessarily perfect, but it has a variety of items and will collect a lot of information with minimum effort on the part of the respondent. Continue to develop your own questionnaire by using the sample as a guide to the kinds of items you may want to include as well as a framework for collecting the information.

Consider the following questions as you analyze the sample questionnaire. Does the order of the questionnaire items help the respondent explain his/her background and feelings effectively? Is the best type of item selected for each type of information? For example, would it be better to use multiple choice items for the first five items? Or were the open-ended items used to save time and space? On item numbers 6, 7, and 19 which are multiple choice types, could you convert them to ranking items and get more information with just about the same amount of time and effort from the respondent? Are all of the responses for the multiple choice items mutually exclusive, especially the salary ranges in item number 17? Are there too many possible responses on any of the items?

Career Questionnaire

1. Title or position:

2. Length of time in your position:

3. How long have you been in advertising?

4. What is your educational background?

5. How many people work in advertising with your company?

6. In which areas do entry-level advertising workers need to improve?

    _____ Professional conduct
    _____ Visualization skills
    _____ Copywriting skills
    _____ Knowledge of the field
    _____ Creativity
    _____ Computer skills
    _____ Overall appearance
    _____ Other_____

7. Which of the following degrees would you prefer for an entry-level associate in advertising?

    _____ B.A. in Communication or Journalism
    _____ B.A. in Advertising
    _____ B.A. in Marketing or Business
    _____ B.S.
    _____ M.A.
    _____ Degree is not important
    _____ Other_____

8. Which of the following types of courses would you recommend for a student interested in advertising as a career:

    _____ Marketing   _____ Sociology
    _____ Psychology   _____ Accounting
    _____ Business/Management   _____ Communication/Journalism/Public Relations
    _____ Anthropology   _____ Other, such as_____

9. Indicate your opinion about this statement: "Practitioners in international advertising MUST have cross cultural experience." (circle one)

Strongly agree   Agree   No opinion   Disagree   Strongly disagree

10 What percentage of time is spent in each of the following areas of advertising:

_____ copywriting	_____ creating ad concepts
_____ strategic planning	_____ writing creative platforms
_____ ad research	_____ marketing research
_____ ad layouts	_____ media planning
_____ ad budgets	_____ coordinating ideas with clients
_____ study in advertising	_____ coordinating ad production
_____ reading current events	_____ advertising plan evaluation
_____ Other activities, such as_____	

11. Rank the following personality traits in order of importance for advertising, with 10 being the most important, 9 next in importance, etc.

_____ Reliability	_____ Sensitivity to others
_____ Enthusiasm	_____ Creativity
_____ Aggressiveness	_____ Organized
_____ Able to work independently	
_____ Other, such as_____	

12. What do you enjoy most about your job and why?

13. What do you enjoy least about your job and why?

14. The salary range usually paid to an entry-level advertising associate in your company is:

a. Less than $12,000
b. $12,000-$15,000
c. $15,001-$18,000
d. $18,001-$21,000
e. $21,001-$24,000
f. Over $24,000

15. How well prepared do you think college students are who enter advertising?

Well prepared ___ ___ ___ ___ ___ ___ ___ Unprepared

16. What is the most common way your organization comes in contact with prospective employees?
a. recommendations by colleagues
b. unsolicited resumes
c. college recruitment
d. employment placement firms
e. personal employment ads in trade publications
f. applications in response to classified employment ads
g. other _____

12 Media Buying

Chapter Objectives and Summary

- **Explain how media buying is different from media planning and how it complements media planning.**
- **Understand the major duties of a media buyer: research analyst, expert evaluator, negotiator, and troubleshooter.**
- **Explain how buyers translate media plan objectives into target-directed advertising schedules.**
- **Understand why negotiation skills more important today to advertising strategies than ever before.**

The media buyer is trying to find desired space or broadcast positions for the lowest available price so that advertisers can get the largest possible target audience for each dollar. Media planning and media buying are not mutually exclusive. Rather, these functions overlap to a certain degree. This shared responsibility between planners and buyers is just one of the features of a professional media department.

Media-buying functions include providing inside information to the media planner, selecting media vehicles, negotiating media prices, monitoring vehicle performance, and providing postcampaign analysis. An essential part of media buying is choosing the best media vehicles to fit the target audience's aperture. The media buyer performs these functions through a variety of special skills including: expert knowledge of media opportunities, knowledge of media pricing, media vehicle selection and negotiation, and maintaining media plan performance.

Media buyers develop narrow but deep expertise in one medium, media content, audience characteristics, and research evaluation. The buyer must also be aware of media innovations. A new medium must do two things: It must show how the opportunity fits in, and it must offer something that other opportunities do not. They must be familiar with media content and audience tastes. Audiences' media preferences are neither stable nor consistent. Buyers must carefully judge the accuracy and fairness of media audience research.

The buyer's media price training begins with an understanding that the advertiser and the media are adversaries when it comes to media pricing. Marketers need the lowest possible price, and the media want to charge as much as they can. Buyers know there is a very important balance to maintain between cost and value. Talented buyers will not sacrifice impact for a cheap price. Media buyers must develop skills in three cost areas, charting media cost trends, learning to use media rate cards, and balancing audience to price.

The media buyer works within the dollar allocation of the advertising budget. Allocations of dollars will determine how much money each medium will receive, how much is spent per month or per week, how many dollars each geographic area will receive, and so on. Target audience research from the media plan will often reveal a relative importance of each profile characteristic. Target audience weighting is common because many advertisers have either more than one prospect audience or one audience with several profile traits. Media buyers may disperse their messages to increase their reach. The media buyer uses timing, continuity, and gross rating point levels as measures to guide decisions.

Media buying is entering a new era of negotiation because so many media companies can offer all sorts of combinations. Negotiation considerations include vehicle performance, unit costs, and extra support offerings. The pursuit of special promotional support sometimes called "value-added services" has become a major focus for negotiation. The pressure on media buyers to gain extra leverage has grown enormously.

A media buyer's responsibility to a campaign does not end with the signing of space and time contracts. The buyer is responsible for monitoring audience research as well as fixing any schedule problems.

Key Terms and Concepts

allocations	Divisions or proportions of advertising dollars among the various media.
average cost trends	A history of changes in the average unit (per message) prices for each medium that is used in cost forecasting.
closings	Clearly set deadlines for magazines and newspapers.
CPM trend analysis	Longitudinal (long-term) history of average cost-per-thousand tendencies of advertising media that is used to assist in forecasting future CPM levels.
guarantees	Agreements in which the medium promises to compensate the advertiser should the audience fall below a specified level.
makegoods	Compensation given by the media to advertisers in the form of additional message units that are commonly used in situations involving production errors by the media and preemption of the advertiser's programming.
open pricing	Method of media pricing in which prices are negotiated on contract-by-contract basis for each unit of media space or time.
preempting	Moving advertisers out of a program in favor of another advertiser who pays a higher price.
preferred positions	Sections or pages of magazine and newspaper issues that are in high demand by advertisers because they have a special appeal to the target audience.
program preemptions	Interruptions in local or network programming caused by special events.
rate card	Published format which includes the price for each message unit (size or length), the types of incentive discounts available, and scheduling and production requirements.

rebate	Discounts received in a lump sum at the end of the schedule contract.
short rate	The difference between the discount taken and the discount earned.
value-added services	Special promotion support such as contests, special events, merchandising space at stores, etc. offered in negotiations by media to get media buyers to purchase placements.

True/False

Circle the appropriate letter.

T   F   1.   An essential part of media buying is choosing the best media vehicles to get the target audience's aperture.

T   F   2.   Local television stations either don't use a published price schedule or only provide a broad range of prices when they do because audience size and composition of the different programs change constantly.

T   F   3.   Target audience weighting is common in media buying because it simplifies media buyer's decisions.

T   F   4.   Media buying and media planning functions are completely separate functions that have nothing to do with each other.

T   F   5.   The greatest fear that media buyers have about too much emphasis on negotiating the lowest possible price is that it may diminish the effectiveness of the media campaign.

T   F   6.   A major focus in price negotiations with media in the pursuit of "more bang for the buck" in media buying has recently become the request for free time or space in return for a media purchase.

T   F   7.   The media buyer's responsibility for a media purchase ends with the signing of the space and time contracts.

T   F   8.   The cardinal rule of media buying is never buy off the rate card.

T   F   9.   Rating point levels are primarily for guidance with the budget.

T   F   10.   Media time and space charges make up the smallest portion of the advertising budget.

T   F   11.   The boundaries of media negotiations are set by the creative strategy.

T   F   12.   A major function of the media buyer is determining media objectives.

T   **F**   13. The only factor more important to the media buyer than securing the lowest possible price is fitting the target audience's aperture.

T   **F**   14. The relationship between the advertiser and the media is cooperative.

T   **F**   15. Network television has shifted to fixed pricing.

True/False Answers

1.	T	9.	T
2.	T	10.	F
3.	F	11.	F
4.	F	12.	F
5.	T	13.	T
6.	F	14.	F
7.	F	15.	F
8.	T		

Completion

Fill in the missing word or words in the blanks provided.

1. The advertising effort that takes the largest portion of the advertising budget is _____.

2. The kind of media options that have the best opportunity for aperture are: _____ media.

3. Media buyers are presented with large amounts of research and analysis on media and media audiences. _____ and _____ are the media buyer's concerns with this information.

4. The three ways that average cost trends can be compiled are: _____ , _____ , and _____.

5. In media buying, "weighting" is: setting different priorities for each _____.

6. _____ is the basis for determining the relative importance of each audience profile characteristic for the media buyer.

7. The media buyer uses _____ as a guideline to judge the effectiveness of the schedule of media insertions or broadcast positions which the buyer will purchase.

8. _____ means that reach is to have priority over frequency in a media buying policy.

9. _____ allows the media buyer to deal with the uncertainty associated with television buying decisions.

10. _____ pricing was rejected by television because it limited profit potential.

11. The two factors that must be considered and balanced in price negotiations in media buying are: _____ and _____.

12. For spot television buys, _____ and _____ allow the media buyer to check program performance.

13. For major users of billboards, the media buyer checks the billboards by _____.

14. The boundaries of media negotiation are set by the _____.

15. Suppose that consumer research done for an airline indicates that occupation is twice as important as age. When buyers assign weights to each feature, occupation figures would be multiplied by _____ and age figures are multiplied by _____.

Completion Answers

1. media time and space charges
2. fresh and interesting
3. accuracy, fairness
4. nationally for each medium, key market, particular media vehicles
5. target audience or target audience characteristic
6. target audience research
7. gross rating points
8. maximum dispersion
9. extensive research
10. fixed
11. cost, media objectives
12. Arbitron, Nielsen Station Index
13. ride through and look
14. advertising plan
15. two, one

Matching

Match the terms and concepts with the appropriate statements. Each term or concept may be used only once; there are more terms and concepts than statements.

Terms and Concepts

a. allocations
b. CPM trend analysis
c. dispersion
d. fixed pricing
e. guarantees
f. makegoods
g. open pricing
h. preempting
i. preferred positions
j. rate card
k. rebate
l. hold
m. ride the showing
n. short rate
o. weighted audience values
p. long rate
q. closed pricing
r. fold

Statements

_____ 1. A formal, published price schedule which includes the price for each message unit (size or length), the types of incentive discounts available, and scheduling and production requirements.

136

_____ 2. When the advertisers receive the discounts as a lump sum at the end of the schedule contract.

_____ 3. The difference between the discount taken and the discount earned.

_____ 4. Moving advertisers out of a program for an advertiser who pays a higher price.

_____ 5. A longitudinal (long-term) history of average cost-per-thousand tendencies of advertising media that is used to assist in forecasting future CPM levels.

_____ 6. Dividing of advertising dollars among the various media.

_____ 7. Numerical values assigned to different audience characteristics that help advertisers assign priorities when devising media plans.

_____ 8. In media buying, reserving a media vehicle purchase at a negotiated price for a given time period.

_____ 9. The use of as many different stations and programs as possible to avoid duplicating the message audience.

_____ 10. Traditional pricing where rates are published and applied equally to all advertisers.

_____ 11. A method of media pricing in which prices are negotiated on a contract-by-contract basis for each unit of media space or time.

_____ 12. Sections or pages of magazine and newspaper issues that are in high demand by advertisers because they have a special appeal to the target audience.

_____ 13. Agreements in which the medium promises to compensate the advertiser should the audience fall below a certain level.

_____ 14. Sending buyers to check the condition of the billboards is called:

_____ 15. The compensation given by the media to advertisers in the form of additional message units that are commonly used in situations involving production errors by the media and preemption of the advertiser's programming.

Matching Answers

1.	j	9.	c
2.	k	10.	d
3.	n	11.	g
4.	h	12.	i
5.	b	13.	e
6.	a	14.	m
7.	d	15.	f
8.	l		

Multiple Choice

Place the letter of the correct answer in the blank provided.

_____ 1. Where does the negotiation of media prices begin?
  a. last year's price
  b. well below the published price
  c. the price on the rate card
  d. wherever the media buyer wishes
  e. none of the above

_____ 2. Which of the following has shown the least willingness to negotiate advertising prices?
  a. television
  b. magazines
  c. radio
  d. out-of-home
  e. none of the above

_____ 3. Agreements in which the medium promises to compensate the advertiser should the audience fall below a specified level are called:
  a. guarantees.
  b. preemptions.
  c. preferred positions.
  d. rebate contracts.
  e. makegoods.

_____ 4. When dividing the media geographically, the gross impression allocation method is often used. What is the advantage of the gross impression allocation method?
  a. ensures that the dollars of the media plan budget are evenly distributed across areas
  b. provides for focusing more gross impressions where needed
  c. allows the media buyer flexibility in determining allocation of gross impressions
  d. ensures that markets with more expensive media do not get a larger share of exposures
  e. all of the above

_____ 5. What phenomenon is adding extra impetus to the demand for "value-added services" by media buyers?
  a. drive for the lowest possible price
  b. move to integrated marketing communication
  c. pressures on media buyers
  d. decreased use of fixed pricing
  e. none of the above

_____ 6. Sections or pages of magazine and newspaper issues that are in high demand by advertisers because they have a special appeal to the target audience are called:
   a. preemptions.
   b. preferred positions.
   c. makegoods.
   d. guarantees.
   e. prime positions.

_____ 7. What job is often seen as an entry-level position for becoming a media planner?
   a. media research
   b. account executive
   c. media supervisor
   d. media buyer
   e. all of the above

_____ 8. When media buyers check to see that outdoor ads run as intended, this is called:
   a. riding the showing.
   b. making good.
   c. preempting.
   d. evaluation.
   e. none of the above

_____ 9 What has caused price negotiation to become more important?
   a. rapidly increasing media prices
   b. decreasing effectiveness of advertising messages
   c. rapidly increasing costs of creating ads
   d. media shift from fixed to flexible pricing
   e. all of the above

_____ 10. What is the greatest fear that media buyers have about too much emphasis on negotiating the lowest possible price?
   a. hurt future negotiations with the medium
   b. cost them their media buyer's license
   c. diminish the effectiveness of the media campaign
   d. damage the viability of the media
   e. reduce the quality of the media vehicle eventually

_____ 11. In media buying, a rebate is:
   a. when advertisers receive discounts as a lump sum at the end of the schedule contract.
   b. the difference between the discount taken and the discount earned.
   c. compensation given in the form of additional message units.
   d. kickbacks to media buyers.
   e. all of the above

12. For what are gross rating points used in media buying?
    a. to determine what media vehicles to purchase
    b. to determine when the campaign media objectives have been met
    c. a budget guideline to develop schedules to meet reach and frequency objectives
    d. to decide what the media objectives should be
    e. to assign different priorities to different target audience segments

13. In media buying, a short rate is:
    a. when advertisers receive discounts as a lump sum at the end of the schedule contract.
    b. the difference between the discount taken and the discount earned.
    c. compensation given in the form of additional message units.
    d. kickbacks to media buyers.
    e. all of the above

14. The cardinal rule of media buying is:
    a. "always buy off the rate card."
    b. "buy off the rate card only in cities with populations under 2 million."
    c. "never buy off the rate card."
    d. "only buy off the rate card with the advertising director's approval."
    e. none of the above

15. Which of the following is a major function of the media buyer?
    a. providing inside information to the media planner
    b. negotiating media prices
    c. monitoring media vehicle performance
    d. media vehicle selection
    e. all of the above

Multiple Choice Answers

1. c	6. b	11. a
2. b	7. d	12. c
3. a	8. a	13. b
4. d	9. d	14. c
5. b	10. c	15. e

Career Exercise -- Cover Letter for Career Questionnaire

The cover letter for the career questionnaire is a key part of the data collection process. You must briefly and clearly explain why you are asking for this particular person's help, provide them with a good reason to give you their time, tell them simply and clearly how to respond, and express your appreciation. Each part of the cover letter should be deftly interwoven just as in any other professional writing. The most important point about the letter is keep it brief -- absolutely no more than one page. Be simple and straightforward. Don't try to cover your lack of preparation with a lot of puffery. Say whatever you have to say in as few words as possible, but make them count.

The first step is the answer to the question -- why me? This is what letter writers sometimes call the "referent allusion." That's fancy talk for the reason-why. The simplest explanation why you are sending them your questionnaire is that they have the information you need. In order for the professional to understand that point, you need only be able to provide them with your career objective "in 25 words or less." However, you can interweave the referent allusion with the reason they should help you. If you identify your information sources ahead of time, as you should, instead of sending the questionnaire cold to various organizations, you could call each professional ahead of time and ask permission to send them your questionnaire. (Of course, this works best if you met them previously at a professional meeting, at school, at a social function, at a convention, etc. Perhaps you're beginning to see a trend here.) Then, the referent allusion is a simple two-step execution. Refer to the telephone conversation, and remind them about your career objective that you mentioned when you called.

With the telephone contact and its mention in the letter, you have begun the second part of the letter -- explaining why the professional should spend the time completing the questionnaire. If they have already committed, you're well on your way. A key point in this part of the letter is to make it clear how much of their time that you need. If you have followed the guidance on preparing the questionnaire and kept it to a couple of pages dominated by closed-ended items, you can tell them that it will only take 5-10 minutes to complete the questionnaire. There are any number of reasons to which you might appeal additionally, but ego-stroking ranks right at the top of any list. Remind them that they represent what you aspire to be some day and that they hold a key to your future. You consider them to be good examples of what you want to be like when you grow up. In addition, if you happen to hold student membership in professional organizations in which they are also members, that also will offer them a significant rationale for helping you. When all else fails, and sometimes in addition to the others, appeal to your college activities such as work in a specific advertising class or simply your degree preparation.

Finally, you want to tell them clearly how to respond. First, you need to tell them about the self-addressed, stamped envelope that you have included with the questionnaire. Second, you need to tell them by what date you would like to have the information. Usually, ask for the response two weeks from the date of the letter. Then, all they need to do is complete the questionnaire and put it in the envelope and throw it in the mail. Of course, always close by thanking for their help. You might also consider offering to provide them with a brief summary of the results of your research.

The following is an example of a cover letter used with a career questionnaire. Use it as a starting point for your cover letter.

(Date)

Professional's Name
Mailing Address
City, State, ZIP

Dear (Last Name):

Thank you for taking the time to speak to me on the phone Monday about advertising in your organization. I realize that you are very busy and so I appreciate your willingness to help me. It was very encouraging.

I am enclosing the questionnaire that I spoke to you about. Completing the questionnaire should only take 5-10 minutes of your time. This project is a requirement for the Introduction to Advertising course that I am taking at First Class University, but it also represents a sincere interest on my part to learn about the field. I am fascinated by my studies but need some concrete data to help understand what happens in advertising in an international advertising agency.

I am including a self-addressed, stamped envelope for your convenience in responding by (month-day). Again, thank you for your assistance.
Respectfully,

Your Name

13 The Creative Side of Advertising

Chapter Objectives and Summary

- List various characteristics of creative people.
- Explain what advertisers mean by a creative concept.
- Describe the various stages involved in creating an advertisement.
- Understand how the various elements in an advertisement work together to create impact.
- Distinguish between effective copywriting and adese.

Behind every good advertisement is a creative concept, a "Big Idea" that makes the message distinctive, attention-getting, and memorable. Usually the concept is developed by a copywriter/art director team. You cannot just run the strategy statement because it is not distinctive, attention-getting, and memorable. The focus of creativity is the end result. The creative leap is what sets the advertisement apart. Advertising has to be creative, but it must also be strategic, that is, it must produce a result. Advertising is a disciplined, goal-oriented field. The goal is persuasion that results in either opinion change or sales. Ideas have to mean something important to the audience; they must have relevance. Having a likeable idea is not enough. The purpose of advertising is first and foremost to sell the product, service, or idea.

Creativity in advertising requires empathy, a keen awareness of the audience. An advertising idea is considered creative when it is novel, fresh, unexpected, and unusual. The essence of a creative idea is that no one else has thought of it before -- originality. The idea must also have impact. Most ads just wash over the audience. A commercial with impact can break through the screen of indifference and focus the audience's attention upon the message and the product. Several factors can hinder effective creativity including strategy hypnosis, bureaucracy, specialization, time clocks, and the risk-aversive nature of many large organizations.

The creative personality is one that is able to combine complex and unrelated ideas and solve problems. Characteristics associated with the creative problem-solving personality include: soaking up experiences, independence, self-assertive, self-sufficient, persistent, self-disciplined, high tolerance for ambiguity, risk taking, powerful ego, internally driven, less conventional, less interest in interpersonal relationships, skeptical, curious, watchful, observant, mentally playful, reach conclusions through intuition, abrasive, hard to deal with, withdrawn, and have good visual imagination. Creative thinking uses a psychological technique called free association. Creative people tend to be right-brain, rather than left-brain, dominant. These differences correspond roughly to divergent versus convergent thinking.

Most people who are good at thinking up new ideas will tell you that the creative process is hard work. The stages of the creative process do not occur in a systematic and orderly manner. Nonetheless, the creative process can be described meaningfully as a series of steps including at least the following: preparation, incubation, illumination, and verification. Understanding the creative process is the biggest step in learning to be more creative. Hard work is one path to becoming more creative. You must accumulate a great deal of information to produce good ideas. Another way is to develop your associative skills. The creative mind is a muscle than can be strengthened.

The creative side of a message strategy involves figuring out what to say and how to say it. This is referred to as message strategy. There are two essential approaches to message design: the hard sell is a rational, informational approach while the soft sell is an emotional approach. The hard sell is direct and emphasizes tangible product features and benefits. The soft sell is designed to touch the heart and create a response based on feelings. Most advertising messages use a combination of two basic literary techniques: lecture and drama. Both techniques are used in broadcast advertising. Print advertising makes less use of drama and more use of an anonymous voice engaged in presenting a written lecture. Lectures are still the dominant commercial message format. Advantages of lectures include less cost to produce, more compact, and efficient. Dramas have a distinct advantage because they encourage the audience to draw their own conclusions from the action of the play. In addition to the basic approaches, advertisers also use straightforward and factual messages, demonstrations, comparisons, humor, problem-solution, slice of life, and spokesperson.

Words and visuals are the key components of the advertising message. Words and visuals are both important, and the best advertising uses the two to reinforce each other. However, they do tend to do different things. Visuals are thought to be better at getting attention, communicating faster, and easier to remember. The most important functions of the visual are to capture attention and illustrate the benefit. Other functions include narration, illustration, demonstration, and symbolization. Words are best for complicated messages, high-involvement products, and intangible ideas such as quality, economy, value, and flexibility. Good advertising writing is characterized as simple, specific, concise, conversational, personal, and informal. Advertising writers avoid brag-and-boast copy and adese.

Key Terms and Concepts

adese	Formula writing that uses cliches, generalities, stock phrases, and superlatives.
art director	Person who is primarily responsible for the visual image of the advertisement.
brag-and-boast copy	Advertising that is written from the company's point of view to extol its virtues and accomplishments.
brainstorming	Creative thinking technique using free association in a group environment to stimulate inspiration.
cliche	A trite expression or an over-used idea.
convergent thinking	Thinking that uses logic to arrive at the "right" answer.
copywriter	Person who writes the text for an advertisement.
creative brief	A strategic platform that presents and explains the logic behind an ad message, the creative message, and the executional details that bring the idea to life.
creative concept	"Big Idea" that is original and dramatizes the selling point.

144

creative process	The problem-solving process through which innovative ideas emerge and which includes problem identification, preparation, incubation, illumination, and verification.
divergent thinking	Thinking that uses free association to uncover all possible alternatives.
empathy	Understanding the feelings, thoughts, and emotions of someone else.
free association	An exercise in which you describe everything that comes into your mind when you think of a word or an image.
hard sell	An approach to designing an advertising message that will touch the mind and create a response based on logic.
idea	Mental representation created by combining thoughts.
impact	The effect that a message has on the audience.
left-brain thinking	Logical thinking and controls speech and writing. This thinking is associated with people such as the accountant.
originality	No one else has thought of the idea before and which is the essence of the creative idea.
product-as-hero	Problem-solution version of the dramatic format of advertising message in which the message begins with some problem and the product is presented as the solution to that problem.
relevance	The quality of an advertising message that makes it important to the audience.
right-brain thinking	Intuitive, nonverbal and emotional thinking. This thinking is associated with people such as the artist.
slice-of-life	Advertising message format in which the problem-solution message is built around some common, everyday situation.
soft sell	Message designed to touch the heart and create a response based on feelings and attitudes.
strategy hypnosis	An extreme concentration on strategy that can stifle creative thinking.
symbolism	Words and images that represent or cue something else.

synectics	Creative thinking technique that trains people to use analogies and metaphors to approach problem-solving.
testimonial	Advertising format in which a spokesperson describes a positive personal experience with the product.
visualization	The ability to see images in the mind, to image how an ad or a concept will look when it is finished.

True/False

Circle the appropriate letter.

T   F   1.   The essence of the creative idea in advertising is relevance.

T   F   2.   Originality is that quality of an advertising message that makes it important to the audience.

T   F   3.   The primary purpose of impact in creative advertising is to break through the screen of indifference of the target audience.

T   F   4.   The secret to successful brainstorming is to defer judgment on the effectiveness of the ideas generated during brainstorming.

T   F   5.   A person can become more creative simply by working around creative people.

T   F   6.   The source of the power of drama in advertising is the audience's involvement.

T   F   7.   The key problem in using humor in advertising is that the humor may overpower the selling message.

T   F   8.   The account executive usually develops the creative concept for an advertising campaign.

T   F   9.   Right-brain thinking is logical thinking.

T   F   10. Convergent thinking uses logic to arrive at the right answer.

T   F   11. Understanding the feelings, thoughts, and emotions of someone else is called intuition.

T   F   12. Marketing myopia is an extreme concentration on strategy that can stifle creative thinking.

T   F   13. The dominant advertising format is demonstration.

T   F   14. In advertising the ability to see pictures in the mind is called imagination.

T   F   15. The key to getting an audience involved in an advertising drama is reality.

True/False Answers

1.	F	9.	F
2.	F	10.	T
3.	T	11.	F
4.	T	12.	T
5.	F	13.	F
6.	T	14.	F
7.	T	15.	T
8.	F		

Completion

Fill in the missing word or words in the blanks provided.

1. A "Big Idea" that is original and dramatizes the selling point is called _____.

2. The _____ usually develops the creative concept for an advertising campaign.

3. _____, _____, and _____ represents the characteristics of the creative idea.

4. _____ is not a characteristic of the creative personality.

5. _____ is logical thinking and controls speech and writing. This thinking is associated with people such as the accountant.

6. _____ is intuitive, nonverbal and emotional thinking. This thinking is associated with people such as the artist.

7. _____ uses logic to arrive at the "right" answer.

8. _____ uses free association to uncover all possible alternatives.

9. _____ is a creative thinking technique using free association in a group environment to stimulate inspiration.

10. _____ is an approach to designing an advertising message that will touch the mind and create a response based on logic. The approach is direct and emphasizes tangible product features and benefits.

11. A message designed to touch the heart and create a response based on feelings and attitudes is called _____.

12. _____ is the dominant advertising message format.

13. The most important functions of the visual in the advertisement are: _____ and _____.

14. The person who writes the text for an advertisement is called _____.

15. The four steps in the creative process as named in 1926 by an English sociologist are:
_____, _____, _____, and _____.

Completion Answers

1. creative concept
2. copywriter/art director team
3. impact, relevance, originality
4. logical
5. left-brain thinking
6. right-brain thinking
7. convergent thinking
8. divergent thinking
9. brainstorming
10. hard sell
11. soft sell
12. lecture
13. capture attention, illustrate the benefit
14. copywriter
15. preparation, incubation, illumination, verification

Matching

Match the terms and concepts with the appropriate statements. Each term or concept may be used only once; there are more terms and concepts than statements.

Terms and Concepts

a. adese
b. art director
c. empathy
d. free association
e. impact
f. incubation
g. problem-avoidance
h. product-as-hero
i. slice-of-life
j. straightforward factual
k. strategy hypnosis
l. synectics
m. testimonial
n. verification
o. visualization
p. invitational
q. problem-acceptance
r. contact

Statements

_____ 1. Understanding the feelings, thoughts, and emotions of someone else.

_____ 2. The effect that a message has on the audience.

_____ 3. An extreme concentration on strategy that can stifle creative thinking.

_____ 4. The ability to see images in the mind, to imagine how an ad or a concept will look when it is finished.

_____ 5. In the creative process, the stage where the creative person allows the subconscious mind to take over the problem-solving effort.

148

_____ 6. In the creative process, the stage where the creative person steps back and looks at the solution objectively and asks whether it is creative, understandable, etc.

_____ 7. A creative thinking technique that trains people to use analogies and metaphors to approach problem-solving.

_____ 8. Advertisements that are usually factual and convey information without any gimmicks or embellishments. They are rational rather than emotional.

_____ 9. A problem-solution version of the dramatic format of advertising message in which the message begins with some problem and the product is presented as the solution to that problem.

_____ 10. A problem-solution version of the dramatic format of advertising message in which the problem is avoided because of product use.

_____ 11. An advertising format in which a spokesperson describes a positive personal experience with the product.

_____ 12. An exercise in which you describe everything that comes into your mind when you think of a word or an image.

_____ 13. An advertising message format in which the problem-solution message is built around some common, everyday situation.

_____ 14. The person who is primarily responsible for the visual image of the ad.

_____ 15. Formula writing that uses cliches, generalities, stock phrases, and superlatives.

Matching Answers

1.	c	9.	h
2.	e	10.	g
3.	k	11.	m
4.	o	12.	d
5.	f	13.	i
6.	n	14.	b
7.	l	15.	a
8.	j		

Multiple Choice

Place the letter of the correct answer in the blank provided.

_____ 1. What is the first and primary purpose of advertising?
   a. to be creative
   b. to deliver the message to the right audience
   c. to get a response from the target audience
   d. to sell the product or service
   e. to entertain the target audience

_____ 2. The creative concept of an advertising campaign:
   a. dramatizes the selling point.
   b. is the big idea that drives the campaign.
   c. makes the message distinctive, attention-getting, and memorable.
   d. is the springboard for the execution of the advertisement.
   e. all of the above

_____ 3. In advertising creativity ROI refers to:
   a. relevance, originality, and impact.
   b. research, originality, and ideas.
   c. resonance, opportunity, and influence.
   d. reality, opinion, and ideas
   e. relevance, opportunity, and influence.

_____ 4. The form taken by the finished advertisement is called the:
   a. creative concept.
   b. execution.
   c. message.
   d. tactic.
   e. big idea.

_____ 5. In terms of the risk involved in creating advertising ideas, what must the nature of the relationship be between the advertising agency and the client?
   a. the client should encourage the agency to take risks
   b. the agency should encourage the client to take risks
   c. the agency and client should share the risk
   d. the agency and the client must avoid taking risks
   e. all of the above

_____ 6. Advertising work done for free or for a very small fee for nonprofit groups and firms too small to have much of an advertising budget is called:
   a. charity advertising.
   b. public service advertising.
   c. social responsibility advertising.
   d. pro bono advertising.
   e. free advertising.

_____7. In the communication process, what is the most important component?
  a. source
  b. message
  c. channel
  d. receiver
  e. none of the above

_____8. Creative people tend to be:
  a. right-brain dominant.
  b. left-brain dominant.
  c. both right- and left-brain dominant.
  d. neither right- nor left-brain dominant.
  e. none of the above

_____9. Which of the following represents the two basic literary techniques used in advertisements?
  a. hard sell and soft sell
  b. slice-of life and demonstration
  c. lecture and drama
  d. humor and emotion
  e. discussion and lecture

_____10. The two basic sales approaches used in advertising are:
  a. adese and brag-and-boast.
  b. reason-why and problem-solution.
  c. lecture and drama.
  d. comparison and demonstration.
  e. hard sell and soft sell.

_____11. Which of the following is a common advertising format?
  a. demonstration
  b. slice of life
  c. spokesperson
  d. problem-solution
  e. all of the above

_____12. Which of the following is **NOT** an advantage of words in an advertisement?
  a. delivering complicated messages
  b. for high involvement products
  c. for technical explanations
  d. communicate faster
  e. for well-considered purchase decisions

_____13. Which of the following is **NOT** an advantage of visuals in an advertisement?
  a. communicate faster
  b. easier to remember
  c. for undifferentiated products with low-inherent interest
  d. for high involvement products
  e. getting attention

_____14. How does the advertising creative team decide whether to emphasize words or pictures?
   a. words are always the focus because they carry the selling message
   b. consider the strategy for the advertisement
   c. visuals are always the focus because they work more efficiently
   d. consider the cost of the advertisement
   e. determine the relative strengths of the creative team

_____15. Which of the following is a characteristic of effective advertising writing?
   a. personal
   b. conversational
   c. informal
   d. concise
   e. all of the above

Multiple Choice Answers

1.	d	9.	c
2.	e	10.	e
3.	a	11.	e
4.	b	12.	d
5.	c	13.	d
6.	d	14.	b
7.	d	15.	e
8.	a		

Career Exercise -- Career Media Plan

As in any media planning process, the point is to get the message to the target audience at the time and place the message has the greatest probability of influencing the target audience. Your problem is to identify media and media vehicles that can contribute to your communication objectives.

The first point to remember is the nature of the marketing communication in career planning. Advertising under most circumstances won't be much of a factor. Most career planning communication will concentrate on public relations and personal selling with sales promotion playing a minor role just like advertising. Highly specialized media have become the core of career communications. Nonetheless, you will have to make the usual decisions about selecting media, considering timing, and analyzing cost.

The traditional media in career planning are direct response, personal, and special media. In direct response, job seekers have used direct mail campaigns for years to contact prospects. Personal letters and telephone calls have been traditional methods for contacting career target audiences. Professional organizations and their meetings and conventions are also very productive channels for making contacts. Special media vehicles developed for career planning include the resume, the portfolio, and the business card. In your career media planning, you need to be both creative and very careful in your use of these media. You need to do research on the particular career area you are targeting to ensure that your use of these media vehicles finds a receptive audience.

Your career research must provide you with a detailed target audience description so that you can locate your target audience in the media that you will use. For example, a very ordinary situation is where to sit at a professional meeting. To have the maximum chance to reach your target audience, you must be able to identify by name and position the people you need to meet.

In career media planning, it is very easy to handicap your effort through inappropriate use of the special career media. For example, it may seem sensible to take resumes to a professional meeting and pass them out directly to the professionals there. However, you may find that the professionals do not appreciate the intrusion. While they are willing to talk and answer questions, even exchange business cards, they may think that it would be more professional for you to send them a copy of your resume at their place of business. What makes career media planning so interesting is the fact that not every professional will view this situation the same. Some respond to the sheer aggressiveness of the new professional pushing for a contact. You simply have to find ways to understand the position of your target audience on such issues.

While continuity, reach, and efficiency cannot be measured in the same manner as in a mass media campaign plan, you still must consider the issues. Under what circumstances would reach be a major consideration in career planning? How many times must a contact be exposed to a career message to make an impression? Why do most pre-professionals use a form of pulsing in their career plans? How could a flighting strategy be employed in career media planning?

Begin preparing a career media plan by considering how you will use the media available to you; how you will use the special vehicles available such as the resume, the portfolio, interviews, business cards, etc.; and what kind of continuity schedule would be most appropriate for your plan.

14 Creating Print Advertising

Chapter Objectives and Summary

- **Distinguish between the key features of newspaper and magazine advertising.**
- **List the various elements of a print ad and their function.**
- **Understand the process by which print ads are created.**
- **Distinguish between letterpress, offset, gravure, and silk-screen printing.**

Local newspapers are unusual in that most people see newspaper advertising as a form of information. In fact, newspaper advertising is one of the few forms of advertising that is not considered intrusive. The advertisements don't have to compete as entertainment. Newspaper reproduction has traditionally been rather low-quality printing. Newspapers are printed at high speed on an inexpensive, rough-surfaced, spongy paper, called newsprint that absorbs ink on contact. Photographs, delicate typefaces, and color all reproduce poorly in the newspaper. Modern high-tech publications led by *USA Today*, which has pioneered much better quality reproduction for daily newspapers, are working to change the perception of newspaper production. Many newspapers are upgrading their production technology to catch up with *USA Today*.

Magazine advertising that ties in closely with the magazine's special audience interest may be valued as much as the articles. Magazine ads are often more informative and carry longer copy than do newspaper ads. Magazines have traditionally led the way in graphic improvements. The paper is usually better; it is normally slick, coated and heavier. Excellent photographic reproduction is a big difference between advertising in newspapers and magazines.

When writing copy for print ads, there are two categories of copy: display and body copy, or text. Display copy includes all text in larger type size that is designed to get attention and to stop the viewer's scanning. Body copy is the text of the advertising message. Most experts agree that in print advertising the headline is the most important display element. The headline is the most important element because most people who are scanning read nothing more. Researchers estimate that only 20 percent of those who read the headline go on to read the body copy. A headline must select the right prospect, stop the reader, identify the product and brand, start the sale, and lure the reader on into the body copy. They select the audience with a strong benefit, promise, or reason why. They identify the product category, and they link the brand with the benefit. Direct headlines are highly targeted. An assertion is used to state a claim or a promise. Indirect headlines are not as selective and may not provide as much information, but they may be better at luring the reader into the message. They are provocative and intriguing and compel people to read on to find out the point of the message, and they use curiosity and ambiguity to get attention and build interest. Subheads, captions, slogans, and taglines are other important display elements.

The body copy develops the sales message and provides support, states the proof, and gives the explanation. Straightforward, narrative, and dialogue are different types of body copy. Pictures and words must work together to create impact and meaning. Write to a particular person. Write the way people talk. Rewrite it until it sounds like something you would say. Thoughts are usually best expressed in short, succinct expression. Use the present tense, active voice, and simple sentence constructions. Short paragraphs are easier to read and less intimidating. Avoid using the corporate. Avoid using a pedantic, preaching, or negative tone of voice.

The art director takes the creative concept that has been developed by the copywriter and visualizes how the final ad will look. The layout is a plan that imposes order and at the same time creates an arrangement that is aesthetically pleasing for an ad. A layout is a map, the art director's equivalent of a blueprint. It serves as a guide for the production people who will eventually handle the typesetting, finished art, photography, and pasteup. In some cases the layout acts as a guide for the copywriter who writes copy to fit the space. The layout is also used for cost estimating. The most common ad layout format is one with a single dominant visual that occupies about 60 to 70 percent of the area. Underneath the dominant visual is a headline and a copy block. The logo or signature finishes the message at the bottom. The thumbnail, rough layout, semicomp, and comprehensive are types of layout.

The functional side of a layout makes the message easy to perceive; the aesthetic side makes it attractive and pleasing to the eye. The last stage in the production process is the development of mechanicals, also called keylines. The key aspects of layout are organization, visual path or direction, dominant element, unity, white space, contrast, balance, proportion, and simplicity.

Color is used in advertising to attract attention, provide realism, establish moods, and build brand identity. Research has consistently shown that ads with color get more attention than ads without color. Art refers to the graphics, whether an illustration or a photograph.

Print production largely involves creating words or art. The words will either take the form of hand-drawn letters, handwriting, or typesetting. Good typesetting doesn't call attention to itself because its primary role is functional--to convey the words of the message. The basic objective of type selection is legibility -- to convey the words as clearly as possible. Factors that influence typeface selection include categories of type, family variations, size, and alignment. There are two general types of images that have to be reproduced in print: line art and continuous tone images. Continuous tone images must be converted to patterns of dots to create the illusion of shades of gray through what is called the halftone process. The quality of the image depends on the screen used. The other major problem in print production is color reproduction. The problem of producing the full range of colored hues is solved through a series of halftone images using four distinct shades of ink called process colors. The process used to reduce the original color image to four halftone negatives is called color separation. The primary printing processes used are letterpress, offset lithography, gravure, flexography, and silk screen.

Key Terms and Concepts

art	Visual elements in art advertising, including illustrations, photos, type, logos and signatures, and the layout.
balance	State of visual equilibrium.
bleed	Advertisement in which the printed area runs to the trim edge of the page.
body copy	The text of the message.
captions	Short descriptions of the content of a photograph or an illustration.

color separation	Process of printing a color image in four images recorded on negatives with each negative representing one of the four process colors.
composition	Process of arranging the elements in a photograph or an illustration.
comprehensive	Layout that looks as much like the final printed advertisement as possible.
copy	Written elements in an advertisement, including headlines, underlines and overlines, subheads, body copy, captions, slogans, and taglines.
digitized	Art that has been broken into tiny grids, each one coded electronically for tone or color.
direct headline	Straightforward and informative headlines.
display copy	Type set in larger sizes that is used to attract the reader's attention.
focal point	First element in a layout that the eye sees.
font	Complete set of letters in one size and face.
formal balance	Symmetrical, left to right. Everything is centered.
free-lance artist	Independent artists who work on individual assignments for an agency or advertiser.
gravure	Type of printing that uses an image that is engraved, or recessed, into the surface of the printing plate.
greeking	Nonsense type often used in the preparation of print advertisements.
Gutenberg diagonal	Visual path that flows from the upper left corner to the lower right.
halftones	Image made up of a pattern of dots so that it gives the illusion of a continuous range of shades from light to dark.
headline	Title of an ad; it is set in large type to get the reader's attention.
in register	A precise matching of colors and images within an advertisement.

indirect headline	Provocative and intriguing, they compel people to read on to find out the point of the message.
informal balance	Asymmetrical and creates a more visually exciting or dynamic layout.
italic	Type variation that uses letters that slant to the right.
layout	Drawing that shows where all the elements in the advertisement are to be positioned.
legibility	Conveys words as clearly as possible.
letterpress	Type of printing that prints from an image onto a raised surface.
line art	Art in which all elements are solid with no intermediate shades or tones.
mechanical	Finished pasteup with every element perfectly positioned that is photographed to make printing plates for offset printing.
newsprint	An inexpensive but tough paper with a rough surface, used for printing newspapers.
offset	Type of printing that prints from a flat surface on the printing plate. The image is transferred to a rubber blanket that carries the impression to the paper.
optical center	Point slightly above the mathematical center of a page.
pica	Unit of type measurement used to measure width and depth of columns.
points	Used to measure the height of type; there are 72 points in an inch.
process colors	Four basic inks--magenta, cyan, yellow, and black--are mixed to produce the full range of colors found in four-color printing.
proportion	Aesthetic and mathematical principle that concentrates on the relative sizes of the elements.
reverse type	Typesetting in which letters appear to be white against a darker background.
rough	Layouts done to size but not with any great attention to how they look.

sans serif	Typeface that does not have the finishing stroke on the main strokes of the letters.
semicomp	Layout drawn to exact size that depicts the art and display type; body copy is simply ruled in.
serif	Typeface with a finishing stroke on the main strokes of the letters.
silk screen	Form of printing where the non-image areas, represented by a "block-out" film or lacquer, are adhered to a porous fabric, while ink is forced through the image areas that aren't blocked out.
subheads	Sectional headlines used to break up masses of type.
surprinting	Printing type over some other image.
tagline	Memorable phrase that sums up the concept or key point of the ad.
thumbnail	Small preliminary sketch of various layout ideas.
tip-ins	Preprinted advertisements that are provided by the advertiser to be glued into the binding of a magazine.
visual path	Direction in which the reader's eye moves while scanning a layout.

True/False

Circle the appropriate letter.

T   F   1.   The main strength of the indirect headline in print advertising is its ability to lure the reader into the body copy.

T   F   2.   Research in direct mail has shown that changing the headline while keeping other elements constant can double or even quadruple consumer response to print advertising.

T   F   3.   The most common layout format for print advertising is a copy-dominated advertisement where the headline is treated as type art.

T   F   4.   Developing the comprehensive is the final stage of the production process for print advertising.

T   F   5.   A visual path that flows from the upper left corner to the lower right is called the focal path.

T   F   6.   In a layout the first element that the eye sees is called the center of attention.

T   F   7.   The key elements of a print ad are the copy and the art.

T   F   8.   Newspapers are usually more tightly targeted than magazines to readers' special interests.

T   F   9.   The layout should help the reader process the information in the ad.

T   F   10. To reproduce color natural color is photographically separated into three negatives that can be reproduced in three colors of ink.

T   F   11. Advertising is news.

T   F   12. Tell only enough in the headline to lure the reader into the copy.

T   F   13. The illustration catches their eye, but the headline wins their heart.

T   F   14. Long copy should be avoided at all times.

T   F   15. The best use of white space is to use it to unify and frame the elements.

True/False Answers

1.	T	9.	T
2.	T	10.	F
3.	F	11.	T
4.	F	12.	F
5.	F	13.	F
6.	F	14.	F
7.	T	15.	T
8.	F		

Completion

Fill in the missing word or words in the blanks provided.

1.   The written elements in an advertisement, including headlines, underlines and overlines, subheads, body copy, captions, slogans, and taglines are called _____.

2.   The visual elements in art advertising, including illustrations, photos, type, logos and signatures, and the layout are called _____.

3.   _____ is the biggest difference between magazines and newspapers in terms of production quality.

4. _____ is the most important display element in a print advertisement.

5. Type set in larger sizes that is used to attract the reader's attention is called _____.

6. The first element in a layout that the eye sees is called _____.

7. _____ makes one element stand out because it is different.

8. An advertisement that is not in a state of visual equilibrium, or _____, seems to be heavier on one side than the other.

9. A point slightly above the mathematical center of a page is called _____.

10. The color that has the most attention-getting power is _____.

11. A complete set of letters in one size and face is called _____.

12. A typeface with a finishing stroke on the main strokes of the letters is called _____.

13. A typeface that does not have the finishing stroke on the main strokes of the letters is called _____.

14. When the four basic inks--magenta, cyan, yellow, and black--are mixed to produce the full range of colors found in four-color printing, this is called _____.

15. The process of printing a color image in four images recorded on negatives with each negative representing one of the four process colors is called _____.

Completion Answers

1. copy
2. art
3. paper quality
4. headline
5. display copy
6. focal point
7. contrast
8. balance
9. optical center
10. yellow
11. font
12. serif
13. sans serif
14. process colors
15. color separation

160

Matching

Match the terms and concepts with the appropriate statements. Each term or concept may be used only once; there are more terms and concepts than statements.

Terms and Concepts

a. direct
b. formal balance
c. halftone
d. headline
e. in-register
f. indirect
g. line art
h. mechanics
i. offset

j. organization
k. proportion
l. roughs
m subheads
n. tagline
o. underline
p. thumbnail
q. semicomp
r. consistency

Statements

_____ 1. A precise matching of colors and images within an advertisement.

_____ 2. The title of an ad; it is set in large type to get the reader's attention.

_____ 3. Straightforward and informative headlines.

_____ 4. Headlines that are not as selective and often do not provide as much information but may be better at luring the reader into the message and are provocative and intriguing.

_____ 5. A subhead that leads from the headline into the body copy.

_____ 6. Sectional headlines used to break up masses of type.

_____ 7. A memorable phrase that sums up the concept or key point of the ad.

_____ 8. A finished pasteup with every element perfectly positioned that is photographed to make printing plates for offset printing.

_____ 9. Layouts done to size but not with any great attention to how they look.

_____ 10. In advertising design, the pattern of the placement of the elements in a layout.

_____ 11. An aesthetic and mathematical principle that concentrates on the relative sizes of the elements.

_____ 12. A type of printing that prints from a flat surface on the printing plate and the image is transferred to a rubber blanket that carries the impression to the paper.

_____ 13. Layout in which everything is centered and symmetrical, left to right.

_____ 14. Art in which all elements are solid with no intermediate shades or tones.

_____ 15. Image made up of a pattern of dots giving the illusion of shades of gray.

Matching Answers

1.	e	9.	l
2.	d	10.	j
3.	a	11.	k
4.	f	12.	i
5.	o	13.	b
6.	m	14.	g
7.	n	15.	c
8.	h		

Multiple Choice

Place the letter of the correct answer in the blank provided.

_____ 1. What percentage of the readers who read the headline do not read the copy?
   a. 20%
   b. 33%
   c. 50%
   d. 80%
   e. 100%

_____ 2. Which of the following is **NOT** a function of the headline?
   a. stop the reader
   b. start the sale
   c. lure reader into copy
   d. select the right prospect
   e. draw attention to the main illustration

_____ 3. Which of the following is a strength of the direct headline in print advertising?
   a. state a claim or promise
   b. select the audience
   c. identify product category
   d. link the brand with a benefit
   e. all of the above

_____ 4. According to research, in what order do readers tend to scan advertisements?
   a. headline, illustration, copy, logo
   b. illustration, headline, copy, logo
   c. copy, illustration, headline, logo
   d. logo, illustration, headline, copy
   e. illustration, logo, headline, copy

_____ 5. How do most readers of newspapers see advertising?
   a. as a nuisance
   b. as a necessary evil
   c. as useful information just like news
   d. as having no real value
   e. all of the above

_____ 6. Where is the usual starting point for print advertisements?
   a. lower right hand corner
   b. lower left hand corner
   c. center
   d. upper right hand corner
   e. upper left hand corner

_____ 7. Which of the following reduces the legibility of the copy?
   a. reverse copy
   b. copy set in all capital letters
   c. unusual typefaces
   d. surprinting copy over a photo
   e. all of the above

_____ 8. All of the following are considered art **EXCEPT**:
   a. type.
   b. layout.
   c. headline.
   d. illustration.
   e. photograph.

_____ 9. All of the following are considered copy **EXCEPT**:
   a. subhead.
   b. headline.
   c. text.
   d. tag line.
   e. type.

_____ 10. All of the following are stages in developing the layout **EXCEPT**:
   a. thumbnail.
   b. rough.
   c. tagline.
   d. comprehensive.
   e. semicomp.

_____ 11. The effort to convey words as clearly as possible in type is called:
   a. legibility.
   b. clarity.
   c. greeking.
   d. readability.
   e. none of the above

_____ 12. Which of the following is **NOT** a purpose of using color in an advertisement?
   a. provide realism
   b. select the right prospect
   c. establish mood
   d. attract attention
   e. build brand identity

_____ 13. Which of the following is the most commonly used printing process for newspapers and magazines?
   a. letterpress
   b. gravure
   c. silk screen
   d. offset lithography
   e. flexography

_____ 14. What new technology has generated a revolution in print advertising reproduction?
   a. satellite communications
   b. modems
   c. inkjet printing
   d. computerized typesetting
   e. fax machines

_____ 15. A unit of type measurement used to measure the height of type (there are 72 in an inch) is called:
   a. pica.
   b. serif.
   c. milline.
   d. point.
   e. em.

Multiple Choice Answers

1. d	6. d	11. a
2. e	7. e	12. b
3. e	8. c	13. a
4. a	9. e	14. d
5. c	10. c	15. d

Career Exercise -- Internships

The most consistent fact in career planning is that everyone agrees that the internship is the most important factor in finding and securing that first job. Practically every survey of professionals on the subject of finding a first job pinpoints the internship. The significance of the internship, however, goes well beyond its role in landing the first job. The internship is critical in helping you find out about the career area that you are targeting, the people in the area, the skills required, the fit between you and the career, etc. The internship is also important in developing references and identifying entry-level jobs available in the field. The internship is not only your best source of information about the field, it is the best source of information about you for the people in the field.

Because of the importance of the internship in your development, you should not view it just as the final step of your academic career. Instead of thinking in terms one final internship in your senior year, try thinking in terms of a series of mini-internships that lead to one key internship that leads to the first full-time job in the field. In this way the internship becomes a means of preparatory training and fact-finding that help you finalize your decision about the job you want after you graduate. This is the hands-on part of your development from student to professional.

Internships can be found and/or developed everywhere from the university campus to the local media to local businesses to national firms. You start your search with your academic advisor. Your next stop should be the career placement and counseling office on campus. Don't restrict your inquiry to "internships" because many opportunities will pose as part-time jobs. The idea is to work in a real job in a real environment where you can acquire the necessary skills, develop the necessary personal qualities, find out about the nature of the work in the field, and get to know people in the field.

When internships or part-time jobs are not available in the field in which you are interested, create your own. Contact members of the local advertising professional organizations, or if that avenue is not available, contact local advertising businesses or local media. Even on campus, you will be surprised at the number of opportunities available to acquire and hone skills. Most campuses produce phone books, registration schedules, athletic schedules, and special publications such as magazines and programs that will contain advertising and must be produced through normal graphic production processes.

15 Creating Broadcast Advertising

Chapter Objectives and Summary

- Understand the roles of the various people associated with television commercials, including the producer, director, and editor.
- List the various stages in the production of a television commercial.
- Identify the critical elements in radio and television commercials.
- Read and understand a radio script and a television script.
- Compare and contrast radio ads and television commercials.

Television commercials are characterized in two ways: they can achieve high audience acceptance if the commercials are well done but they are also considered to be intrusive. Most people give television more attention than they do radio. Television is a visual medium, and the message is dominated by the impact of visual effects. Good television advertising uses the impact of action and motion to attract attention and sustain interest. Most of the programming on television is storytelling Effective television advertisements also use storytelling both for entertainment value and to make a point. More than any other advertising medium, television has the ability to touch emotions to make people feel things. If you have a strong sales message that lends itself to demonstration, then television is the ideal medium for that message. One of the strengths of television is its ability to reinforce verbal messages with visuals or visual message with verbal.

Various elements work together to create the visual impact of television. A television commercial is the most complex of all advertising forms. The key elements of the television commercial are the video, audio, talent, props (the most important prop is the product), setting, lighting, graphics, and pacing. Today about 90 percent of television commercials are shot on 16mm or 35mm film. In planning a television commercial there are many considerations. The most common length for a commercial on broadcast television is 30 seconds. The storyboard is the visual plan, the layout, of the commercial. It uses selected frames to communicate how the story line will develop. It depicts the composition of the shots as well as the progression of action and the interaction of the audio with the video. A television script is a detailed document that includes everything depicted on the storyboard plus all the descriptions necessary to assist the director or producer in find the location or building the set. The key members of the commercial production team are the producer, the director, the music composer, the music arranger, and the editor. The stages of the commercial production are preproduction, the shoot, and postproduction.

Radio is a theater of the mind in which the story is created in the imagination of the listener. Radio is the most intimate of all media. Successful radio writers and producers have excellent visualization skills and a great theatrical sense. The primary challenge for radio advertisers is to break through the various distractions and get the audience to focus attention on the message.

The radio message is ephemeral. A radio message cannot be reread, The key to success is to evoke visual images. It is important to capitalize on intimacy and the listener's imagination. Radio copywriters write in a conversational style using vernacular language. Word choice should reflect the speech of the target audience. Radio uses three primary tools to develop message: voice, music, and sound effects. Radio commercials are written for a limited time frame. The common lengths are 10, 20, 30, and 60 seconds. Radio commercials are produced in one of two ways: taped and duplicated for distribution or recorded live. The more common form is the taped radio commercial. National radio commercials are produced by an advertising agency and duplicate copies of the tape are distributed to local stations around the country.

The future of broadcasting has a number of interesting trends. Two trends concern television messages: length of ads and zapproofing ads. There are two observable trends in the length of television messages. Network commercials are getting shorter, with 15-second spots becoming more and more common. In alternative media such as cable, videocassettes, and movie theaters, advertising messages are getting longer -- often lasting 2 to 5 minutes. A new term, infomercials, has been introduced to refer to even longer commercials -- some lasting 30 to 60 minutes -- that provide extensive product information. Zapproofing is a concern for creating ads that can deter viewers from using remote controls to avoid commercials. Other trends include computer image manipulation and the development of interactive, viewer controlled media.

Key Terms and Concepts

animatic	Preliminary version of a commercial with the storyboard frames recorded on videotape along with a rough sound track.
animation	Type of recording medium in which objects are sketched and then filmed one frame at a time.
answer print	Final finished version of the commercial with the audio and video recorded together.
arranger	Person who orchestrates the music, arranging it for the various instruments, voices, and scenes.
claymotion	Technique that uses figures sculpted from clay and filmed one frame at a time.
composer	Person who writes the music.
crawl	Computer-generated letters that move across the bottom of the screen.
cut	Abrupt transition from one shot to another in the editing process.
director	Person in charge of the actual filming or taping of the commercial.
dubbing	Process of making duplicate copies of a videotape.
editor	Person who assembles the best shots to create scenes and who synchronizes the audio track with the images.
embed	Placing the television commercial within the regular television programming.

infomercial	Longer commercials--some lasting 30 to 60 minutes--that provide extensive product information.
interlock	Version of the commercial with the audio and video timed together, although the two are still recorded separately.
key frame	Single frame of a commercial that summarizes the heart of the message.
mixing	Combining different tracks of music, voices, and sound effects to create the final ad.
pacing	How fast or slow the action progresses. Some messages are best developed at a languid pace; others work better done upbeat and fast.
photoboard	Type of rough commercial similar to an animatic except that the frames are actual photos instead of sketches.
piggybacking	A strategy where an advertiser buys a 30-second spot and splits it in half for two related products in the line creating two interdependent messages.
producer	Person in charge of all the arrangements for a commercial, including settings, casting, arranging for the music, and handling bids and budgets.
production notes	Describe in detail every aspect of the production. They are important for finding talent and locations, building sets, and getting bids and estimates from the specialists. They are the starting point of the commercial.
release print	Duplicate copies of a commercial that are ready for distribution.
rough cut	Preliminary rough edited version of the commercial.
rushes	Rough versions of the commercial assembled from unedited footage.
set	Constructed setting where the action in a commercial takes place.
stock footage	Previously recorded image, either video, still slides, or moving film, that is used for scenes that aren't accessible to normal shooting.
stop motion	Technique in which inanimate objects are filmed one frame at a time, creating the illusion of movement.

ryboard	Series of frames sketched to illustrate how the story line will develop.
chronize	Matching the audio to the video in a commercial.
nt	People who appear in television commercials.
nacular	Language that reflects the speech patterns of a particular group of people.
ce-over	Technique used in commercials in which an off-camera announcer talks about the on-camera scene.

ue/False

cle the appropriate letter.

F   1.   The script for radio advertising is formatted with two columns with the sound source on the right and the actual content is on the left.

F   2.   Radio advertising is the most complex type of advertising to make.

F   3.   The copywriter writes the actual script, whether it involves dialogue, narrative, lyrics, announcement, or descriptive copy.

F   4.   The 60-second television commercial has become so rare because of the desire for more repetition in media plans.

F   5.   Network television commercials are getting shorter with 15-second spots becoming more common.

F   6.   The effort to "zapproof" television commercials has led to more informative commercials.

F   7.   Demonstrations are persuasive on television because we believe what we see.

F   8.   The script for television advertising is formatted with two columns with the video on the right and the audio on the left.

F   9.   Television uses motion and action to create impact.

F   10. Television is the best medium for demonstration.

F   11. The most common length for a broadcast television commercial is 15 seconds.

F   12. The successful television commercial should capture the viewer's interest within the first 15 seconds.

T   **F**   13. Television commercials lasting 30 or 60 minutes that provide product information are called infomercials.

T   **F**   14. The key frame of a television commercial is the one moment in the commercial that tells the whole story.

T   **F**   15. The most important prop in a television commercial is the product.

True/False Answers

1.	F	9.	T
2.	F	10.	T
3.	T	11.	F
4.	F	12.	F
5.	T	13.	T
6.	F	14.	T
7.	T	15.	T
8.	F		

Completion

Fill in the missing word or words in the blanks provided.

1. The media that is the most personal is _____.

2. _____, _____, and _____ are the primary tools used to develop radio advertising messages.

3. _____ is the most important element in developing radio advertising messages.

4. The _____ time frame for a spot is very common in radio but has almost disappeared in television.

5. The person in charge of all the arrangements for a commercial, including settings, casting, arranging for the music, and handling bids and budgets is called the _____.

6. _____ is the best medium for demonstration.

7. Elements that work together to create the visual impact of the television ad are: _____ talent, _____, video, _____, pacing, _____, and _____.

8. The _____ is the most important prop in a television commercial.

9. Most television commercials today are shot by _____.

10. The most common length for a broadcast television commercial is _____.

1. A single frame of a commercial that summarizes the heart of the message is called
   _____.

2. A series of frames sketched to illustrate how the story line will develop is called _____.

3. The _____ develops the storyboard and establishes the "look" of the commercial, whether realistic, stylized, or fancified.

4. Rough versions of the commercial assembled from unedited footage are called _____.

5. The written form of radio or television commercials is called _____.

Completion Answers

.	radio	9.	film
.	sound effects, voice, music	10.	30 sec
.	voice	11.	key frame
.	60 sec	12.	storyboard
.	producer	13.	art director
.	television	14.	rushes
.	graphics, audio, setting, props, lighting	15.	scripts
.	product		

Matching

Match the terms and concepts with the appropriate statements. Each term or concept may be used only once; there are more terms and concepts than statements.

Terms and Concepts

.	animatic	j.	photoboard
.	animation	k.	piggybacking
	answer print	l.	preproduction
.	cut	m.	release prints
	director	n.	rough cut
	editor	o.	synchronizing
.	infomercials	p.	digitizing
.	interlock	q.	crop
	mixing	r.	script writer

Statements

_____ 1. Combining different tracks of music, voices, and sound effects to create the final ad.

_____ 2. A type of recording medium in which objects are sketched and then filmed one frame at a time.

_____ 3. The technique in which an advertiser buys a 30-second spot and splits it in half for two interdependent messages for two related products in a line.

_____ 4. A preliminary version of a commercial with the storyboard frames recorded on videotape along with a rough sound track.

_____ 5. A type of rough commercial, similar to an animatic except that the frames are actual photos instead of sketches.

_____ 6. The person in charge of the actual filming or taping of the commercial.

_____ 7. The person who assembles the best shots to create scenes and who synchronizes the audio track with images for a commercial.

_____ 8. The matching of the audio to the video in a commercial.

_____ 9. A preliminary rough edited version of the commercial.

_____ 10. A version of the commercial with the audio and video timed together, although the two are still recorded separately.

_____ 11. The final finished version of the commercial with the audio and video recorded together.

_____ 12. Duplicate copies of a commercial that are ready for distribution.

_____ 13. Commercials lasting 30 or 60 minutes that provide extensive product information.

_____ 14. The arrangements that have to made before a commercial can be filmed or taped, such as finding a location, making arrangements with police and other officials to use the site, etc.

_____ 15. An abrupt transition from one shot to another in the editing process.

Matching Answers

1. i   9. n
2. b   10. h
3. k   11. c
4. a   12. m
5. j   13. g
6. e   14. l
7. f   15. d
8. o

Multiple Choice

Place the letter of the correct answer in the blank provided.

_____ 1. Which of the following is a strength of radio advertising?
   a. demonstration
   b. prestige
   c. image advertising
   d. reminder messages
   e. all of the above

_____ 2. Which of the following is a common message strategy in television commercials?
   a. use of emotion
   b. demonstration
   c. storytelling
   d. combining action and motion
   e. all of the above

_____ 3. Which of the following is a strength of television advertising?
   a. intimacy
   b. production costs
   c. reminder messages
   d. demonstration
   e. all of the above

_____ 4. All of the following are usually members of the team responsible for producing a television commercial **EXCEPT**:
   a. account executive.
   b. composer.
   c. editor.
   d. producer.
   e. director.

_____ 5. Which of the following is a key decision involved in planning and producing a television commercial?
   a. key frame
   b. number of scenes
   c. length
   d. whether to use local production
   e. all of the above

_____ 6. How many scenes will a 30-second television commercial usually have?
   a. 1-2
   b. 3
   c. 4-6
   d. 7-9
   e. 10-12

_____ 7. What are the points-of-view possible for a television commercial?
   a. eye-level and bird's eye
   b. subjective and objective
   c. personal and unusual
   d. omniscient and omnipotent
   e. observer and viewer

_____ 8. Why is radio such a difficult environment for which to write?
   a. the need to integrate copy with music
   b. having to write for the human voice
   c. lack of attentiveness of the listener
   d. writer must create visual images without visuals
   e. impersonal nature of radio

_____ 9. Which of the following kinds of messages should radio copywriters avoid?
   a. very short ones
   b. humor
   c. complicated ones
   d. ones with long lists of copy points
   e. all of the above

10. Which of the following kinds of techniques/message strategies should radio copywriters use?
    a. messages that are national in orientation, that cut across geographic locales
    b. live commercials, especially in client presentations
    c. sound effects
    d. shorter commercials
    e. all of the above

11. Which of the following styles of language is preferred for radio commercials?
    a. polished prose
    b. formal
    c. vernacular
    d. grammatically sound
    e. all of the above

12. In a 30-second commercial, how often should the name of the product be mentioned?
    a. 1
    b. 2
    c. 3
    d. 4
    e. 5

13. Which of the following represents the correct percentage of television commercials shot on film?
    a. 10%
    b. 25%
    c. 40%
    d. 70%
    e. 90%

14. Which of the following is **NOT** a standard time frame for radio commercials?
    a. 10 secs
    b. 15 secs
    c. 20 secs
    d. 30 secs
    e. 60 secs

15. A storyboard is:
    a. a series of frames sketched to illustrate how the story line will develop in a commercial.
    b. a preliminary version of a commercial with a series of sketched frames recorded on videotape along with a rough sound track.
    c. a final finished version of a commercial with the audio and video recorded together.
    d. a rough, animated version of a commercial with rough audio and video recorded together.
    e. type of rough commercial in which the frames are actual photos.

Multiple Choice Answers

1.	d	9.	e
2.	e	10.	c
3.	d	11.	c
4.	a	12.	c
5.	e	13.	e
6.	c	14.	b
7.	b	15.	a
8.	d		

Career Exercise -- Resume

Below is a sample resume that you can use as a reference point for developing your own. An example of a pre-professional resume follows. How should a pre-professional resume look compared to a professional resume? What about the two would be the same? What about the two would be different? What strengths and weaknesses do you find in the pre-professional resume? How does it satisfy the layout principles (organization, direction, unity, contrast, balance, proportion, and simplicity) suggested in Chapter 14? Is the design simple? Could the design be simplified? Are the resume points made in a graphically clear manner? The entire resume is set in Times. Do you think that is a professional choice? Would it improve the resume in your opinion if the name and personal information headline and the division subheads were set in another typeface? Does the design of the resume contribute to or hurt the clarity of the information in the resume? Is the resume effectively organized?

Does the content of the resume effectively sell the individual? Should the career objective be included? Is the career objective specific enough? Do the descriptions of the individual's experience leave the reader with the impression that the individual is accomplishment-oriented? Do the descriptions of the individual's experience emphasize what was done in the job or what was accomplished? Should the skills list be included? Should the references about high school and junior college have been included? Should the grade point average be included?

Use the resume example as a starting point for your own resume. Keep in mind that there is only one basis for answering any of the questions raised here. Decisions about the resume should be based on the attitudes of the target audience -- the professionals in the career field that you are targeting. It does not matter what you think, what your professor thinks, what some resume book thinks, or anyone else. You must make a judgment about what will make the best impression on the target audience. You usually find this out by asking them or at least using the information collected when someone else asked them.

Name
Address
City, State ZIP
Phone

Career Objective

Desire opportunity to use skills obtained in college and from job experience to be successful in a position in Public Relations; such skills as public speaking and business writing

Experience

1988 - 1991   *Merchandising Supervisor, Six Flags Over Texas, Arlington, TX.*
Responsible for managing four gift shops with combined cash flows of over $45,000 monthly. Increased profits of two stores by 47% while cutting labor and budget costs by over 31%. Also responsible for creating a quality circle program for employees which has been implemented by the Six Flags Corporation. Programs which fall under my supervision are: Activities, Grievance Committee, Newspaper and Publications, and The Bridge Chemical Dependency Program.

1987 - 1988   *Customer Service Manager, Walmart, Grand Prairie, TX.*
Operated layaway computers, recorded layaway transactions. Trained associates on cash registers and layaway computers, handled money for service desk and cash registers, supervised cashiers.

1986 - 1987   *Office Manager, The Tanning Place, Avon, CN.*

Extracurricular Activities

Big Brothers/Big Sisters Association   Activities director for 1 year in Lubbock.
Parks Home for Retired Individuals   Extensive volunteer work with senior citizens.
Ad-3, University of Texas at Arlington   Treasurer.

Skills and Strengths

Creative, organized and able to follow through on commitments; clerical (including computer); verbal and written; cross cultural experience; good interpersonal skills; work independently, as part of a team, and under pressure; high level of integrity; enthusiastic.

Education

1981-1985   *Monsignor Nolan High School*
1985-1991   *University of Texas at Arlington*
Currently enrolled at the University of Texas at Arlington, working towards a Bachelor of Arts degree in Advertising. Senior status. GPA. 4.0.

16   Creating Direct-Response Advertising

<u>Chapter Objectives and Summary</u>

- **Define direct-response advertising.**
- **Distinguish between direct-response advertising, direct-marketing, and mail order.**
- **Evaluate the various media that direct-response advertising can utilize.**
- **Explain how today's technology has transformed the nature of direct-response.**

Marketing communication is changing from a one-way monologue and increasingly is becoming a one-on-one dialogue using computers, the mail, video, and the touch-tone telephone. New technologies based on computers and databases of information are creating the ultimate in "tight" targeting because the information allows advertisers really to understand consumers and zero in on primary prospects. Where traditional advertising has targeted groups of people, database advertising targets the individual. Direct marketing is interactive in nature and has five components: interactive system, a mechanism for consumer response, exchange not bound to retail store, measurable response, and a database of consumer information. Direct marketing offers the consumer convenience, efficiency, and compression of decision-making time. There are three basic categories of direct marketing: the one-step process, the two-step process, and the negative option.

Direct-response advertising uses databases both to reach consumers and to collect information about them. Direct-response advertising is growing because of social and technological reasons. The increase of women in the workforce and the rise of single-parent homes are two societal factors. The technology that has had the biggest impact is the computer. Technological advances have made direct-response more efficient and more beneficial for consumers. Direct-response uses media to contact a prospect directly and elicit a response without the intervention of a retailer or personal sales. Direct-response advertising is a type of marketing communication that accomplishes an action-oriented objective as a result of the advertising message. The focus of the objectives contrasts with brand or image advertising where the response to the advertising message is typically awareness, a favorable attitude, or a change of opinion. Direct-response advertising is the ultimate form of integrated marketing communication.

The key players involved in direct-response marketing are advertisers, agencies, and consumers. The key to the success of direct-response marketing is managing the database. Designing the direct-marketing message has five key elements: the offer, the medium, the message, timing and sequencing, and customer service. Direct response is a multimedia field. All conventional advertising mass media can be used. Telemarketing (use of the telephone) is the growth area in direct response.

Direct mail provides the historical foundation for the direct-response industry. Direct mail continues to be the main medium of direct-response messages. Direct mail demonstrates more than any other medium how a message can sell a product without the help of a salesperson. The response rates of direct mail are generally higher than those of any other medium used in direct marketing. Because a single mailing package must in one fell swoop do the work of many hundreds of people in a more conventional selling program, the direct response message is more involved and usually longer than in other media. The functions of a direct-mail message are to get the attention of the targeted prospect, create a need for the product, show what it looks like, demonstrate how it is used, answer questions, reassure the buyer, provide critical information about product use, inspire confidence, minimize risk, establish that the company is reputable, make the sale, tell how to buy, tell how to order, tell where to call, tell how to pay or charge the purchase, and offer an incentive to encourage a fast response. The main elements of the direct mail process are the outer envelope, a letter, a brochure, supplemental flyers or folders, and a reply card with a return envelope. The key to the success of direct mail is the mailing list.

A catalog is a multipage direct-mail publication that lists a variety of merchandise. The growth in the catalog field is in the area of specialty catalogs. Catalogs also are becoming available in videocassette and computer disk formats. Catalog, as with all direct-mail advertising, can only be as effective as the mailing list that targets the appropriate customers. The mailing list is really a segmentation tool. There are three types of lists: house lists, response lists, and compiled lists. The most important part of the catalog message is the graphics.

Direct-response ads in the mass media are less directly targeted than are direct mail or catalogs. They can still provide the opportunity for a direct response. Television has become a major medium for direct marketers who are advertising a broadly targeted product and who have the budget to afford the ever increasing costs of television advertising. Cable television lends itself to direct-response commercials because the medium is more tightly targeted to particular interests. Radio has not been a dynamic medium for direct-response advertising. Radio's big advantage is its targeted audience.

More direct-marketing dollars are spent on telephone ads using telemarketing than on any other medium currently. Telemarketing is almost as persuasive, but a lot less expensive, as personal selling. Telemarketing is four to five times as expensive as direct mail. Telemarketing's primary advantage is that it is personal. Two technological changes have spurred the use of telemarketing. The first is the wide area telephone service (WATS line). The other innovation is the incoming WATS line, the 800 number or toll-free number. Most companies that use telemarketing hire a specialized company to handle the solicitations and order taking. The most important thing to remember about telemarketing solicitations is that the message has to be simple enough to be delivered over the telephone. The message also needs to be compelling, provide a strong initial benefit, and be short.

Key Terms and Concepts

broadsheets	Large brochures that unfold like a map.
compiled list	List rented from a broker who represents a company that has a house list for sale or who works for a direct mail company that builds lists.
database	Lists of consumers with information that helps target and segment people who are highly likely to be in the market for a certain product.
direct mail	Advertising medium that uses the postal service to deliver the message.
direct-order/mail-order marketing	Form of marketing using mail or some other personal delivery system to deliver the product.

179

direct-response advertising	Type of marketing communication that achieves action-oriented objective as a result of the advertising message.
direct-response marketing	Type of marketing that uses media to contact a prospect directly and elicit a response without the intervention of a retailer or personal sales.
house list	Customer lists kept by firm, store or association.
list broker	Handle a variety of lists from many different sources and can act as a consultant to help find a list or compile one from several different sources.
list manager	People who work for companies that offer lists of group memberships for purchase.
merging	Process of combining two or more lists.
negative option	Type of direct marketing in which the consumer joins a plan, such as a video or book club, that automatically sends the product unless the consumer mails a response card by a specific date..
one-step process	Type of direct marketing in which the consumer may respond to an ad and receive the product by mail.
purging	Process of deleting repeated names when two or more lists are combined.
response list	Derived from people who respond to something such as a solicitation from group with members similar to the advertiser's target audience.
teaser	Statement or question that might be used to spark curiosity about the product.
response list	Derived from people who respond to something such as a solicitation from a group whose members are similar to the advertiser's target audience.
two-step process	Type of direct marketing in which the consumer must be qualified before ordering the product.
WATS (wide area telephone service)	System for mass telephone calls at discount rates.

True/False

Circle the appropriate letter.

T   F   1.   In direct-response advertising high cost is not as much of a problem as it once was because the personal contact of direct-response advertising makes it worth the cost.

T   F   2.   "Tight targeting" allows the direct marketer to personalize the message more than in any other form of advertising.

T   F   3.   Most direct mail letters are long -- usually 2-4 pages and many even longer -- because people seem to prefer long letters.

T   F   4.   The merge/purge capability of computer-generated mailing lists helps the direct marketer avoid name repetition.

T   F   5.   Computer disk catalogs are the growth area in the catalog business.

T   F   6.   Research on direct mail advertising has found that people with any interest in the product will read an entire letter even if it is long.

T   F   7.   Personal telephone sales calls are very expensive but very persuasive.

T   F   8.   Most people will stay on the telephone longer than 10 to 15 minutes for a sales call.

T   F   9.   Direct-response advertising is one of the fastest-growing segments of the advertising industry.

T   F   10.   Direct-response advertising is different from other types of advertising because it seeks an action-oriented objective such as an inquiry.

T   F   11.   The primary target in database marketing is the individual.

T   F   12.   Past criticisms of direct-response advertising have focused on effectiveness and efficiency.

T   F   13.   Direct mail is the historical foundation of the direct-response industry.

T   F   14.   Direct mail advertising can only be as effective as the mailing list.

T   F   15.   Sales in the direct response field are increasing faster than sales for retail stores.

True/False Answers

1.	F	6.	T	11.	T
2.	T	7.	F	12.	F
3.	F	8.	F	13.	T
4.	T	9.	T	14.	T
5.	F	10.	T	15.	T

Completion

Fill in the missing word or words in the blanks provided.

1. Past criticisms of direct-response advertising have focused on _____ and _____.

2. _____ is where direct-order marketing focuses the attention to the marketer.

3. The _____ has had the biggest impact on direct marketing.

4. _____ is the most important characteristic of direct-response advertising.

5. In _____ advertising the message is most personalized.

6. _____ advertising has the highest cost-per-thousand of any form of advertising.

7. _____ is the form of direct marketing that generally has the highest response rates of any other medium used in direct marketing.

8. The critical decision whether or not to read direct mail pieces is made on the basis of the _____.

9. _____ is the biggest problem with computer-generated mailing lists.

10. Direct mail advertising can only be as effective as the _____.

11. _____, _____, and _____ are the three types of lists available for direct mail advertising.

12. _____ is the most important part of a catalog message.

13. The most important characteristic of the telemarketing message is _____.

14. The direct marketing industry estimates that _____ of the direct mail pieces get read.

15. More direct-marketing dollars are spent on the _____ than any other.

Completion Answers

1. efficiency, cost
2. distribution
3. computer
4. tight targeting
5. direct response
6. direct response
7. direct mail
8. envelope
9. accuracy
10. mailing list
11. house lists, response lists, compiled lists
12. graphics
13. simplicity
14. 3/4
15. telephone

Matching

Match the terms and concepts with the appropriate statements. Each term or concept may be used only once; there are more terms and concepts than statements.

Terms and Concepts

a. bind-ins
b. broadsheets
c. compiled lists
d. database marketing
e. database
f. direct order marketing
g. direct response advertising
h. house lists
i. list brokers
j. list managers
k. merging
l. purging
m. response lists
n. WATS
o. teaser
p. overlapping
q. catalog
r. prospect lists

Statements

_____ 1. Lists of consumers with information that helps target and segment people who are highly likely to be in the market for a certain product.

_____ 2. A special form of direct response marketing that uses databases to collect information on consumers who are highly likely to buy a certain product.

_____ 3. A type of marketing communication that accomplishes the action-oriented objective (such as an inquiry, visiting a showroom, answering a questionnaire, or purchasing a product) as a result of the advertising message and without the intervention of a sales representative or retailer.

_____ 4. A form of marketing that uses mail or some other personal delivery system such as fax, to deliver the product.

_____ 5. The process of combining two or more lists of prospects.

_____ 6. The process of deleting repeated names when two or more lists are combined.

_____ 7. People who work for companies that offer lists of group memberships for purchase.

_____ 8. People who handle a variety of lists from many different sources and can act as a consultant to help find a list or compile one from several different sources.

_____ 9. Lists of customers maintained by a company, store or association.

_____ 10. Type of list derived from people who respond to something such as a direct mail offer or solicitation from a group whose members are similar to the advertiser's target audience.

_____ 11. Type of list that is rented from a direct mail list broker who represents a company that has a house list for sale or who works for a direct mail company that is in the business of building lists.

_____ 12. Cards that are stapled or glued right into the binding of the magazine adjoining the advertisement.

_____ 13. System of mass telephone calling at discount rates.

_____ 14. Large brochures that unfold like a map.

_____ 15. A statement or question used to spark curiosity in a direct mailing.

Matching Answers

1.	e	9.	h
2.	d	10.	m
3.	g	11.	c
4.	f	12.	a
5.	k	13.	n
6.	l	14.	b
7.	j	15.	o
8.	i		

Multiple Choice

Place the letter of the correct answer in the blank provided.

_____ 1. In what way has the nature of marketing communication changed recently for advertisers?
   a. increasingly a one-way monologue with consumers talking to advertisers
   b. increasingly a two-way interaction between consumers and advertisers
   c. increasingly a one-way monologue with advertisers talking to consumers
   d. increasingly a two-way interaction between consumers and computers
   e. has not changed much

_____2. Which of the following is **NOT** a reason for the growth of direct-response advertising?
   a. the number of women in the work force
   b. the credit card
   c. the computer
   d. the general popularity of direct-response advertising
   e. the number of single-parent homes

_____3. Which of the following is **NOT** a use for computers in direct marketing?
   a. consumers use computers to find ads in which they are interested
   b. advertisers use computers to sort prospects by characteristics
   c. advertisers use computers to manage lists of names
   d. advertisers use computerized shopping carts to show store maps and advertising specials
   e. consumers use personal computers to shop

_____4. Traditional advertising targets _____ while database advertising targets _____ .
   a. the individual . . . groups
   b. groups . . . retailers
   c. individuals . . . retailers
   d. groups . . . the individual
   e. consumers . . . retailers

_____5. What is the biggest direct-response area?
   a. radio
   b. the computer
   c. telemarketing
   d. direct mail
   e. television

_____6. What is the most important thing to remember about telemarketing solicitations?
   a. keep it simple
   b. demonstrate the product
   c. don't be afraid of complicated messages
   d. people will stay on the phone longer than most marketers think
   e. none of the above

_____7. Which of the following is **NOT** a function of the direct mail message?
   a. make the sale
   b. explain how to order
   c. get the attention of the target
   d. demonstrate the product
   e. provide a means for feedback

_____8. Direct marketing always involves what kind of relationship with the prospect?
   a. impersonal
   b. hostile
   c. one-on-one
   d. adversarial
   e. complementary

_____9. What is the key to the use of any medium for direct-response advertising?
   a. data base
   b. response device
   c. electronic transmission
   d. list
   e. all of the above

_____10. Which of the following is a problem with print media as direct response advertising media?
   a. permanence
   b. flexibility
   c. less targeted
   d. complex message
   e. coupons

_____11. Which of the following is an advantage to the consumer of direct marketing?
   a. compression of decision-making time
   b. efficiency
   c. convenience
   d. all of the above
   e. none of the above

_____12. Which of the following is NOT an important characteristic of direct-response advertising?
   a. interactive
   b. action objectives
   c. uses target audiences
   d. measurability
   e. less waste circulation

_____13. Which of the following is one of the types of lists available for direct mail advertising?
   a. compiled lists
   b. house lists
   c. response lists
   d. all of the above
   e. none of the above

_____14. According to a 1991 study, what percentage of the public consider direct mail to be an invasion of privacy?
   a. 10%
   b. 25%
   c. 50%
   d. 75%

_____15. What potential legal problem is increasingly a concern with the growth of direct marketing?
   a. privacy issues connected to information in data bases
   b. unauthorized purchases
   c. failure to deliver merchandise
   d. harassment involved in intrusive direct-marketing programs
   e. theft of computerized information

Multiple Choice Answers

1.	b	9.	b
2.	c	10.	c
3.	a	11.	d
4.	d	12.	c
5.	c	13.	d
6.	a	14.	b
7.	e	15.	a
8.	c		

Career Exercise -- Resume Graphics

The major considerations in the design of the resume are simplicity, clarity, and organization. Simplicity in the resume involves a number of different elements of the resume. First, most professionals will tell you they would prefer to see a resume that is limited to one page, especially for the pre-professional and beginning professional. This limitation does not mean that you must figure out how to cram everything you want to say into one page. Rather, you should simplify. Find a way to find the key information and to tell enough in one page to capture the attention of the target and to generate enough interest to make the target seek more information. Second, keep the visual look of the resume simple and professional. A common violation of this principle is in the selection of type. Choose a readable, professional font and stick to it. Never use more than two fonts -- one for text and one for display type. Always use a serif font, such as Times, Palatino, Optima, etc., for the copy of the resume. If you need type variations for emphasis, use style variations such as italic, boldface, all caps, underline, etc.

Hopefully, simplicity helps move us toward clarity in the resume. Starting with paper selection, everything about the design of the resume should help make your points clear. Choose a white, bond paper or at least a neutral paper such as a cream, light sepia, smoke, etc. You want the information to jump off the page with a sharp contrast between the type and the background. Also, use white space effectively in the design in order to isolate important elements for the reader. Make sure that the reader can find key points and make sure that like information appears to go together and unlike information is clearly separated.

In addition, the organization of the resume should be simple and clear. First, start the resume with your strongest selling point. Don't bury your best quality in some textbook or other formula about how to design a resume. Use clear, obvious divisions that expose the reader effectively to the qualities that will elicit interest. The divisions of experience, education, activities/organizations, awards/honors, and special skills are obvious and best. Keep it simple is always the best policy.

Extraordinary design is almost always an apparent admission of insufficiency of experience or skill, even if in fact this is not true.

A final consideration is the production of the resume. Today, it is pointless not to use the computer to write and produce the resume. At least the computer should be used for word-processing and basic design. Many professionals recommend that the resume must be typeset in order to achieve the appearance required to make the best impression. However, other professionals who have used computer production through desktop publishing software and laser printing argue that there is no appreciable difference between typesetting and laser printing, if the laser printing is done well and uses the proper fonts. In order to achieve anything close to a typeset quality with laser printing, you must use a laser font. Experience has shown, for example, that text set in Times 10 point type on Microsoft Word® on a Macintosh SE computer on an Apple LaserWriter IINTX laser printer is virtually indistinguishable from typeset text.

More is involved than just appearance though. The process involved with typesetting also destroys flexibility. Using computer design and laser printing allows fast changes to the content of the resume that can be very useful in tailoring the resume to different jobs. For example, the career objective needs to be very specific -- almost written specifically for a particular job in order to be persuasive. Computer design and laser printing allow this kind of honing of the career message.

17   Creating Directory and Out-of-home Advertising

<u>Chapter Objectives and Summary</u>

- **Understand how consumers use the Yellow Pages to search for information about stores, products, and services.**
- **Describe the characteristics of a well-written and well-designed Yellow Pages ad.**
- **Understand the effect of a moving audience on the design of a billboard.**
- **Explain the difference between interior and exterior transit advertisements.**
- **Identify innovative media to use to deliver sales, reminder, and action messages.**

Yellow Pages advertising is directional advertising because it tells people where to go to get the product or service. It reaches prospects -- people who already know they have a need for the product or service. Directory advertising is the only form of advertising that is actively consulted by prospects who need or want to buy something. Yellow Pages advertising is the most widely used form of directory advertising. It is the most universal of advertising medium. For some small businesses, the Yellow Pages ad is their only source of advertising. More than 88 percent of Yellow Pages advertising is generated from local businesses. Yellow Pages advertising is consulted by consumers who are interested in buying something. A Yellow Pages ad is the last step in the search for a product or service by a committed consumer. The Yellow Pages are used primarily for comparison shopping.

Although the advertisement doesn't have to attract the attention of an indifferent audience, it does have to stand out in a competitive environment. The decision about which store to call or visit will be based on certain criteria, the size of the ad being the first. Larger ads get more attention than small ones. Other decision factors include convenience, range of products or services, and the reputation or image of the store. The most important feature of Yellow Pages advertising is the category system. Certain information is critical to Yellow Pages ads including location, hours of operation, and telephone number. The key design elements of the Yellow Pages ad are size, image, and graphics. A recent development in directory advertising is the electronic Yellow Pages, a database accessed by computer.

Out-of-home advertising is a large, prevalent segment of the advertising industry. Out-of-home includes outdoor, transit, painted walls, taxi signs, airport/bus terminal displays, blimps, and much more. The main types of out-of-home media are billboards, transit, and movie advertising. Billboards take two forms: posters and painted bulletins. A poster is a large placard or sign that is posted in a public place to announce or publicize something. Painted bulletins are prepared by artists working for the local outdoor advertising company. They are hand-painted either on location or in the shop on removable panels that can be hoisted up and attached to the billboard frame. The primary objectives of outdoor advertising are awareness, announcement, and reminder. Detailed explanations are not possible, and there is no time for elaborate copy points. Impact billboard advertising is big, colorful and hard to ignore. Billboard advertising delivers messages to moving audiences using "quick impact" techniques such as strong graphics and short, catchy phrases. Effective billboard advertising is built on a strong creative concept that can be easily understood. The most important message characteristic is brevity. The best copy for billboard advertising is a short, catchy phrase. Because billboards must make a quick and lasting impression, design is critical to effectiveness. The most important feature of billboard design is high visibility.

Transit advertising is primarily an urban advertising form that uses vehicles to carry the message to people. Transit advertising is reminder advertising. It provides a high-frequency medium that lets advertisers get their name in front of a local audience. There are two types of transit advertising: interior and exterior. Interior advertising can be studied; exterior advertising must be seen at a glance. Transit messages can be targeted to specific audiences if the vehicles follow a regular course.

Theater advertising called trailers are similar to television commercials but are usually longer and better produced. The important audience factor is the attention and concentration generated by the theater environment. Theater advertising is the most compelling form of advertising because of the larger-than-life images on the big screen. However, some people resent the compelling nature of the message. The critical feature of theater advertising is that it must function as entertainment. People in theaters have a low tolerance for hard sell messages.

Key Terms and Concepts

car card	Small advertisements that are mounted in racks inside a vehicle.
cutout	Irregularly shaped extensions added to the top or side of standard outdoor boards.
directional advertising	Directs the buyer to the store where the product or service is available.
exterior transit advertising	Advertising posters that are mounted on the sides, rear, and top of vehicles.
holography	Technique that produces a projected three-dimensional image.
indicia	Postage label printed by a postage meter.
interior transit advertising	Advertising on posters that are mounted inside vehicles such as buses, subway cars, and taxis.
kinetic board	Outdoor advertising that uses moving elements.
kiosk	Multisided bulletin board structures designed for public posting of messages
painted bulletin	Hand-painted by artists either on location or in the shop on removable panels that can be hoisted up and attached to the billboard frame.
poster	Large placard or sign that is posted in a public place to announce or publicize something.
spectacular	Billboards with unusual lighting effects.

trailer   Advertisements that precede the feature film in a movie theater.

True/False

Circle the appropriate letter.

T   F   1.   The key characteristic of directional advertising is that it reaches prospects who already know they need the product.

T   F   2.   The breakup of AT&T caused a boom in the Yellow Pages advertising business.

T   F   3.   Sixty percent of the Yellow Pages advertising is generated from local businesses.

T   F   4.   For maps to be used efficiently in Yellow Pages ads, they need to be simple.

T   F   5.   The most recent innovation in directory advertising is the electronic Yellow Pages.

T   F   6.   The regional Bell companies have not become involved in the electronic directory/Yellow Pages publishing business because their participation is prohibited by U.S. government.

T   F   7.   The key to the location of an outdoor advertising poster is what the people who see the poster are doing when they see it.

T   F   8.   A design for a typical newspaper or magazine advertisement does transfer well to a billboard because the design would be too complicated.

T   F   9.   The category system is the most important feature of Yellow Pages advertising.

T   F   10.   Yellow Pages is the most universal advertising medium.

T   F   11.   Impact is the main purpose of transit advertising.

T   F   12.   It is more difficult to perceive the message being carried by exterior transit advertising than billboards because the vehicle carrying the message, as well as the reader, may be in motion.

T   F   13.   According to a Gallup survey, the primary use for the Yellow Pages is comparison shopping.

T   F   14.   The primary difference between a poster and a painted bulletin is that the poster is prepared by a printer and the painted bulletin is hand painted.

T   F   15.   As used by the outdoor advertising industry, a gross rating point is 10 percent of the total population exposed to the message one time.

True/False Answers

1.	T	9.	T
2.	F	10.	T
3.	F	11.	F
4.	T	12.	T
5.	T	13.	T
6.	T	14.	T
7.	F	15.	F
8.	F		

Completion

Fill in the missing word or words in the blanks provided.

1. Yellow pages advertising is _____ advertising.

2. _____ is the primary use for the Yellow Pages, according to a Gallup survey.

3. When people use the Yellow Pages, the first criteria in the decision about which store to call or visit is _____.

4. _____, telephone number and _____ represents the critical pieces of information that must be included in Yellow Pages advertisement.

5. According to the text, _____, _____, and _____ are the key design elements of Yellow Pages advertisements.

6. The image of a store is communicated to a customer in the design of a Yellow Pages advertisement by use of type, _____, headline, and _____.

7. The type of illustration that works best in Yellow Pages advertisements is _____.

8. The primary objectives of outdoor advertising messages are: _____, _____, and _____.

9. _____, _____, and _____ are the main formats of outdoor advertising.

10. _____ is the key element to most posters.

11. What major advertising medium has the lowest cost-per-thousand?

12. The most important characteristic in outdoor advertisement copywriting is _____.

13. _____ is the most important feature of billboard design.

14. In media strategy, _____ is the primary value of transit advertising.

15. _____ is the critical factor of theater advertising.

Completion Answers

1. directional
2. comparison shopping
3. size of the advertisement
4. location, hours of operation
5. image, graphics, size
6. layout, illustration
7. line drawings
8. announcement reminder, awareness
9. billboards, posters, printed bulletins
10. dominant visual
11. outdoor
12. brevity
13. visibility
14. high frequency
15. entertainment

Matching

Match the terms and concepts with the appropriate statements. Each term or concept may be used only once; there are more terms and concepts than statements.

Terms and Concepts

a. 10 ft. x 22 ft.
b. 30-sheet
c. billboards
d. directional
e. exterior transit advertising
f. holography
g. interior transit advertising
h. kinetic board
i. kiosk
j. painted bulletins
k. poster
l. posters
m. spectaculars
n. trailers
o. transit advertising
p. 8 ft. x 20 ft.
q. 20-sheet
r. 40-sheet

Statements

_____ 1. Advertising that directs the buyer to the store where the product or service is available.

_____ 2. Type of advertising that has been called the oldest form of advertising.

_____ 3. A large placard or sign that is posted in a public place to announce or publicize something.

_____ 4. The standard size for an outdoor advertising poster.

_____ 5. The size of a standard outdoor advertising poster.

_____ 6. A multisided bulletin board structure designed for public posting of messages.

_____ 7. Large structures erected on highways and roads for the display of huge advertising posters.

_____ 8. Advertising structures that are hand-painted by artists either on location or in the shop on removable panels that can be hoisted up and attached to a frame.

_____ 9. Billboards with unusual lighting effects.

_____ 10. A lighting technique that produces a projected three-dimensional image.

_____ 11. An outdoor advertising that uses moving elements.

_____ 12. Advertising posters that are mounted on the sides, rear, and top of vehicles.

_____ 13. Advertisements on posters that are mounted inside vehicles such as buses, subway cars, and taxis.

_____ 14. Advertisements that precede the feature film in a movie theater.

_____ 15. Urban advertising form that uses vehicles to carry the message.

Matching Answers

1.	d	9.	m
2.	l	10.	f
3.	k	11.	h
4.	b	12.	e
5.	a	13.	g
6.	i	14.	n
7.	c	15.	o
8.	j		

Multiple Choice Answers

Place the letter of the correct answer in the blank provided.

_____ 1. What is the only source of advertising for some small businesses?
  a. newspaper
  b. Yellow Pages
  c. direct mail
  d. radio
  e. sign

_____ 2. What is the most compelling type of advertising?
  a. outdoor
  b. Yellow Pages
  c. theater
  d. transit
  e. billboards

_____ 3. Which of the following is a reason consumers use the Yellow Pages?
   a. to locate the closest business
   b. for comparison shopping
   c. for local maps
   d. to check hours of operation
   e. all of the above

_____ 4. Which of the following is a key design element for a Yellow Pages ad?
   a. graphics
   b. size
   c. image
   d. all of the above
   e. none of the above

_____ 5. What should be the focus of the message of a poster?
   a. the visual
   b. copy
   c. headline
   d. lighting
   e. all of the above

_____ 6. Which of the following is an example of an innovative medium?
   a. blimps
   b. grocery carts
   c. telephones
   d. garbage cans
   e. all of the above

_____ 7. Directional advertising is:
   a. advertising that embraces all advertising that is displayed outside the home.
   b. advertising that directs buyer to store where product or service is available.
   c. advertisements that proceed the feature film in a movie theater.
   d. advertising that achieves an action-oriented objective.
   e. none of the above

_____ 8. What are the two basic categories of the audience for Yellow Pages advertising?
   a. current and former customers
   b. comparison shoppers and transient shoppers
   c. cash and credit card customers
   d. those who know the product and those looking for what the product offers
   e. frequent and infrequent customers

_____ 9. What is the key to searching for something in the Yellow Pages?
   a. headings
   b. visuals
   c. color
   d. layout
   e. all of the above

_____ 10. Which of the following is **NOT** an advantage of outdoor advertising?
   a. cost
   b. availability
   c. long message life
   d. reminder
   e. trigger impulse

_____ 11. What has slowed the expected conversion of directories from print to electronic?
   a. high costs associated with electronic publishing
   b. lack of interest shown by users
   c. decreases in printing costs
   d. recent innovations in print directory formats
   e. all of the above

_____ 12. Which of the following is a characteristic of outdoor copywriting?
   a. no more than 6 to 7 words
   b. short words
   c. short phrases
   d. no wasted words
   e. all of the above

_____ 13. Which of the following is a characteristic of outdoor layout?
   a. simple visual path
   b. integrated headline and art
   c. catchy headline
   d. strong graphic
   e. all of the above

_____ 14. If three posters in a community of 500,000 achieve a daily exposure of 250,000, how many GRPs have been achieved?
   a. 20
   b. 200
   c. 50
   d. 500
   e. 12.5

_____ 15. What is the method used in the outdoor advertising industry to measure frequency of exposure to outdoor advertising?
   a. travel diaries
   b. traffic analysis
   c. traffic observation
   d. map recall
   e. all of the above

1.	b	6.	e	11.	c
2.	c	7.	b	12.	e
3.	e	8.	d	13.	e
4.	d	9.	a	14.	c
5.	a	10.	b	15.	d

Career Exercise -- Resume Content

Resume content should be a direct outgrowth of the creative platform. The message delivered to the target audience through the resume should be the culmination of your career research. The resume needs to talk to the target audience about the things that these people want to hear and in ways they want to hear it -- just as they told you in response to such vehicles as the career questionnaire. At the core should be the inherent concepts of achievement and professionalism.

Keep in mind that the person who reviews your resume may be looking at anything from several to hundreds of resumes for a given job. Your resume must be brief, readable, and accurate. Those are the minimum criteria just to play the game. If the resume is too long, is difficult to understand, or has a mistake such as a spelling error; the resume will frequently be rejected out of hand.

But these are the minimum criteria. In order to compete, the resume must be relevant to the requirements of the job and must separate you from the crowd. Standing out usually must come after the initial evaluation. Excessive length and unusual design normally fall in the initial screening. So most of the standing out must rely on the content of the resume. Can you do something that the other applicants cannot? You usually prove this through what you have already done. Many get confused at this point and assume employers are only interested in those who have done the job before. That is just the easy way to determine if someone can do a job. In a field such as advertising where creativity and ultimately originality play such a pivotal role, employers are willing to look at all facets of your background to determine if you have ever done anything that suggests that you might do the advertising job well. Look to every aspect of your professional, social, or academic background to show how you perform when you work. The best beginning professional salary I ever saw a student get was the direct result of the work, knowledge, and experience gained in a cultural association of which he was a member. This was in spite of the fact that he already had more than 10 years of professional experience. Find your best evidence that you can excel wherever you can and deliver it as forcefully as you can. Don't let rules or "normal" guidelines keep you from emphasizing your best experiences and abilities.

Many types of content raise considerable debate just on whether they should even be included in the resume. The best examples are the career objective and personal information. Many pros will tell you not to include a career objective unless it is specific enough that the reader can get a clear view of where you are heading in your career or at least in your next job. Statements such as "anything that pays well" or "a job that will let me develop" are not very stimulating. The objective should tell the employer that you want the specific job for which you are applying. Unfortunately, that means needing only a different objective for every job. The computer helps, but the only solution is a thorough knowledge of where you are going in your career.

Another problem content area is personal information such as health, marital status, religion, etc. A good rule of thumb here is don't include anything on a resume that can't help you and don't include anything that could have the potential to hurt you. Also, don't include nonsense. For example, many resumes include a statement that the applicant is in good health. If an applicant was mentally defective, would this same person note that his or her mental health was not good? If your current health status is not specifically requested and has no direct bearing on your application, don't include it. This analysis eliminates most personal information and raises serious questions about the usefulness of personal information sections on resumes. Include your name, address, and telephone number, and let the rest take care of itself.

The heart of the resume must be the description of previous experience. As noted above, this should not necessarily be restricted to work experience, but of course your selling job will be much easier when you reach the point that work experience can carry the load. Emphasis should be on the most recent and relevant experience -- not just the most recent. A classic example of this is in the area of education. As soon as you reach the four-year college level in your education, it is not necessary to refer to your high school and junior college background.

When describing your work experience, focus on how well you did the job not just on the tasks that you performed. For jobs that the employer would likely be familiar, such as those within the career field and routine jobs such as a cashier, don't bother reiterating the job tasks. Rather, concentrate on the experiences that you had that were out of the ordinary and tell about things that you created or added to the normal job. For example, you were a checker at a grocery store but participated in a customer survey performed by the store, or you started a store newsletter for employees. What makes you different in the way you approach your work? Most people see this type of thing when they consider it and work hard to remember what they have done. If you find that you are a "nine-to-fiver" who just puts in his time, then you may want to consider a product modification on yourself -- a change of attitude.

18 Sales Promotion

Chapter Objectives and Summary

- **Distinguish between sales promotion and advertising.**
- **Explain how promotion and advertising work together within the marketing mix.**
- **List the several types of promotions, both for consumers and for resellers.**
- **Understand why advertisers are spending increasing sums of money on sales promotion.**
- **Explain the advantages and disadvantages of sales promotion as compared to advertising.**

Sales promotion offers an "extra incentive" for consumers to take immediate action. Sales promotion has three goals: to increase immediate customer sales, to increase support among the marketer's sales force, and to gain the support intermediaries (resellers) in marketing the product. Current trends suggest that more promotional dollars are being spent on sales promotion than advertising. Virtually all major advertising agencies have acquired a sales promotion subsidiary or have brought sales promotion in-house.

The reasons for the growth of sales promotion include pursuit of short-term profit solutions, need for accountability, economic factors, consumer behavior, lack of new-product categories, the pricing cycle, and the increasing power of retailers. There is a drive for immediate profits and progress, which sales promotion satisfies. Another reason for the growth of sales promotion is the fact that it is relatively easy to determine whether a given sales promotion strategy accomplished its objectives, and this assessment can be done quickly. Also, escalating media costs have forced marketers to look for alternatives. Furthermore, shoppers are better educated, more selective, and less loyal to brand names. A lack of new product categories has also contributed. Sales promotion is often the most effective strategy for increasing share and volume. Moreover, consumers have become more price sensitive at least partially because of the introduction of low-priced private-label brands. Finally, the increasing power of retailers has allowed them to demand more sales promotion support from manufacturers.

Sales promotion has three primary objectives: to stimulate demand, to improve market performance of resellers, and to supplement and coordinate advertising, personal selling, and public relations activities. Sales promotion is both different from and similar to advertising. The major differences concern their methods of appeal. Advertising is interested in creating an image and will take time to do so. Sales promotion is interested in creating immediate action. Advertising promotes this perception of the benefit through informational and transformational executions. Sales promotion enhances the message by offering coupons as part of the ad, mailing free samples, and conducting a contest. The specific objectives of each are quite similar. They share the roles of increasing the number of customers and increasing the use by current customers. They both try to get customers to try a new product, encourage increased spending in certain periods, and encourage present customers to use the product more often. Both try to create an awareness that the product offers some clear benefit.

Sales promotion strategies are divided into three primary types: consumer, trade, and sales-force. Consumer sales promotions are directed at the ultimate end user. They are intended to "presell" consumers so that when they go into a store they will be looking for a particular brand. The primary strengths of consumer sales promotions are their variety and flexibility. Consumer sales promotion techniques include price deals, coupons, contests and sweepstakes, refunds, premium offers, specialty advertising, continuity programs, and consumer sampling. Price deals are commonly used to encourage trial, to persuade existing users to buy more, or to convince new users to try an established product. They are effective only if price is an important factor in brand choice or if consumers are not brand loyal. The primary advantage of coupons is that it allows the advertiser to lower prices without relying on cooperation of the retailer. Disadvantages associated with coupons include serious coupon clutter, low redemption rate, high cost, and misredemption and fraud. A good contest or sweepstakes generates high degree of consumer involvement. Refunds have proven to be very effective. Research indicates that money refund offers generate five times as much business as product coupons of comparable values.

Trade sales promotions are intended to accomplish four goals: stimulate in-store merchandising or other trade support, manipulate levels of inventory, expand product distribution to new areas or new classes of trade, and create a high level of excitement about the product among those responsible for its sale. Trade sales promotions include point-of-purchase displays, dealer contests and sweepstakes, trade shows, trade incentives, and trade deals. Trade shows allow demonstrating the product, providing information, answering questions, comparing competing brands, and writing orders.

Sales-force promotions are simply activities directed at the firm's salesforce, which are intended to motivate salespeople to strive to increase their sales levels in one of two ways. The first includes programs that better prepare salespeople to do their jobs. The second is concerned with efforts or incentives that motivate salespeople to work harder.

Key Terms and Concepts

advertising allowance	Manufacturer pays the wholesaler or retailer a certain amount of money for advertising the manufacturer's product.
bonus packs	Contain additional amounts of the product free when a standard size is purchased at the regular price.
banded packs	One or more units of a product are sold at a reduced price compared to the regular single-unit price.
contests	Sales-promotion activities that require participants to compete for a prize on the basis of some skill or ability.
continuity plan	Requires the customer to save coupons or special labels attached to the product that can be redeemed for merchandise.
coupons	Legal certificates offered by manufacturers and retailers that grant specified savings on selected products when presented for redemption at the point of purchase.
dealer loader	Premium given to a retailer by a manufacturer for buying a certain quantity of product.

direct premium	Awards the incentive immediately, at the time of purchase.
display allowance	A direct payment of cash or goods to the retailer if the retailer agrees to set up the display as specified.
free-in-the-mail premium	Customer mails in a purchase request and proof-of-purchase to the advertiser.
game	Type of sweepstakes that requires the player to return to play several times.
mail premium	Requires the customer to take some action before receiving the premium.
manufacturer-sponsored coupons	Coupons that can be redeemed at any outlet distributing the product.
point-of-purchase display	Display designed by the manufacturer and distributed to retailers in order to promote a particular brand or line of products.
premium	Tangible reward received for performing a particular act, such as purchasing a product or visiting the point of purchase.
price deal	Temporary reduction in the price of a product.
price-pack deal	Provides the consumer with something extra through the package itself.
push money	Monetary bonus paid to a salesperson based on units sold over a period of time.
refund	An offer by the marketer to return a certain amount of money to the consumer who purchases the product.
retailer-sponsored coupons	Coupons that can only be redeemed at the specified retail outlet.
sales promotion	Marketing activities that add value to the product for a limited period of time to stimulate consumer purchasing and dealer effectiveness.
sampling	An offer that allows the customer to use or experience the product or service free of charge or for a very small fee.
self-liquidator	Requires that some proof-of-purchase and payment be mailed in before receiving the premium.

sweepstakes	Sales-promotion activities that require participants to submit their names to be included in a drawing or other type of chance selection.
trade advertising	Directed at wholesalers and retailers and can be effective in providing resellers with important information.
trade deal	An arrangement in which the retailer agrees to give the manufacturer's product a special promotional effort in return for product discounts, goods, or cash.
trade incentive	When a contest is not appropriate or the goal may be to gain extra shelf space or increase use of promotional material rather than to increase sales.
trade sales promotion	Techniques such as price discounts, point-of purchase displays, and advertising allowances that help to gain shelf space.
trade show	Allows product demonstration, provides information, answers questions, compares competing brands, and writes orders.

True/False

Circle the appropriate letter.

T F 1. The goals of sales promotion are to gain reseller support, to increase sales force support, and to increase sales.

T F 2. Current expenditures on advertising are about the same as expenditures on sales promotion.

T F 3. Sales promotion is good for building brand loyalty.

T F 4. Price deals are effective when coordinated with coupon programs.

T F 5. The primary advantage of the coupon is that it allows the advertiser to lower prices without the cooperation of the retailer.

T F 6. The redemption rate for coupons is high.

T F 7. The ideal specialty advertising item is something entertaining.

T F 8. Sampling is most effective when done in a retail store where the product can be demonstrated.

T   F   9. Consumer sales promotion is most effective if the product or service is presold by advertising.

T   F   10. The ultimate measure of the success of reseller sales promotions is a reduction in inventory levels.

T   F   11. In general, retailers and manufacturers maintain that sampling can boost sales volume by 5 to 10 times during a product demonstration.

T   F   12. Sales promotion is less expensive than advertising.

T   F   13. One area in which advertising and sales promotion work well together is the introduction of new products and services.

T   F   14. The distinction between sales promotion and advertising is increasingly blurred because advertising is frequently the vehicle for carrying sales promotions.

T   F   15. Convenience goods usually employ a push sales promotion strategy.

True/False Answers

1.	T	9.	T
2.	F	10.	F
3.	F	11.	T
4.	F	12.	T
5.	T	13.	T
6.	F	14.	T
7.	F	15.	F
8.	F		

Completion

Fill in the missing word or words in the blanks provided.

1. Marketing activities that add value to the product for a limited period of time to stimulate consumer purchasing and dealer effectiveness are called _____.

2. The main purpose of sales promotion is to _____.

3. Sales promotions try to induce action on the part of the target audience by using _____.

4. According to a study by United Marketing Services, the most popular sales promotion technique is _____.

5. According to a study by United Marketing Services, _____ were most effective in producing a brand change within a product category.

6. _____ is often the most effective strategy in producing immediate increases in market share.

7. _____ convinces consumers of the value of a product, and they will go to their supermarkets and demand that the product be stocked.

8. _____ is used to convince members of the distribution network to carry and market a certain product.

9. The 3 primary types of sales promotion strategies are: _____, _____, and _____.

10. _____ and _____ are the two types of sales-force sales promotion activities.

11. Legal certificates offered by manufacturers and retailers that grant specific savings on selected products when presented for redemption at the point of purchase are called _____.

12. _____ is the most important advantage of specialty advertising.

13. _____ and _____ are the primary strengths of consumer sales promotions.

14. _____ is the most important reseller sales promotion technique.

15. Money refund offers generate _____ times as much business as product coupons for comparable value, according to Shopper's Pay Day.

Completion Answers

1. sales promotion
2. stimulate action
3. extra incentive
4. coupons
5. coupons
6. sales promotion
7. pull
8. push promotion strategy
9. trade, sales force, consumer
10. help to improve sales performance; motivational incentives
11. coupons
12. long life
13. variety, flexibility
14. trade deal
15. five

Matching

Match the terms and concepts with the appropriate statements. Each term or concept may be used only once; there are more terms and concepts than statements.

Terms and Concepts

a. buying allowance
b. dealer loader
c. direct premium
d. display allowance
e. game
f. point-of-purchase display
g. premium
h. price deal
i. push money

j. retailer-sponsored coupon
k. sampling
l. sweepstakes
m. trade deal
n. trade incentive
o. trade show
p. bonus packs
q. coupons
r. contests

Statements

_____ 1. A temporary reduction in the price of a product.

_____ 2. Sales-promotion activities that require participants to submit their names to be included in a drawing or other type of chance selection.

_____ 3. A type of sweepstake that requires the player to return to play several times.

_____ 4. A sales promotion activity in which a tangible reward is received for performing a particular act, such as purchasing a product or visiting the point of purchase.

_____ 5. A sales promotion activity in which the incentive is awarded immediately at the time of purchase.

_____ 6. A sales promotion trade deal that involves a direct payment of cash or goods to the retailer if the retailer agrees to set up the display as specified.

_____ 7. A sales promotion offer that allows the customer to use or experience the product or service free of charge or for a very small fee.

_____ 8. A sales promotion display designed by the manufacturer and distributed to retailers in order to promote a particular brand or line of products.

_____ 9. A sales promotion event that allows the producer to demonstrate the product, provide information, answer questions, compare competing brands, and write orders.

_____ 10. Sales promotion activity in which money is offered directly to reseller by marketer for doing such things as providing premium shelf space, special displays, and so on.

_____ 11. A sales promotion activity in which a monetary bonus is paid to a salesperson based on units sold over a period of time.

_____ 12. A sales promotion activity in which a premium is given to a dealer by a manufacturer for buying a certain quantity of product.

_____ 13. A sales promotion arrangement in which the retailer agrees to give the manufacturer's product a special promotional effort in return for product discounts, goods, or cash.

_____ 14. A coupon that can only be redeemed at the specified retail outlet.

_____ 15. Sales promotion trade deal in which a manufacturer pays a middleman a set amount of money for purchasing a certain amount of the product during a specified time period.

Matching Answers

1.	h	9.	o
2.	l	10.	n
3.	e	11.	i
4.	g	12.	b
5.	c	13.	m
6.	d	14.	j
7.	k	15.	a
8.	f		

Multiple Choice

Place the letter of the correct answer in the blank provided.

_____ 1. The pressure from top management to produce immediate profits and progress has resulted in:
   a. increased use of advertising and increased use of sales promotion.
   b. increased use of advertising and decreased use of sales promotion.
   c. decreased use of advertising and increased use of sales promotion.
   d. decreased use of advertising and decreased use of sales promotion.
   e. no noticeable change

_____ 2. What is the best marketing communication tool for launching a new product?
   a. advertising
   b. sales promotion
   c. public relations
   d. packaging
   e. none of the above

_____ 3. What is the only form of marketing communication that brings all the elements of the sale together at the same time?
    a. advertising
    b. publicity
    c. point-of-purchase displays
    d. public relations
    e. coupons

_____ 4. Which of the following is a reason sales promotion is growing so rapidly?
    a. sales promotion is less expensive than advertising
    b. sales promotion offers the manager short-term solutions
    c. sales promotion responds to the new power acquired by modern retailers
    d. extent to which sales promotion has achieved objectives can be assessed
    e. all of the above

_____ 5. Which of the following is **NOT** a type of consumer sales promotion?
    a. coupons
    b. point-of-purchase displays
    c. refunds
    d. specialty advertising
    e. sampling

_____ 6. When a manufacturer pays a wholesaler or retailer a certain amount of money for advertising the manufacturer's product, this is called:
    a. display allowance
    b. buying allowance
    c. advertising deal
    d. advertising allowance
    e. display loader

_____ 7. A temporary reduction in the price of the product in sales promotion is called a/an:
    a. price deal.
    b. refund.
    c. premium.
    d. push money.
    e. trade deal.

_____ 8. A sales promotion activity which requires participants to submit their names to be included in a drawing or other type of chance selection is called:
    a. contest.
    b. continuity plan.
    c. trade deal.
    d. trade show.
    e. sweepstakes.

_____ 9. Which of the following statements about coupons is **TRUE?**
    a. the primary advantage is that it allows the advertiser to increase prices without relying on cooperation from the retailer
    b. the redemption rate is high
    c. distribution is very expensive
    d. coupon clutter is not a problem
    e. all of the above

_____ 10. Which of the following is a goal of sales promotion?
    a. increase sales force support
    b. gain reseller support
    c. increase sales
    d. all of the above
    e. none of the above

_____ 11. Which of the following statements about specialty advertising is **FALSE:**
    a. It is inexpensive.
    b. Cost per prospect is high.
    c. It is very flexible.
    d. The most important advantage is its low waste circulation.
    e. Recipients have a positive attitude toward it.

_____ 12. Which of the following is **NOT** a type of reseller sales promotion?
    a. coupons
    b. point-of-purchase displays
    c. trade shows
    d. trade deals
    e. trade premiums

_____ 13. Which of the following is a primary type of sales promotion strategy?
    a. consumer
    b. sales force
    c. trade
    d. all of the above
    e. none of the above

_____ 14. Which of the following is one of the goals of reseller sales promotions?
    a. to get greater cooperation from retailers
    b. to get customers to try a new product
    c. to encourage present customers to use the product in greater quantities
    d. to increase the amount of impulse buying
    e. all of the above

_____ 15. How does sales promotion try to induce action on the part of its target audience?
    a. by informing the audience
    b. by providing an extra incentive
    c. by entertaining the audience
    d. by enhancing the brand image of the product
    e. through product benefits

Multiple Choice Answers

1.	c	6.	d	11.	d
2.	a	7.	a	12.	a
3.	c	8.	e	13.	d
4.	e	9.	c	14.	e
5.	b	10.	d	15.	b

Career Exercise -- Letter of Application

The letter of application should concentrate on explaining precisely why the applicant is the perfect candidate for the job. The letter should explain briefly, clearly, and forcefully what experiences, knowledge, and personal traits the applicant has that meet the requirements of the job. Writing a letter of application comes down to matching your abilities to the requirements of the job. All of this should be covered in the resume but not as directly as in the letter of application.

In order to accomplish this, the letter of application must address two major points: why you have come to apply for the job and how you match the requirements of the job. The first of these points is the letter writer's "referent allusion," noted in the Chapter 12 career exercise on cover letters for questionnaires. The point of the referent allusion is basically to explain how you found out about the job. Immediately in the first sentence explain that you are responding to an ad from a specific publication or that a mutual professional friend suggested that you apply -- whatever simply describes your reason, even if you are sending the employer an unsolicited application.

The second part of the letter depends upon very detailed information about the nature and needs of the job. You must either gather the information directly from the employer or you will have to infer the job requirements from the job description. The more accurate and specific your information -- the less you have to infer -- the better your letter can be. Whatever is the case, make sure that you state your experience, skills, traits, and knowledge as forcefully as you can, but never exaggerate or go beyond your actual experiences or training. In the process of explaining how you satisfy the job requirements, you will need to substantiate your claims. The best proof is a third person known by both who can verify the experience. The next best proof is an example or examples of actual work. However, submit examples of your work with a letter of application only if requested.

Close the letter simply with appreciation and a clear means of contacting you when a decision has been made. Usually, a mailing address is best.

19 Public Relations

Chapter Objectives and Summary

- Understand what public relations is, how it differs from advertising, and what its advantages are.
- Explain how public relations, advertising, and other marketing communications can work together to achieve greater benefit for an organization.
- Identify the areas in which public relations operates and some of the activities performed in those areas.
- Understand the value and importance of measuring the results of public relations efforts.

The goodwill of the public is the greatest asset any organization can have. A public that is well-informed and factually informed is not only important, but it is critical to the survival of an organization. Informing the public is the responsibility of public relations. Its audiences (publics) may be external and also internal. Public relations, advertising, and sales promotion together present the marketing communication strategy of an organization. What a company's advertising says, how it says it, and what medium it uses have a direct bearing on the company's public relations strategy and vice-versa.

In an integrated marketing communication program, advertising and public relations should be complementary, but they are not always. Although advertising should complement a total public relations program, it is really a separate function. Public relations practitioners, for example, have a different approach to the media than do advertisers. Whenever possible, they avoid purchasing time or space to communicate messages. Instead, they seek to persuade media "gatekeepers" to carry their information. Publicity is cost-free because there are no direct media costs. There are indirect costs, however, such as getting the cooperation of the gatekeepers. When public relations people do use paid media, the nature of the message tends to be general with little or no attempt to sell a brand or product line. The goal is to change the attitudes of the public in favor of the sponsoring organization. This is referred to as corporate or institutional advertising.

Amount of control is the second inherent difference between advertising and public relations. The public relations strategist is at the mercy of the media representative. In contrast, advertising is paid for, so there are many checks to ensure that the message is accurate and appears when scheduled. The difficulty in measuring the results of public relations is another problem. Public relations, however, does offer a credibility not usually associated with advertising.

Public relations, like advertising, is a managed activity. It begins with a thorough understanding of its publics and is guided by objectives. Managing a public relations image begins with a plan. Public relations should align the organization's interests with the public interest so that both are served. The public relations strategist researches the answers to two primary questions. First, which publics are most important to my organization? Second, what do these publics think? Public opinion is the label used to describe what people think. Public opinion is defined as a "belief, based not necessarily on fact but on the conception or evaluation of an event, person, institution, or product." Despite the critical need to understand public opinion, there is still no one continuous system of measurement of the "climate of public opinion." One approach to measuring public opinion contends that opinion evolves through seven stages: dawning awareness, greater urgency, discovering the choices, wishful thinking, weighing the choices, taking a stand intellectually, and making a responsible judgment morally and emotionally.

The techniques available to the public relations practitioner can be broadly classified as controlled and uncontrolled media. Controlled media techniques include house ads, public service announcements, corporate (institutional) advertising, in-house publications, and visual presentations such as speakers, photographs, film, displays, exhibits, and staged events. Controlled media are generally paid for by the sponsoring organizations. These techniques give the organization control over how and when the messages appear. Two exceptions to the paid-for criteria are house ads and public service announcements.

When public relations uses uncontrolled media the organization has no direct control over how the media will report on corporate activities. The news release is the primary medium used to deliver public relations messages to various media editors and reporters. Another uncontrolled technique is the press conference. Handling bad news is the responsibility of public relations. This is usually referred to as crisis management. The public relations strategist must anticipate the possibility of a crisis and establish a mechanism for dealing with it and ensuring that it will not happen again.

Noncommercial advertising is advertising that is sponsored by businesses or organizations that are not motivated by the maximization of profits. The emphasis in this type of advertising is on changing attitudes or behaviors relative to some idea or cause. Advertising sponsored by nonprofit organizations falls into one of six categories: political advertising, social-cause advertising, charitable advertising, government advertising, private nonprofit advertising, and association advertising

Measuring the effectiveness of public relations has been a problem, which is a major reason that public relations has not been accepted as an efficient and effective approach to behavior change. One of the major differences between evaluating advertising and public relations is the lack of control public relations practitioners exercise over whether their message appears in the media and what it will look like if it does appear. Public relations measurement may be divided into two categories: process evaluation and outcome evaluation (effect on the audience). Process evaluation examines the success of the public relations program in getting the message out to the target audiences. It is difficult to assess the public relations contribution within a larger marketing communications mix. The modest effects normally associated with public relations are very difficult to isolate and measure. "Success" is ambiguous and hard to ascertain. Even if a positive change in awareness and attitudes is achieved, it is difficult to know whether these changes will lead to desired behaviors.

Key Terms and Concepts

controlled media

Media that are generally paid for by the sponsoring organizations and give the organization control over how and when the messages appear.

corporate identity advertising

Advertising used by firms that want to enhance or maintain their reputation among specific audiences or to establish a level of awareness of the company's name, and the nature of its business.

corporate/institutional advertising

Advertising used to create a favorable public attitude.

house ad	Ad that is prepared by the organization for use in its own publication or a publication over which it has some control.
in-house publications	Publications provided by organizations to their employees and other publics.
news release	Primary medium used to deliver public relations messages to the various media editors and reporters.
noncommercial advertising	Advertising sponsored by businesses or organizations that are not motivated by the maximization of profits.
outcome evaluation	Measures effect of public relations efforts on publics.
press conference	Public gathering of media people for the purpose of establishing a company's position or making a statement.
press kit	Provides all the important background information to members of the press before they arrive or when they arrive at the press conference.
process evaluation	Measuring the effectiveness of media and nonmedia efforts to get the desired message out to the target audience.
public	Groups or individuals who are involved within an organization, including customers, employees, competitors and government regulators.
public opinion	People's beliefs, based on their conceptions or evaluations of something rather than on fact.
public relations	Management function enabling organizations to achieve effective relationships with various audiences through an understanding of audience opinions, attitudes, and values.
public relations/advocacy advertising	Involves creating advertisements and purchasing space to deliver a specific message.
public service announcement (PSA)	Type of public relations advertising that deals with public welfare issues and is typically delivered by the media free of charge.
publicity	Marketing communication considered "cost free" because there are no direct media costs.

uncontrolled media			Media with which the organization has no direct control over whether or how the media will convey their message.

True/False

Circle the appropriate letter.

T F 1. Programs for advertising, sales promotion, and public relations must be coordinated carefully.

T F 2. Public relations' basic approach to media is the same as advertising.

T F 3. Public relations has about the same control over the content of the messages as advertising.

T F 4. The risk involved in using advance press kits for a press conference is that the press conference may become unnecessary.

T F 5. Marketing has responsibility for handling bad news that results from crises.

T F 6. The reason that government gives "nonprofit" organizations a special status for business and tax purposes is only a tradition. They have not been taxed; so, the government has just continued the tradition.

T F 7. In cases where advertising is not permitted or is considered inappropriate, public relations becomes the primary means of reaching and persuading target audiences.

T F 8. Unless a public relations effort is directly aimed at changing a specific audience behavior, such as product purchase, the "success" of the effort is difficult to determine.

T F 9. In most companies and other organizations the public relations function is clearly defined and staffed.

T F 10. Public relations has no role to play in integrated marketing communications.

T F 11. In promoting products and services, public relations can play only a minimal role.

T F 12. In the last several years, the definition of public relations has been clarified and is now universally agreed upon.

T F 13. Although advertising is becoming more common among physicians, dentists, lawyers, architects, and other professionals, public relations remains the primary means of communicating these services.

T   F   14. A message from an organization that is accepted by a medium and worked into its editorial, news, feature, or program content has greater credibility because of the power of media "endorsement."

T   F   15. The greatest asset any organization can have is the goodwill of the people upon whom it depends for its success.

True/False Answers

1.	T	9.	F
2.	F	10.	F
3.	F	11.	F
4.	T	12.	F
5.	F	13.	T
6.	F	14.	T
7.	T	15.	T
8.	T		

Completion

Fill in the missing word or words in the blanks provided.

1. Management function that enables organizations to achieve effective relationships with their various audiences through an understanding of audience opinions, attitudes, and values is called _____.

2. Those groups or individuals who are involved with an organization, including customers, employees, corporations, and government regulators are called _____.

3. People's beliefs, based on their conceptions or evaluations of something rather than on fact, are called _____.

4. _____ and _____ are the two categories of communication tools available to the public relations practitioner.

5. _____, _____, and _____ are examples of controlled media used in public relations.

6. _____ produces virtually all public service announcements that appear on network television.

7. The type of public relations technique used when NBC broadcasts an advertisement about a new television program is called _____.

8. Pamphlets, newsletters, information racks and bulletins are examples of _____.

9. Open houses and plant tours are examples of _____.

10. _____ and _____ are examples of uncontrolled media.

11. _____ is the primary medium used to deliver public relations messages to media editors and reporters.

12. A public gathering of media people for the purpose of establishing a company's position or making a statement is referred to as a _____.

13. A _____ is normally in a folder and provides all the important background information to members of the media at a press conference.

14. _____ and _____ are the two categories of public relations evaluation measurement.

15. The greatest asset any organization can have is _____.

Completion Answers

1. public relations
2. publics
3. public opinion
4. controlled and uncontrolled media
5. house ad, PSA, corporate ad, in-house publication
6. Advertising Council
7. house ad
8. in-house publication
9. staged events
10. news release, press conference, crisis management
11. news release
12. press conference
13. press kit
14. process evaluation and outcome evaluation
15. goodwill of the public

Matching

Match the terms and concepts with the appropriate statements. Each term or concept may be used only once; there are more terms and concepts than statements.

Terms and Concepts

a. advocacy advertising
b. controlled
c. corporate advertising
d. corporate identity advertising
e. crisis management
f. display
g. exhibits
h. house ad
i. noncommercial advertising

j. outcome evaluation
k. press agentry
l. press kit
m. process evaluation
n. public service announcement
o. publicity
p. special events
q. issue advertising
r. public

Statements

_____ 1. The goal of this type of advertising is to change the attitudes of the public in favor of the sponsoring organization with little or no attempt to sell a brand or product line.

_____ 2. Type of marketing communication which is considered "cost-free" because there are no direct media costs.

_____ 3. A type of advertising that involves creating advertising and purchasing space to deliver a pointed message on a topic or cause that is important to the interest of the organization.

_____ 4. Media that give the organization total control over how and when the message is delivered.

_____ 5. Ad that is prepared by the organization for use in its own publication or a publication over which it has some control.

_____ 6. A type of public relations advertising that deals with public welfare issues and is typically delivered by the media free of charge.

_____ 7. A type of advertising used by firms that want to enhance or maintain their reputation among specific audiences or to establish a level of awareness of the company's name and the nature of its business.

_____ 8. A picture of a new store being built or a presentation of a company's product line at a regional fair.

_____ 9. Large presentations which may have moving parts, sound, videos, and are usually manned by a company representative.

_____ 10. Advertising designed to promote a cause rather than to maximize profits.

_____ 11. Measuring the effectiveness of media and nonmedia efforts to get the desired message out to the largest audience.

_____ 12. Measuring the ultimate effect of the public relations effort on the target audience.

_____ 13. Group involved with or within an organization, including customers, employees, competitors, and government regulators.

_____ 14. The medium used to deliver public relations messages directly to individual media editors and reporters.

_____ 15. Public relations activity involving handling product recalls, hostile takeovers, bankruptcies, factory accidents, or contaminated product incidents.

Matching Answers

1.	c	9.	g
2.	o	10.	i
3.	a	11.	m
4.	b	12.	j
5.	h	13.	r
6.	n	14.	l
7.	d	15.	e
8.	f		

Multiple Choice

Place the letter of the correct answer in the blank provided.

_____ 1. Public relations is:
   a. working to get positive publicity for organizations.
   b. management function that helps organizations develop relationships with people upon whom the organization depends by considering their interests.
   c. managing crisis situations for organizations.
   d. activity that tries to create a positive image for the organization in spite of what the organization may do.
   e. putting the right "spin" on whatever the organization does.

_____ 2. What advantage does public relations offer over advertising or sales promotion?
   a. greater credibility
   b. more control over the content of messages
   c. more control of the timing of the placement of messages
   d. easier to determine success
   e. all of the above

_____ 3. Which of the following statements about public relations is **TRUE**?
  a. Public relations is more expensive than advertising.
  b. What public relations should be doing is universally agreed upon.
  c. Public relations is only concerned with getting information about the organization and its product into the news media.
  d Public relations is a managed activity.
  e. all of the above

_____ 4. Which of the following is a difference between public relations and advertising?
  a. amount of control in delivering messages through the media
  b. credibility of messages
  c. amount of control of the content of messages
  d. purchase of media time and space
  e. all of the above

_____ 5. In public relations which of the following is an important dimension for categorizing media?
  a. cost
  b. delivery
  c. control
  d. support
  e. none of the above

_____ 6. Which of the following is the universally accepted definition of public relations?
  a. management function that helps organizations develop relationships with people upon whom the organization depends by considering their interests
  b. the use of information to influence public opinion
  c. management function that enables organizations to achieve effective relationships with their various audiences through an understanding of audience opinions, attitudes, and values
  d. the art and social science of analyzing trends, predicting their consequences, counseling organizational leaders, and implementing planned programs of action which will serve both the organization and the public interest
  e. none of the above

_____ 7. A type of public relations in which media time or space is purchased to present a company's point of view is called a/an:
  a. advertorial.
  b. infomercial.
  c. press agentry.
  d. institutional advertisement.
  e. none of the above

_____ 8. What is the essential difference between public relations as a marketing tool as opposed to public relations as a management tool? As a marketing tool, it focuses on _____ while as a management tool it focuses on _____ .
   a. all publics . . . product
   b. profit . . . product
   c. product . . . all publics
   d. all publics . . . profit
   e. product . . . employees

_____ 9. Publicity is:
   a. paying for the use of media time and space to relay messages through media gatekeepers.
   b. using the media to relay messages to publics.
   c. using advertising to create a favorable public attitude toward the sponsoring organization.
   d. cost-free public relations that relays messages through media gatekeepers.
   e. all of the above

_____ 10. With the development of scientific methods of research and attitudinal analysis, determining the success of public relations has:
   a. become a precise science.
   b. is still difficult to determine precisely.
   c. is totally impossible to measure.
   d. all of the above
   e. none of the above

_____ 11. A public is:
   a. the group at which the public relations program is aimed.
   b. a specific group to whom public relations messages are directed.
   c. groups or individuals who are involved with an organization.
   d. the group to whom the organization is trying to sell its product or service.
   e. the mass of people to whom the mass media direct messages.

_____ 12. Today the move toward public relations integrated marketing communications:
   a. is faltering.
   b. is gaining momentum.
   c. has completely stopped.
   d. has reversed.
   e. is an established fact.

_____ 13. Which of the following is one of the categories of communication tools available to the public relations practitioner?
   a. uncontrolled media
   b. sponsored media
   c. direct media
   d. special media
   e. personal media

_____ 14. All of the following are public relations activities **EXCEPT**:
    a. house ads.
    b. speakers bureau.
    c. public service announcement.
    d. product publicity.
    e. product advertising.

_____ 15. All of the following are media channels used by public relations **EXCEPT**:
    a. classroom education.
    b. speeches.
    c. telephone.
    d. newsletters.
    e. none of the above

Multiple Choice

1. b	6. e	11. c
2. a	7. a	12. b
3. d	8. c	13. a
4. e	9. d	14. e
5. c	10. b	15. e

Career Exercise -- Public Relations and the Mentor or Sponsor

Public relations has been defined as the planned effort to create a human environment necessary to the success of an organization, person, or idea through socially responsible and acceptable behavior based on mutually satisfactory two-way communication. People are critical to the success of a career marketing effort. The idea of the human environment is used to encourage thinking broadly about the people who are involved. At the core of the definition is the idea that your behavior must be acceptable to this human environment if you want to have success. In order to know whether your behavior is acceptable, it is necessary to engage in two-way communication, which is simply listening as well as talking with the members of this human environment. In other words, you need to adapt yourself to a certain extent to what they want if you want their help.

The key elements of the career human environment are the potential employers in your field, personal and professional references, and your contemporaries in the field. The role of employers should be obvious. References use what they know about you to influence others to think more favorably about you. Your contemporaries mostly extend your range of abilities and knowledge. By tapping their abilities and knowledge, you can become more effective. These are the groups of people who can most influence your success or failure in getting and performing a job. In career planning the process of identifying and contacting these key people is often referred to as networking. This is basically another name for the human environment. Networking is creating a connected framework of people who help you contact and keep in touch with the people in your professional field. A career is fed on the ideas and attitudes of the people that you interact with. What people know about you is the life-blood of your career.

At the core of your human environment/network should be what is commonly called a mentor or sponsor. A mentor is a professional in your field who takes the responsibility of helping you design and develop your career. The mentor must be someone who is well established in the field and already has a well-developed human environment/network. The mentor should be in a position to provide the detailed advice that you need to guide your career. This information can only come from an established position within the field. The mentor should have firsthand knowledge of the needs and expectations of the people in your field. From this core of information, the mentor can provide the insight that you need to make crucial career decisions.

You don't choose the mentor; the mentor doesn't choose you. The choice must be a mutual one. The relationship is a very close one, such that you can entrust some of the most important decisions of your career to this person. Finding a mentor is a very important step in your career development but cannot be rushed. You must be prepared to trust this person's judgment over your own in very important career choices. The mentor is more than just a matter of a trusted confidant or someone who is admired and respected. The mentor role is seen by many professionals as one of great responsibility. Most will not enter into the relationship lightly. It is a relationship that must be nurtured very carefully, and if offered, should be considered very carefully before you accept or reject the offer.

Begin the process of developing your human environment/network by identifying 10 people in each of the three key categories -- employers, references, and contemporaries. You already have begun to examine the expectations of the employers and references in your career planning and research. You want your references to provide information to the employers. Most often this takes the form of a letter of reference. Try writing a letter of reference to a potential employer for yourself. You should make it as persuasive as possible. This is what you want the reference to do. If you cannot write the letter, how can you expect to communicate to the reference what you want said? You will find that many references will appreciate a draft letter of recommendation from you to start them on the letter they will write. Be prepared to provide this kind of support.

Next, what do you need to know and do to develop effective relationships with your contemporaries? What do your contemporaries think about you? What would they need to think about you in order for them to offer you help if you needed it to get a project completed? What do you offer them for their support? What kinds of contemporaries would be most helpful in your career?

20   The Advertising Campaign

<u>Chapter Objectives and Summary</u>

- **Understand the role of the situation analysis in identifying key problems to be solved by the advertising.**
- **Understand how the basic strategy decisions are developed for an advertising campaign.**
- **Analyze how the message strategy solves the key problem.**
- **Explain how the media plan relates to advertising objectives and message needs.**
- **Explain how the effectiveness of an advertising campaign is evaluated.**

The advertising campaign is designed strategically to meet a set of objectives and to solve some critical problem. It is a short-term plan that usually runs for a year or less. A campaign plan summarizes the marketplace situation and the strategies and tactics for the primary areas of creative and media, as well as the supporting areas of sales promotion, direct marketing, and public relations. It is also summarized in a written document called a plansbook.

The first section of most campaign plans is a situation analysis that summarizes all the relevant information the agency has compiled on the product, the company, the competitive environment, the industry, and the consumers. The situation analysis is sometimes called a business review. This information is obtained using primary and secondary research techniques. One approach to managing the information compiled in this process is the use of a SWOT analysis, which stands for Strengths, Weaknesses, Opportunities, and Threats. The Orlando/Orange County Convention and Visitors Bureau campaign is used as an extended case study to explain the elements and steps in campaign planning. Orlando/Orange County is the home of Disney World and is a major tourist and convention destination. The Bureau's primary function is, first, to book conventions and, second, to manage the exchange of information and business leads to and from members. The bureau's business is divided into two basic groups: tourists and conventioneers. The bureau found that consumers buy vacations much like they buy other products by searching for information, shopping around, and comparing costs and features. For tourists the decision is a family decision with the female head of household collecting the information. For conventioneers the decision process is more complicated with intermediaries such as conference planners and travel agents influencing the decision. The bureau found that competition in the tourism business is intense. New destinations and attractions compete with the more established locations. The Orlando area has an advantage in having both and has continued to grow in spite of the intense competition.

The concluding section of the Situation Analysis is the SWOT analysis, where the significance of the research is analyzed. A major strength of the Orlando bureau is the support of local business for tourism. A major threat to tourism in the Orlando area is the economic downturn of the early 1990s. Another threat is the perception of crime in Florida. A final threat is the emergence of new tourism attractions that compete with the Orlando area for repeat visitors. An important opportunity is the World Cup Soccer matches of 1994. Another opportunity is the excess inventory of rooms and restaurant capacity which allows for room to grow. Orlando's ability to get people to return is a key strength reflected in the fact that 85 percent of all visitors return to Orlando. The bureau identified four challenge areas for the 1994 campaign: compete effectively with limited resources and increased competition, avoid decrease in nonsoccer visitors as a result of hosting World Cup Soccer, increase visitation among first-time and repeat visitors, and implement convenient methods for distributing information to consumers.

After the Situation Analysis and the SWOT analysis, most advertising campaign plans focus on the key strategic decisions that will guide the campaign. The decisions include objectives, targeting, geographical strategies, and positioning. The objectives for the bureau focus on increasing demand and maintaining its important relationships with members, the travel trade, and its previous customers. In general the targeting strategy focuses on the visitor because in nine out of ten instances the destination decision is made by the visitor. The primary external target audience is the potential consumer visitor who makes up 80 percent of the Orlando business. Other important external targets are convention planners, delegates, and the trade. Finally, because the bureau is an association, members form a primary internal target audience. Orlando's position is built on its perception as a premiere leisure and business destination. Walt Disney World is linked very closely with this position. The connection has been reflected in the past in the "Orlando--Go for the Magic" slogan. While people in the Orlando area appreciate the role of Disney World, they also want to move beyond the "shadow of the ears." The bureau has an interesting positioning problem in trying to satisfy these desires while not losing the advantage of the Disney connection. A new slogan has been commissioned to broaden the position.

A campaign is a complex communication program that is tightly interwoven with all of an organization's marketing efforts. The total communication program reaches all stakeholders, all audiences, and all publics with the same theme. For the Orlando Bureau, the two-pronged message focused on the fun of tourism and the quality of a convention experience in the Orlando area. A campaign is a series of ads built around one central theme. The various ads are designed to be different in order to speak to different audiences or address different copy points. A strong umbrella theme holds the various ads together and creates synergy. The Orlando logo and the "Go for the Magic" theme have been used throughout all bureau communications for ten years. The Orlando message is delivered through advertising media, direct-response media, member relations, consumer promotions, trade activities, and public relations. For advertising media, the media planning and buying are handled by a freelance media planner. Consumer advertising tries to create awareness of the Orlando area in U.S. and Canadian newspapers and magazines. The plan uses cost effective co-op advertising. The bureau responds to more than 500,000 information requests with a consumer mailing package. Trade activities include sales literature, trade shows, sales missions, and familiarization trips. Most of the bureau's activities involve public relations in one way or another through publications, publicity, or special event planning. Because of the increase in tourist assaults in Florida, the focus of the bureau's communication program shifted from an aggressive marketing stance to one reflecting more of a public relations orientation.

The Orlando/Orange County Convention and Visitors Bureau operates a total communication program that involves a variety of different marketing communication areas, target audiences, media, and messages. In a sense the bureau is a victim of its own success because it suffers from a nearly chronic shortage of materials. The bureau uses a number of different indicators to measure its success: customer evaluations of bureau personnel, the number of leads for member business resulting from answered requests for information, as well as the amount of publications distributed. But the real measure of the program's success is brand equity, entailing high levels of both name recognition and customer loyalty.

Key Terms and Concepts

advertising campaign   A comprehensive advertising plan for a series of different but related ads that appear in different media across a specified time period.

campaign strategy   Specifying the objectives, targeting the audience, identifying the competitive advantage, and locating the best position for the product or brand.

competitive advantage   Areas where a product or brand is strong and the competition is weak.

plansbook   A written summary of an advertising campaign plan that is presented to the client.

situation analysis   A section of an advertising campaign plan that summarizes the relevant research finds about the company, the product, the competition, the marketplace, and the consumer.

True/False

Circle the appropriate letter.

T   F   1. The term "campaign" used in advertising planning was borrowed from business planning terminology.

T   F   2. The situation analysis includes findings about the organization, its product, the competition, the marketplace, and consumers.

T   F   3. The SWOT analysis summarizes the situation in terms of strategy, work, objectives, and targets.

T   F   4. The strategy section of a campaign plan includes a theme, or creative concept, and executions for various media, situations, and audiences.

T   F   5. A goal of campaign evaluation is to try to predict when the message is no longer having any effect on the audience.

T   F   6. When a campaign is dropped by an advertiser, so is the agency that produced the campaign.

T   F   7. When the Orlando area holds a place in the consumer's mind as the "home of Walt Disney World's Magic Kingdom," this is called a position.

T　　F　　8.　Competitive advantage is a unique product feature that gives a product a selling advantage over the competition.

T　　F　　9.　A campaign should try to cover every possible consideration and still be flexible enough to be able to move in new directions.

T　　F　　10.　The SWOT analysis of the situation analysis of a campaign plan should analyze the brand's situation in the marketplace.

T　　F　　11.　The ultimate point of evaluation for the Orlando tourism campaign (as well as any advertising campaign) is the number of products sold.

T　　F　　12.　The strategy section of the campaign plan serves as a transition that leads directly into key decisions that form the foundation of the plan.

T　　F　　13.　The advertising objectives would be found in the strategy section of the campaign plan.

T　　F　　14.　Competitive advantage is based on a competitor weakness.

T　　F　　15.　An increase in assaults on tourists in Florida would be a weakness in the situation analysis of the Orlando campaign.

True/False Answers

1.	F	9.	T
2.	T	10.	T
3.	F	11.	F
4.	F	12.	F
5.	T	13.	T
6.	T	14.	F
7.	T	15.	F
8.	F		

Completion

Fill in the missing word or words in the blanks provided.

1.　A comprehensive advertising plan for a series of different but related ads that appear in different media across a specified time period is called _____.

2.　A section of an advertising campaign plan that summarizes the relevant research findings about the company, the product, the competition, the marketplace, and the consumer is called _____.

3.　The usual timeframe for an advertising campaign plan is _____.

4.　The term "campaign" was borrowed from the _____ area of planning.

5. A written summary of an advertising campaign plan that is presented to the client is called a
_____.

6. In the _____ of the advertising campaign plan, you would find primary and secondary
research findings about the company, the product, the competition, the marketplace, and the
consumer.

7. In the _____ section of the situation analysis the advertising planner would consider the
attitudes, interests, motivations and lifestyles of the ultimate users of the product.

8. In the _____ of the advertising campaign plan, you would find the objective for the
campaign.

9. In the _____ of the advertising campaign plan, you would find a detailed description of
the target audience selected for the campaign.

10. According to the text, the most important part of the advertising plan is the _____.

11. _____, _____, and _____ are the key points in determining whether a
product has a "competitive advantage" for a given feature.

12. When an advertising campaign is described as having one message and a coordinated strategy
from situation analysis to media planning to graphic design, the campaign is said to be
_____.

13. _____ and _____ are the two pieces of information you expect to find in the
media objectives of the media plan of an advertising campaign plan.

14. A situation analysis is obtained using _____ and _____ research techniques.

15. A product feature that is important to the consumer and is a strength of the product and is a
weakness of the competition is _____.

Completion Answers

1.	advertising campaign	9.	campaign strategy
2.	situation analysis	10.	creative plan
3.	1 year or less	11.	important to consumer, product strength, competitor weakness
4.	military	12.	seamless
5.	plansbook	13.	target audience and reach-frequency emphasis
6.	situation analysis	14.	primary, secondary
7.	consumer analysis	15.	"competitive advantage"
8.	campaign strategy		

Matching

Match the terms and concepts with the appropriate statements. Each term or concept may be used only once; there are more terms and concepts than statements.

Terms and Concepts

a. campaign strategy
b. campaign strategy
c. campaign strategy
d. campaign strategy
e. campaign strategy
f. competitive advantage
g. creative plan
h. industry trends
i. media plan

j. perception of company
k. position
l. product
m. scope of the project
n. seamless
o. strengths, weaknesses, opportunities, and threats
p. zipless
q. marketing summary
r. evaluating the plan

Statements

_____ 1. Section in the situation analysis that would be involved when the planner considers the time-frame and the amount of effort needed to solve critical problems. The planner would look at the problems and consider the overall marketing planning changes needed in order to see how these would impact advertising planning.

_____ 2. Section of the situation analysis where the advertising planner documents the size of the industry, industry price trends, and industry growth trends.

_____ 3. Section of the situation analysis where the advertising planner documents consumer brand awareness, brand imagery, distributor attitudes, and company reputation.

_____ 4. Section of the situation analysis where the advertising planner documents the characteristics of the company's products and services, benefits provided to consumers, problems associated with product use, and the sociological and psychological factors involved in use of the product.

_____ 5. Section of the situation analysis where the significance of the kinds of research described is analyzed. This section serves as a transition that leads directly into the key strategic decisions that serve as a foundation for the campaign plan.

_____ 6. Section of the advertising campaign plan where you would find the advertising objectives, the target audience, the competitive advantage, and the position.

_____ 7. Section of the advertising campaign plan where the advertising planner would document the key decisions that will guide the campaign. These include setting objectives, targeting the audience, identifying the competitive advantage, and locating the best position for the product.

_____ 8. Section of the advertising campaign plan where you would find the selling strategy for the campaign.

_____ 9. Section of the advertising campaign plan where you would find an explanation of the position of the product for which the campaign is designed.

_____ 10. Section of the advertising campaign plan where you would find an explanation of the product's competitive advantage.

_____ 11. Term used to refer to how a product is seen in the marketplace by the target audience. This is the product's place in the consumer's mind relative to the competition.

_____ 12. When a product feature is important to consumers and the product is strong on this feature and the competition is weak.

_____ 13. Section of the advertising campaign plan where you would find the campaign theme, the creative concept and executions for different media, situations, and times of the year.

_____ 14. Reach and frequency objectives would be found in this part of the advertising campaign plan.

_____ 15. Term that means that campaign has one message and a coordinated strategy from situation analysis to media planning to graphic design.

Matching Answers

1. scope of the project
2. industry trends
3. perception of company
4. product
5. strengths, weaknesses, opportunities, and threats
6. campaign strategy
7. campaign strategy
8. campaign strategy

9. campaign strategy
10. campaign strategy
11. position
12. competitive advantage
13. creative plan
14. media plan
15. seamless

Multiple Choice

Place the letter of the correct answer in the blank provided.

_____ 1. What is the first section of the advertising campaign called?
   a. marketing objectives
   b. product history
   c. situation analysis
   d. organization mission statement
   e. none of the above

_____ 2. Which of the following is **NOT** part of the campaign strategy section of the advertising campaign plan?
   a. campaign theme
   b. competitive advantage and positioning
   c. selling strategy
   d. objective
   e. target audience

_____ 3. Which of the following is a part of the creative plan of the advertising campaign plan?
   a. campaign theme
   b. creative concept
   c. message strategy
   d. executions
   e. all of the above

_____ 4. What problem plagues American business planning as well as advertising planning?
   a. short-term thinking
   b. marketing myopia
   c. not enough concern for the consumer perspective
   d. long-term thinking
   e. none of the above

_____ 5. What are the two points of view of the situation analysis?
   a. short-term and long-term
   b. present and future
   c. competitor's and organization's
   d. past and present
   e. consumer's and management's

_____ 6. Which of the following is **NOT** part of the integrated marketing communication section of the advertising campaign plan?
   a. public relations
   b. selling strategy
   c. special promotions
   d. sales support
   e. merchandising and dealer support

_____ 7. In the situation analysis, internal factors involve:
   a. weaknesses that make the brand vulnerable to threats from outside.
   b. consumer perceptions of the brand.
   c. employee attitudes.
   d. strengths that lead to opportunities.
   e. all of the above

_____ 8. In the situation analysis, external factors involve:
   a. weaknesses that make the brand vulnerable to threats from outside.
   b. consumer perceptions of the brand.
   c. social issues that impact on the brand.
   d. strengths that lead to opportunities.
   e. all of the above

_____ 9. What research techniques are used to collect the information for the situation analysis?
   a. qualitative and quantitative
   b. formal and informal
   c. primary and secondary
   d. personal and group
   e. consumer and product

_____ 10. How much information is necessary for the situation analysis?
   a. enough
   b. all you can get
   c. an amount sufficient to guide the entire campaign
   d. provides the key answer to the strategy
   e. all of the above

_____ 11. Which of the following would you **NOT** expect to find in the strengths, weaknesses, opportunities, and threats section of the situation analysis of the advertising campaign plan?
   a. analysis of the brand's situation in the marketplace
   b. identification of the major weakness of the brand
   c. comparison of the product to the competition
   d. detailed description of the target audience
   e. description of the key strength of the brand

_____ 12. What was the problem associated with the current Orlando campaign slogan, "Orlando--Go for the Magic?"
   a. had grown stale from 10 years of use
   b. over-emphasis on Walt Disney World
   c. decreasing effectiveness of the slogan to attract tourism to the Orlando area
   d. dissatisfaction expressed by tourists and conventioneers
   e. unfortunate association of the slogan with the increasing crime against tourists in Florida

_____ 13. What makes the Orlando program a campaign as opposed to just a series of ads?
   a. amount of money spent on the effort
   b. use of integrated marketing communication
   c. use of a variety of media and communication approaches
   d. use of the "Go for the Magic" theme in every ad
   e. all of the above

14. In evaluating the Orlando/Orange County Convention and Visitors Bureau campaign, what was used as indicators of success?
    a. customer evaluations of bureau personnel
    b. the number of leads for member business resulting from answered requests for information
    c. the amount of publications distributed
    d. brand equity, reflected in high levels of both name recognition and customer loyalty
    e. all of the above

15. What caused a shift in the Orlando communication program from an aggressive marketing stance to one reflecting more of a public relations orientation?
    a. increase in tourist assaults in Florida
    b. decrease in tourists coming to the Orlando area
    c. dissatisfaction expressed by members of the Orlando bureau
    d. loss of conventions for the Orlando area
    e. problems with local business dissatisfaction with the over-emphasis on Walt Disney World

Multiple Choice Answers

1.	c	9.	c
2.	a	10.	e
3.	e	11.	d
4.	a	12.	b
5.	d	13.	d
6.	b	14.	e
7.	d	15.	a
8.	a		

Career Exercise -- Interviewing

The key to a successful interview is to keep in mind that you are trying to sell yourself to the interviewer. Keep in mind that the interview is the personal sales element of the career marketing communication mix. The point is to make a sale -- that is, land the job. While the interview is a communication effort, it is more than a give and take of information. The interview is persuasive communication. The point is to finish the transaction with the interviewer convinced that you are a better choice than the other candidates.

There are three significant points to remember in the interview: overall impression, sales messages, and personal research. Perhaps the most important facet of the interview is the impression left with the interviewer. Many of the specific messages delivered may not be retained, but there certainly will be an overall impression. The impression is determined by three factors: appearance, energy, and enthusiasm. Your appearance must be acceptable to the interviewer but must also help you convey confidence and control. It is more important for you to appear neat and comfortable than to make some kind of fashion statement. When you get right down to it, the only real mistake to be made in the area of appearance is for your appearance to be noticed. You should look professional and normal. You should hope not to look dressed up or dressed down. You want to appear to be confident and comfortable in the normal business attire of the field.

When you are nervous, it can be difficult to create a feeling of energy. The best advice is to allow the nervous energy to work for you. Work to channel your nervous energy into your responses to questions just as you would do in a public speaking situation. Don't sit on your hands and methodically answer questions. Allow yourself some movement. Gesture normally and change positions. Don't lock yourself in a chair and grab hold of the arms. This kills any physical energy that you might generate. Try to speak clearly and forcefully -- that is, normally.

Energy and enthusiasm often go hand-in-hand. You want to communicate that you are excited about the field and the job at hand. Don't be reluctant to tell the interviewer how much you want to work in the field and to have the job. The enthusiasm must be real. If you are not excited about what you hope to do, you won't convince the interviewer. However, just because you are excited does not mean the interviewer will feel that enthusiasm. You need to show some fire and hunger.

When you go into the interview, be prepared to make definite points with the interviewer. You will probably find it useful to approach this in much the same fashion as a creative platform. Decide ahead of time exactly what points you want the interviewer to remember about you. Keep it simple -- one or two is probably best. For example, you are a proven achiever; or you have proven creative abilities. Once you have decided what points to emphasize, you need to determine the best specific proof that you have to document the points -- through training, skills, experiences, references, etc. When you get into the interview, you look for opportunities to make your points and to prove them. You answer the questions asked, but you are always looking for opportunities to make your points and to repeat the points.

Finally, keep in mind that you should also be collecting information of your own in the interview to make certain that this job is for you. You must be careful. Interviewers are turned off by people who appear to be too self-serving -- that is, those who seem to be only interested in what does the job offer me in terms of salary, benefits, and opportunity. The interview is probably best used to find out about the nature of the responsibilities and opportunities offered by the job and the organization. Make sure you know as much as possible about the organization offering the job. Even if you have legitimately not had time to research the organization, you probably would want to be very careful with questions about the organization.

When preparing for an interview, keep in mind that the interviewer will be trained to look for indications of confidence, drive, enthusiasm, verbal facility, listening comprehension, persuasiveness, human relations skills, credibility, technical competence, conceptual skills, organization skills, growth potential, functional interests, job match, and location preferences/limits. Be prepared to answer open-ended questions such as the following: why have you chosen a career in advertising; how would you define the role of advertising in the marketing process; tell me how you go about solving a business problem; or how do you handle conflict situations?

As an exercise in preparing for interviews, become an observer of personal behavior. Observe your friends and teachers as they talk and speak. Which ones do you think show high energy when they talk? What indicates energy to you? Who do you think shows enthusiasm? What indicates enthusiasm to you?

21 Evaluative Research

Chapter Objectives and Summary

- **Explain why advertisers devote time and money to evaluative research.**
- **Distinguish between evaluative and diagnostic research.**
- **Identify the eight major evaluative research methods and what each one claims to test.**
- **Evaluate the strengths and weaknesses of various forms of testing.**
- **Understand the concerns surrounding the issues of validity and reliability.**

Faced with questions of the effectiveness of advertising, many advertisers turn to evaluative research to make final go, no-go decisions about finished or nearly finished ads. Evaluative research must be distinguished from strategic research (described in Chapter 6), which is used to test strategies and different versions of a concept or approach. Ideally the results of evaluative research would become available before large sums of money have been invested in finished work. Failing that, the best alternative would be a test that predicts effectiveness before millions of media dollars have spent. Copy-testing methods fall into eight categories: memory tests, persuasion tests, direct-response counts, communication tests, focus groups, physiological tests, frame-by-frame, and in-market tests. Of these, memory, persuasion, communication, and focus groups are the most widely employed.

Memory tests are based on the assumption that if an advertisement is to affect behavior, it must leave a mental "residue" with the person who has been exposed to it. Memory tests in turn fall into two major groups: recall tests and recognition tests. Recall tests require that the respondent link a specific brand name or, at least, a specific product category to a specific commercial. If the commercial fails to establish a tight connection between the brand name and the selling message, the commercial will not get a high recall score. Recall test results are analyzed by examining the verbatim responses to determine how many viewers remembered something specific about the ad. Across a range of product categories, the average recall score for a 30-second commercial is about 20 percent. The advantages of recall tests include the fact that advertisers are accustomed to using them and that there are accumulated norms available. Although recall tests are not perfectly reliable, they are more reliable than most tests. Validity means there is a strong, positive relationship between an ad's overall recall score and some later assessment of its sales effectiveness. When an advertiser uses a recall test, the advertiser is assuming that the recall score is a valid indication of the advertisement's sales effectiveness. Many researchers, and most of advertising's creative leaders, however, believe that this assumption is incorrect. Recall tests are not inexpensive. On the average, television tests cost from $9,000 to $17,000 per commercial; print recall tests cost from $7,000 to $13,000 per ad. The most fundamental reason that advertisers continue to use recall tests is that they help them make decisions.

One way to assess an advertisement's effectiveness is to ask people to recall it. Another way is to show the advertisement to people and ask them if they remember having seen it. This is the recognition test. One of the most popular recognition tests is the Starch Test. The Starch test can test only print ads that have already run. The questions are easier. It is relatively fast and cheap. Starch tests cost $500 per ad. Like the recall tests, the Starch test has accumulated norms. It is an unusually reliable measure of something. The trouble is that it probably measures the attractiveness of the ad. Another recognition test is the Bruzzone Test. The Bruzzone test is a television analogue of the Starch test. The scores it produces are quite reliable. It is relatively inexpensive and has accumulated norms. It cannot be used until after all the costs of final production and placement in the media have already been incurred.

The persuasion test is a measure of attitude-change. Results are analyzed to determine whether intention to buy has increased as a result of exposure to the advertisement. The validity of a persuasion test depends in part on whether participants in the experiment constitute a good sample of the prospects the advertiser is trying to reach. Another threat to validity is the highly artificial testing environment. Also, when the advertisement being tested is for a well-known brand, the amount of change created by one exposure to one commercial is almost always very small, and small changes tend to be unreliable. Persuasion tests are relatively expensive. A typical persuasion test costs between $11,000 and $15,000, but the cost can go much higher.

Direct-response counts are direct measures of advertisement effectiveness through sales results usually. Sometimes "split run" tests are used to compare different ads. The advertiser gets a reading of which ad produces the best response. Compared to recall and recognition tests, the direct response has few reliability and validity problems. Direct response counts cannot be used effectively when the purchase is a retail purchase. The direct connection between ad and purchase is lost.

Communication tests are used to find out whether an ad delivered the intended message or perhaps some unintended message, and how the target audience members reacted to the message. Communication tests do not give single scores, but rather patterns of findings, which require detailed analysis and interpretation of consumers' reactions to the advertisement. It increases the unreliability caused by subjective interpretation, but it provides richer, more detailed information about how consumers reacted to the ad.

Focus groups are useful because the results can be virtually instantaneous. Three or four groups can be conducted and reported in less than a week. Focus groups are also relatively inexpensive -- usually less than $5,000 per ad. However, focus groups can be extremely unreliable and can be of questionable validity, depending on how well the groups were conducted.

Physiological tests try to get around the problems inherent in verbal response. Physiological measurements might pick up responses that the person was unable or unwilling to report. Several physiological measurements have been tried including heart rate, pupil dilation, galvanic skin response, and electroencephalographic (EEG) response. Validity has been a problem because physiological reactions are often caused by incidents that have little or nothing to do with the content of the ad. Most physiological tests require that respondents report to a laboratory, a setting that is hardly conducive to natural responses. Requirements reduce the representativeness of samples because many potential respondents cannot be persuaded to submit to such unusual and possibly threatening tasks. They also reduce the representativeness of the environment in which the advertisement is shown. No one is entirely sure how to interpret any of the physiological reactions. Although physiological tests continue to attract intermittent attention and interest, they are not now in general use in evaluative research.

The frame-by-frame tests can be useful because they provide some guidance as to how a commercial might be improved. It provides direct clues as to which parts of the commercial need further work. Reliability and validity are difficult to establish. It provides an opportunity to look inside a commercial, and it offers clues as to what scenes produce what kind of response. The PEAC test combines the advantages of moment-to-moment response with an opportunity to ask and discuss questions about the respondents' reactions. The PEAC test is relatively expensive -- $17,000 per ad. This combination provides useful diagnostic information that cannot be accumulated in any other way.

In-market tests evaluate advertisements by measuring their influence on sales. Full-scale-in-market tests are seldom attempted in evaluating individual ads. Sales of any brand are produced by a tightly interwoven net of factors, including economic conditions, competitive strategies, and all of the marketing activities in which the advertiser is engaged. They are very costly and time-consuming. The effect of a single advertisement may be entirely lost. By the time sales figures become available, most of the important investments have already been made. Some of those problems can be avoided by using simulated test markets. In spite of the artificiality of a simulated test market, research companies that conduct them have developed formulas using trial-and-repeat numbers which have proved to be remarkably accurate predictors of later in-market success. A single simulated test market costs from $50,000 to $75,000.

Another major substitute for a full in-market test, the research company conducting the test arranges to control the television signal received by the households in a community. The test collects exact records of what every household purchases. Because exposure records and purchasing records come from the same household, the data collected in this way are known as single-source data. Single-source data can produce exceptionally dependable results. The method is, however, very expensive -- $200,000 to $300,000. The method usually requires more than 6 months to produce usable results.

Key Terms and Concepts

direct-response counts	Evaluative tests that count the number of viewers or readers who request more information or who purchase the product.
evaluative research	Research intended to measure the effectiveness of finished or nearly finished advertisements.
frame-by-frame test	Test that provides some guidance as to how the commercial might be improved by providing an opportunity to look inside a commercial and offering clues as to what scenes produce what kind of response.
in-market test	Test that measures the effectiveness of advertisements in measuring actual sales results in the marketplace.
persuasion test	A test that evaluates the effectiveness of an advertisement by measuring whether the ad affects consumers' intentions to buy a brand.
physiological test	Test that measures emotional reactions to advertisements by monitoring reactions such as pupil dilation and heart rate.
recall test	A test that evaluates the memorability of an advertisement by contacting members of the advertisement's audience and asking them what they remember about it.
recognition test	A test that evaluates the memorability of an advertisement by contacting members of the audience, showing them the ad, and asking if they remember it.

reliability	A characteristic that describes a test that yields essentially the same results when the same advertisement is tested time after time.
simulated test market	The research procedure in which respondents are exposed to advertisements and then permitted to shop for the advertised products in an artificial environment where records are kept of their purchases.
single-source data	Data such as exposure records and purchasing records collected from the same household.
validity	The ability of a test to measure what it is intended to measure.

True/False

Circle the appropriate letter.

T F 1. Evaluative research is most valuable in the advertising process before large sums of money have been spent on finished work.

T F 2. Evaluative research is well-accepted in the advertising industry with clients, creative directors, and agency managers all agreeing on its value.

T F 3. Memory tests are based on the assumption that an advertisement leaves a mental residue with the person exposed to it.

T F 4. The research company most associated with day-after recall tests is Gallup and Robinson In-View Service.

T F 5. A fill-in-the-blank item is an example of aided recall.

T F 6. Favorable scores on recall tests are good indicators of sales success as a result of an advertising campaign.

T F 7. The major problem with persuasion tests is that the change produced by one exposure to an advertisement may be too small to measure.

T F 8. No copy test is reliable, valid, affordable, and fast.

T F 9. Even when conducted properly, the results of persuasion tests have not shown a clear correlation with sales effectiveness.

T F 10. The key advantage of direct-response counts is that they provide a direct measure of the effectiveness of advertisements.

T F 11. Communication tests are not used much because they are relatively expensive.

T	F	12.	Focus groups should not be used to make final go/no-go decisions on advertisements.

T	F	13.	Physiological tests are regularly used as evaluative research for advertising.

T	F	14.	The relationship between the results of a frame-by-frame analysis of an ad and the advertisement's ultimate effect is uncertain.

T	F	15.	A major weakness of in-market tests is that the results are only available after the advertisement has been produced and media costs have been incurred.

True/False Answers

1.	T	9.	T
2.	F	10.	T
3.	T	11.	F
4.	F	12.	T
5.	F	13.	F
6.	F	14.	T
7.	T	15.	T
8.	T		

Completion

Fill in the missing word or words in the blanks provided.

1. Research intended to measure the effectiveness of finished or nearly finished advertisements is called _____.

2. _____ test, _____ test, _____, _____ test, _____, _____ test, _____ test, and _____ test are the categories of copy-testing used in evaluative research.

3. Of the types of evaluative research, _____, _____, _____, and _____ are the most widely used.

4. _____ is the research company most commonly associated with memory recall tests.

5. A memory recall test in which the particular brand is not mentioned when the respondent is asked questions about advertising is called _____.

6. A memory recall test in which the particular brand is mentioned in order to increase the likelihood of recall is called _____.

7. The Bruzzone test is most commonly associated with _____.

8. A test that evaluates the memorability of an advertisement by contacting members of the advertisement's audience and asking them what they remember about it is called _____.

9. The average recall score for a 30-second television commercial across a range of product categories is _____.

10. A characteristic that describes a test that yields essentially the same results when the same advertisement is tested time after time is called _____.

11. The ability of a test to measure what it is intended to measure is called _____.

12. A test that evaluates the memorability of an advertisement by contacting members of the audience, showing them the ad and asking if they remember it is called _____.

13. The Starch recognition test is used with the medium of _____.

14. _____ and _____ are the two advantages of the use of focus group interviews for evaluative research.

15. _____ and _____ are the key attributes that advertising decision-makers look for in evaluative research techniques.

Completion Answers

1. diagnostic research
2. memory, persuasion, direct-response counts, communication, focus group, physiological, frame-by-frame, in-market
3. communication, focus groups, persuasion, memory
4. Burke Marketing Services
5. unaided recall
6. aided recall
7. recall testing
8. recall tests
9. about 20%
10. reliability
11. validity
12. recognition test
13. magazines
14. cost, speed
15. reliability, reality

Matching

Match the terms and concepts with the appropriate statements. Each term or concept may be used only once; there are more terms and concepts than statements.

Terms and Concepts

a. $7,000 to $17,000
b. $50,000 to $75,000
c. $200,000 to $300,000
d. about $5,000
e. about $500
f. communication tests
g. direct-response tests
h. frame-by-frame tests
i. in-market tests

j. evaluative research
k. norms
l. persuasion test
m. physiological tests
n. simulated test market
o. single-source data
p. in-house tests
q. evaluation test
r. double-source data

Statements

_____ 1. Research used to make go/no-go decisions about ads.

_____ 2. The price range per ad of a recall test.

_____ 3. The price per ad for the Starch recognition test.

_____ 4. The price per group for a focus group interview.

_____ 5. The price per market for a simulated test-market type of in-market test.

_____ 6. The price per market for a single-source-data type of in-market test.

_____ 7. A test that evaluates the effectiveness of an advertisement by measuring whether the ad affects consumers' intentions to buy a brand.

_____ 8. Evaluative tests that count the number of viewers or readers who request more information or who purchase the product.

_____ 9. A test that seeks to find out whether an ad delivers its intended message or any unintended message and how the target audience reacted to the message.

_____ 10. Tests that measure emotional reactions to advertisements by monitoring reactions such as pupil dilation and heart rate.

_____ 11. Tests that evaluate consumers' reactions to the individual scenes that unfold in the course of a television commercial.

_____ 12. Tests that measure the effectiveness of advertisements by measuring actual sales results in the marketplace.

_____ 13. The research procedure in which respondents are exposed to advertisements and then permitted to shop for the advertised products in an artificial environment where records are kept of their purchases.

_____ 14. Data for advertising exposure as well as purchase records that come from the same household.

_____ 15. The accumulated records of results compiled by research companies on copy tests that serve as batting averages for the tests.

Matching Answers

1. j
2. a
3. e
4. d
5. b
6. c
7. l
8. g

9. f
10. m
11. h
12. i
13. n
14. o
15. k

Multiple Choice

Place the letter of the correct answer in the blank provided.

_____ 1. What is the difference between evaluative and strategic research?
  a. evaluative research tests the concept while strategic research tests the final ad
  b. evaluative research is primary research while strategic research is secondary research
  c. evaluative research tests ideas while strategic research tests ads
  d. evaluative research tests the final ad while strategic research tests the concept
  e. evaluative research is quantitative research while strategic research is qualitative research

_____ 2. Which of the following is **NOT** one of the categories of evaluative research?
  a. physiological tests
  b. survey research
  c. persuasion tests
  d. direct-response counts
  e. in-market tests

_____ 3. What are the two major types of memory tests?
  a. persuasion and communication
  b. primary and secondary
  c. recognition and recall
  d. short-term and long-term
  e. attitudinal and informational

_____ 4. What type of memory test is involved when a multiple-choice question is used?
a. aided recall
b. top-of-mind recall
c. automatic recall
d. unaided recall
e. none of the above

_____ 5. Which of the following is **NOT** an advantage of memory recall tests?
a. reliability
b. advertisers are accustomed to using them
c. recall tests have established norms
d. validity
e. decision making tool

_____ 6. What is the correlation between advertising recall scores and sales?
a. no correlation
b. weak positive correlation
c. strong positive correlation
d. weak negative correlation
e. strong negative correlation

_____ 7. Which of the following is the least expensive?
a. recall test
b. recognition test
c. persuasion test
d. single-source data test
e. simulated test market

_____ 8. What does the persuasion test measure?
a. attitude change
b. information remembered
c. perception of the strategic concept
d. the dynamic of the effect of the message
e. none of the above

_____ 9. What does the communication test measure?
a. attitude change
b. information remembered
c. whether the ad delivered the message intended
d. perception of the strategic concept
e. all of the above

_____ 10. What is the weakness of the analysis provided by the communication test?
a. lacks invalidity compared to other tests
b. offers clues as to what scenes produce what response
c. does not provide a single score but rather a pattern of results
d. test and analysis take a great deal of time
e. very expensive

_____ 11. Of the following, which is the most reliable test?
    a. focus group
    b. recall test
    c. communication test
    d. persuasion test
    e. physiological test

_____ 12. Which type of evaluative research is the most valid?
    a. in market tests
    b. direct response counts
    c. persuasion tests
    d. communication tests
    e. physiological tests

_____ 13. Which of the following is a problem with in-market tests for evaluative research?
    a. cost
    b. time
    c. by the time sales figures are available, most of the important investments have already been made
    d. effect of a single ad is hard to isolate from economic conditions, competitive strategies and all the other marketing activities involved
    e. all of the above

_____ 14. In the final analysis, what is the basic function of research data in advertising decision making?
    a. to make tough decisions for advertising decision makers
    b. replace intuition with logic
    c. to reduce uncertainty
    d. appease cautious business executives
    e. all of the above

_____ 15 What do physiological tests measure?
    a. attitude change
    b. emotional response
    c. information remembered
    d. whether the ad delivered the message intended
    e. perception of the strategic concept

Multiple Choice Answers

1. d	6. a	11. b
2. b	7. b	12. a
3. c	8. a	13. e
4. a	9. c	14. c
5. d	10. c	15. b

Career Exercise -- Professional Appearance

The best rules for professional appearance are observe, observe, and observe. Observe what the professionals in your field wear. Observe the range of variation in dress and grooming. Observe what the professionals who have been in the field for a long time wear versus the newer professionals ... the managers versus the worker bees.

Having observed, ask questions about appearance -- new fashions, hair styles, beards and side-burns for men, make-up for women, shoes, etc. Question a range of people with emphasis on the potential employers and references that you are targeting. If you are already appearance conscious, good; if not, you must at least become conscious of others' reaction to your appearance.

Having observed and asked questions, make your own decisions about your appearance. No one can tell you what is best for you as an individual. Seek advice; read books; collect every scrap of information on the subject that you can get your hands on, but make your own decisions. Appearance is the most personal of all forms of communication, and to be effective appearance must emerge from the informed judgment of an individual who is sensitized to the feelings and reactions of other people.

Two keys stand out in regard to professional appearance. Make choices that are within the range of acceptance of the people with whom you have to deal. Make choices that make you feel confident, comfortable and in control. Your appearance must be acceptable but must also help you convey confidence. It is more important for you to appear neat and professional than to make some kind of fashion statement. Dressing to a current fashion fad seldom results in a successful professional appearance. When you get right down to it, the only real mistake in the area of appearance is for your appearance to be noticed. You should look professional and normal. You should hope not to look dressed up or dressed down. You want to appear confident and comfortable in the normal business attire of the field.

Go to a professional meeting in your area. Observe what the people at the meeting are wearing. Pick out 10 people that you feel make a good professional appearance. Note in as much detail as possible what they are wearing including their basic dress (casual, sporty, business, sophisticated), shoes, socks/stockings, jewelry, glasses, hair styles, make-up, and general grooming (finger nails, beards, etc.). You are looking for details. How long are the pants/skirts? What kinds of materials are worn? What shades of colors are most common? What types of hair styles predominate? What kinds of jewelry are worn?

If you cannot comfortably take notes, you may have to concentrate on just a couple of individuals at a time to recall sufficient detail. Work at getting a picture in your mind of the individual's appearance and then write down what you recall as soon as possible following the meeting. You will find that observation research pays dividends beyond your professional appearance.

22 Business-to-Business and Retail Advertising

Chapter Objectives and Summary

- **Explain business-to-business advertising objectives.**
- **List the different markets in the business arena and the various media used in business advertising.**
- **Understand how local retail advertising differs from national brand advertising.**
- **Understand how cooperative advertising works.**

Business-to-business advertising is directed at people who buy or specify products for business use. Although personal selling is the most common method of communicating with business buyers, business advertising enables a business marketer to reach a large portion of the market at a lower cost. Business advertising objectives center on creating company awareness, increasing overall selling efficiency, and supporting channel members.

The business arena comprises five markets: industrial, government, trade, professional, and agricultural. The industrial market is interested in goods and services that either become part of the final product or facilitate the operation of the business. The largest purchaser of industrial goods in the United States are the federal, state, and local governments. However, advertisements are seldom targeted directly to government agencies. The trade market involves resellers, wholesalers, and retailers.

A purchaser in the business market engages in a decision making process much the same as an individual consumer. Several inherent characteristics differentiate business marketing from consumer marketing including: market concentration, decision makers, strategy, and purchase objectives. The market for a typical business good is relatively small compared to the market for a consumer good. More people tend to be involved in the decision for a business purchase, and they tend to use rational criteria when comparing choices. Thus, business advertising is also used to (1) reach the various influencers involved and (2) communicate the different information needs. Business decision makers tend to be guided by a specific strategy. This strategy eliminates much of the autonomy in decision making. Also, the process can be more time consuming. Finally, purchasing objectives in the business market center on rational, pragmatic considerations. Buyers in the business market are more interested than ordinary consumers with the cost of owning and using the product.

Business-to-business advertising objectives center on creating company awareness, increasing overall selling efficiency, and supporting distributors and resellers. The best business-to-business ads are relevant, understandable, and strike an emotion in the prospective client. However, adjustments must be made for the differences in the nature of the market and the decision makers. Although some business advertisers use traditional media, most rely on general business or trade publications, industrial directories, direct marketing, or some combination thereof. Direct mail has emerged as a primary medium for several business-to-business advertisers in the last decade. There has also been a tremendous growth in business television programming that is targeted at both business people and consumers who are interested in business-related topics. The videocassette industry has also entered the fray as a reliable business-to-business medium. Many people have questioned the effectiveness of business advertising. A 1987 study by the Advertising Research Foundation and the Association of Business Publishers demonstrated that business advertising was effective in increasing sales, generating higher profits, and affecting purchasers' awareness of and attitudes toward industrial products. With a reputation for poor advertising planning and execution, business advertising is being held to new standards of accountability and efficiency, as well as becoming more benefit oriented in its messages.

Retail advertising is often called local advertising because it is targeted at people living in the local community. Just as advertising is part of the marketing mix for nationally promoted products and services, it also plays an important role in the marketing or merchandizing mix for retailers. Retail advertising is designed to promote several functions: selling a variety of products, encouraging store traffic, delivering sales promotion messages, and creating and communicating a store image.

Retail advertising differs from national advertising in that it is targeted at people living in the local community, must support multiple brands, is customized to reflect the local store, and has more inherent urgency. The primary objectives of retail ads is to attract customers and to communicate the store location. With few exceptions, retail advertising is less sophisticated and more utilitarian than national advertising. In addition, retailers can't justify high production costs for advertising. Most retailers have little formal training in advertising and rely more heavily on their media sales representatives. The ads work, but they are usually less creative than national advertising.

One way retailers can compensate for their smaller budgets and limited expertise is to take advantage of cooperative advertising. Cooperative advertising is manufacturers helping retail advertising with the cost of advertising by either funding or creative support. Different types of cooperative support are the ad allowance, the accrual fund, and vendor support programs.

Trends in retail advertising include the relocation of retail activity from city centers to suburbs; demographic changes such as time compression, aging, and market fragmentation; product specialization; nonstore retailing; and focus on price advertising. There are two categories of retail advertising: product and institutional. Product advertising includes nonpromotional, promotional, and semipromotional advertising.

In creating the retail ad, the primary difference between national and retail advertising ad copy is the emphasis on price and store name. Most retail advertising is created and produced by one or a combination of in-house staff, the media, ad agencies, or freelancers. Although some retail ads are created by agencies, this is the most expensive way to produce retail ads. Perhaps the most rapidly changing area in retail advertising is the buying and selling of local media time and space. Retailers are becoming more sophisticated about media. At the same time, local media competition has increased significantly. This has resulted in media selling strategies that focus more on advertising and promotion combinations and less emphasis on just rate cards and circulation. In media strategy, unlike national advertisers, retailers prefer reach over frequency. Newspapers have always made up the bulk of the retailer's advertising. Most retailers that advertise regularly make space contracts with the newspaper. Free-distribution newspapers are becoming increasingly popular. Pre-printed inserts have also become popular as retailers strive for greater market coverage. Broadcast media are used primarily to supplement newspaper advertising. Telephone directories are important advertising media for retailers. Direct response is also used extensively.

Key Terms and Concepts

accrual fund	When a manufacturer automatically sets aside a certain percentage of a retailer's purchases that the retailer may use for co-op advertising at any time within a specified period.
ad allowance	Amount that can change from month to month for each unit of purchase in cooperative advertising.
agricultural advertising	Advertising directed at large and small farmers.
assortment advertising	When the theme of retail advertising centers on the complete collections of available products and on merchandise events.
business-to-business advertising	Advertising directed at people who buy or specify products for business use.
cooperative advertising	Form of advertising in which the manufacturer reimburses the retailer for part or all of the advertising expenditures.
data sheets	Advertising that provides detailed technical information.
dealer tag	Time left at the end of a broadcast advertisement designed for co-op advertising that permits identification of the local store.
geomarketing	Attempting to develop offers that appeal to consumers in different parts of the country as well as in different neighborhoods in the same suburb.
horizontal publications	Publications directed to people who hold similar jobs in different companies across different industries.
industrial advertising	Advertising directed at businesses that buy products to incorporate into other products or to facilitate the operation of their businesses.
nonpromotional advertising	Retail advertising in which themes center around merchandise that is new, exclusive, and of superior quality and designs.
professional advertising	Advertising directed at people such as lawyers, doctors, and accountants.
promotional advertising	Retail advertisement in which the sale price dominates.

retail advertising	Advertising used by local merchants who sell directly to consumers.
semipromotional advertising	Retail advertising in which sales items are interspersed with regular-priced items.
space contract	Agreement in which the retailer agrees to use a certain amount of space over the year and pay a certain amount per line, which is lower than the paper's open rate for the same space.
tear sheet	Page from a newspaper on which a co-op advertisement appears.
trade advertising	Advertising used to influence resellers, wholesalers, and retailers.
vendor support program	Special supplements developed by retailers in which manufacturers are offered the opportunity to buy ad space.
vertical publications	Publications directed to people who hold different positions in the same industries.
zone edition	Versions of a newspaper which go to particular counties or cities and greatly reduce the waste circulation often associated with large newspapers.

True/False

Circle the appropriate letter.

T   F   1.   A major difference between purchase decisions made for businesses and decisions made for consumer purchases is that business buyers don't gather information for the decision.

T   F   2.   Advertising people in business advertising departments are typically more involved in the actual creation and placement of ads than in consumer organizations because most business advertising is not commissionable to advertising agencies.

T   F   3.   The Robinson-Patman Act prohibits manufacturers from offering a price incentive to one retailer and not to another in the same area.

T   F   4.   Consolidation of ownership in retailing has resulted in more emphasis on price and quality comparisons in retail advertising.

T   F   5.   Business-to-business advertising is the most common method of communicating with business buyers.

T   F   6.   Business-to-business advertising is used to reach the various influencers involved in the business purchase decision and to communicate the different information needs.

T   F   7.   A 1987 study by the Advertising Research Foundation and the Association of Business Publishers found that business advertising as currently practiced had little effect on purchasers' awareness of and attitudes toward industrial products.

T   F   8.   Decision making for business purchases tends to be done using more rational criteria than in consumer decision making.

T   F   9.   Decision making for business purchases tends to be done faster than for consumer purchases.

T   F   10. As in consumer advertising, the best business-to-business ads are relevant, understandable, and strike an emotion in the prospective client.

T   F   11. In targeting consumers for retail advertising, a retailer's first concern is geography.

T   F   12. Consumer media, because of their wasted circulation, have not been found to be useful for business-to-business advertising.

T   F   13. Retail advertising tends to have more copy and to include more specifics.

T   F   14. Unlike national advertisers, retailers generally prefer frequency over reach.

T   F   15. Retailers compensate for their smaller budgets and limited experience by taking advantage of cooperative advertising opportunities provided by manufacturers.

True/False Answers

1.	F	9.	F
2.	T	10.	T
3.	T	11.	T
4.	F	12.	F
5.	F	13.	T
6.	T	14.	F
7.	F	15.	T
8.	T		

Completion

Fill in the missing word or words in the blanks provided.

1.   _____, _____, _____, _____, and _____ are the markets for the business-to-business advertiser to reach.

2. _____ is the largest group of purchasers of industrial goods in the United States.

3. _____, _____, _____, and _____ are the types of information that is sought by the trade market from the advertising directed to it.

4. The four types of business decision makers identified in a study sponsored by the Australia Post are _____, _____, _____, and _____.

5. _____ spend the most on advertising as a percentage of sales.

6. Products advertised at or below cost in order to build store traffic are called _____.

7. A form of advertising in which the manufacturer reimburses the retailer for part or all of the advertising expenditures is called _____.

8. In targeting consumers for retail advertising, _____ is a retailer's first concern.

9. _____ is the main objective of retail advertisements.

10. _____ is the most costly way to produce retail advertising.

11. Professional retail ads are created by _____, _____, _____, and _____.

12. _____ is a key advantage to using freelancers to create retail advertising.

13. In media strategy for retail advertising, _____ is generally emphasized.

14. Certain versions of the paper which go to particular counties or cities and greatly reduce the wasted circulation often associated with large newspapers are called _____.

15. _____ have always made up the bulk of the retailer's advertising.

Completion Answers

1. trade, government, professional, agricultural, and industrial
2. federal, state, and local government
3. expected profit margins, advertising support, major selling points, support activities
4. hesitants, innovators, information makers, and doubters
5. department stores
6. loss leaders
7. cooperative advertising
8. geography
9. attract customers
10. advertising agencies
11. advertising agencies, freelancers, in-house staff, local media
12. lower cost
13. reach
14. zone editions
15. newspapers

Matching

Match the terms and concepts with the appropriate statements. Each term or concept may be used only once; there are more terms and concepts than statements.

Terms and Concepts

a. accrual fund
b. advertising allowance
c. assortment advertising
d. business-to-business
e. corporate image
f. data sheets
g. dealer tag
h. geomarketing
i. horizontal

j. promotional advertising
k. retail
l. space contract
m. tear sheet
n. trade
o. vertical
p. industrial
q. brand
r. profit margin

Statements

_____ 1. Advertising directed at people who buy or specify products for business use.

_____ 2. Advertising used to influence resellers, wholesalers, and retailers.

_____ 3. Type of advertising that is used more than government advertising to influence purchases in the government market.

_____ 4. Publications directed to people who hold similar jobs in different companies across different industries.

_____ 5. Publications directed to people who hold different positions in the same industries.

_____ 6. Advertising that provides detailed technical information.

_____ 7. Advertising used by local merchants who sell directly to consumers.

_____ 8. The type of advertising in which the sale price dominates.

_____ 9. The type of advertising in which the theme centers on the complete collections of available products and on merchandise events.

_____ 10. In co-op advertising the amount that can change from month to month for each unit of purchase.

_____ 11. When a manufacturer automatically sets aside a certain percentage of a retailer's purchases that the retailer may use for co-op advertising at any time within a specified period.

_____ 12. The page from a newspaper on which a co-op advertisement appears.

13. The time left at the end of a broadcast advertisement designed for co-op advertising that permits identification of the local store.

14. Retailer's attempt to develop offers that appeal to consumers in different parts of the country as well as in different neighborhoods in the same suburb.

15. An agreement in which the retailer agrees to use a certain amount of space over the year and pay a certain amount per line, which is lower than the paper's open rate for the same space.

Matching Answers

1.	d	9.	e
2.	n	10.	b
3.	e	11.	a
4.	i	12.	m
5.	o	13.	g
6.	f	14.	h
7.	k	15.	l
8.	j		

Multiple Choice

Place the letter of the correct answer in the blank provided.

_____ 1. Business-to-business advertising is:
   a. advertising directed at businesses that buy products to incorporate in other products.
   b. advertising directed at influencing government purchases.
   c. advertising directed at people who buy or specify products for business use.
   d. advertising used to influence resellers, wholesalers, and retailers.
   e. all of the above

_____ 2. Which of the following is **NOT** a market for business-to-business advertising to reach?
   a. consumer
   b. industrial
   c. trade
   d. professional
   e. agricultural

_____ 3. Which of the following is **NOT** an objective of business-to-business advertising?
   a. increase customer interest in a supplier's product
   b. decrease overall personal selling costs
   c. increase selling efficiency by reaching hard to identify influentials
   d. creates customer awareness of a supplier's product
   e. supplements personal selling by providing information to distributors and resellers

_____ 4. Which of the following is a difference between business versus consumer advertising?
   a. there will typically be more decision-makers for a business purchase decision
   b. business purchases tend to be made by professionals with technical knowledge of the products being purchased
   c. the business purchase decision typically takes a lot longer than a consumer purchase decision
   d. market for a typical business good is relatively small compared to the market for a consumer good
   e. all of the above

_____ 5. Which of the following is one of the types of business decision makers?
   a. innovators
   b. information seekers
   c. hesitants
   d. doubters
   e. all of the above

_____ 6. Which of the following is a purchase objective in the business market?
   a. assurance of supply
   b. services
   c. price
   d. quality
   e. all of the above

_____ 7. The cost per thousand of reaching only those in a target audience is called:
   a. relative cost.
   b. target CPM.
   c. adjusted CPM.
   d. CPM.
   e. absolute cost.

_____ 8. What advertising mechanism has emerged as a primary medium for business-to-business advertisers during the last decade?
   a. direct mail
   b. newspapers
   c. radio
   d. television
   e. all of the above

_____ 9. Which of the following is considered retail advertising?
   a. advertising for banks
   b. advertising for real estate organizations
   c. advertising for financial services
   d. all of the above
   e. none of the above

10. What brand is the focus of the retailer?
    a. the cheapest
    b. the one that is selling the best
    c. the store brand
    d. the national brand
    e. all of the above

11. Which of the following is correct concerning modern changes in retailing?
    a. retailers are placing more emphasis on price in all promotional activities
    b. retail activity has shifted from suburbs to city centers
    c. ownership consolidation in retailing has weakened retailers' bargaining power
    d. nonstore retailing is not as popular as it once was
    e. product specialization is decreasing in retailing

12. Which of the following is an objective for building and maintaining retail store traffic?
    a. convince consumers that products and services are high quality
    b. create consumer understanding of products and services offered
    c. build store awareness
    d. convince consumers
    e. all of the above

13. Which of the following is **NOT** an objective of retail advertising?
    a. increase the amount of the average sale
    b. attract new customers
    c. build and maintain store traffic
    d. build brand awareness
    e. help counter season sales lows

14. What is a problem in using an advertising agency to create retail advertising?
    a. lack of creativity
    b. cannot guarantee a consistent look
    c. lack of skill in print media
    d. cannot respond promptly to frequent changes
    e. all of the above

15. Which of the following is **NOT** an advantage of newspapers for retail advertising?
    a. immediacy
    b. prestige
    c. geographic coverage
    d. cost
    e. participative medium often read for advertising

Multiple Choice Answers

1.	a	6.	e	11.	a
2.	b	7.	b	12.	b
3.	b	8.	c	13.	e
4.	b	9.	d	14.	d
5.	d	10.	d	15.	d

Career Exercise -- Portfolio and Business Card

After the resume and the interview, the two most common special media vehicles in career planning are the portfolio and the business card.

The portfolio is a collection of examples of your best work. It is not all your work. As a pre-professional, you may have to include virtually everything you have done, but that should be a temporary situation. One of the things that a professional who examines your portfolio will look for is the quality of your judgment regarding professional work. The portfolio is a primary tool in convincing an employer of your talent and skills. Everything about the portfolio should be as professional as you can make it.

Start by investing in a quality container. Your university bookstore, art supply shops, and luggage stores are good sources of high quality, professional portfolio cases. You may or may not need an over-sized case, depending on the size of your work samples. It is important to be able to display the samples in full size -- unfolded and professionally mounted.

Mount every sample. At least place copy, ad layouts, brochures, etc. on art paper so that the sample stands out and reflects a real concern on your part. Somewhere on the mounting, provide an explanation of the origin of the work, including for whom it was done, when it was prepared, how it was prepared (for example, an ad layout done using Illustrator on a Macintosh SE-30 computer), and the basic strategy behind the work. If there are apparent flaws/weaknesses in the work, explain why they appear in the final product and what could be done to correct them.

The business card should become a standard career communication tool for pre-professionals just as the resume has become a standard. It is a sign of the sophistication of the modern university student/pre-professional that a frequent question today is, should a student have a business card? The answer is an unqualified yes. They are easy to develop. They are inexpensive. And most important, they impress professional contacts. The business card should be the ultimate in simplicity -- name, address, title (if applicable), and phone number.

The student has one disadvantage in the use of the business card with which a professional does not usually have to be concerned. Since the student frequently is not employed, the student usually must use a home address and phone number. In modern society, handing out your home address and phone number is not always rational behavior. There are a number of ways around the problem. The simplest answer is not to include the address. Giving out your phone number can be troublesome but not as dangerous as the address. Other alternatives require more ingenuity. One approach is to become the officer of a campus organization and to use the campus address and phone number of the organization as your business contact point. Sometimes, you can use a part-time job or internship as the business reference point.

The business card should not be expected to do more than it was intended for. Its purpose is simply a means of exchanging names along with addresses and phone numbers in a social or business context. The business card was never intended to carry messages concerning your abilities, experiences, etc. Some professionals use them inappropriately to include other information. Keep it simple and professional. You just want a convenient way to give someone your name if they ask for it. Because of the simplicity of the business card, any quick-service print shop can produce them readily and inexpensively. Most have standard format designs that you can choose from so that you do not even have to design the card yourself.

23　International Advertising

Chapter Objectives and Summary

- **Distinguish between local, regional, international, and global brands.**
- **Explain how international advertising is created and executed.**
- **Understand how international agencies are organized.**
- **List the special problems that international advertisers face.**
- **Observe changes in Eastern Europe advertising with greater comprehension.**

In most countries markets are composed of local, regional, and international brands. A local brand is marketed in one specific country. Regional brands operate in the market blocs of North America, Europe, Latin America, or Asia-Pacific. An international brand is available in most parts of the world -- at least in two or more of the four major regional blocs. A global brand has the same name, same design, and same strategy everywhere in the world.

International advertising is a relatively recent development within international commerce -- not until the late 19th century. International marketing emerged when the emphasis changed from importing products to exporting products. Advertising was used to introduce, explain, and sell the benefits of a product in markets outside the home country. The current patterns of international expansion emerged in the 20th century. International expansion starts with a product that begins to reach saturation in its home market and cannot grow faster than the population. At this point, management seeks to recapture the sales gains of the growth period by either introducing new products or expanding into foreign markets. Foreign expansion involves the following steps: (1) production of goods in the home country; (2) export of goods; (3) transfer of management to on-site management in the export country; (4) local manufacture of the imported products; (5) coordinated regional manufacturing, marketing, and advertising; and (6) coordinated global marketing.

A global perspective directs the advertising of a product to a worldwide market. The achievement of a global perspective requires internationalizing the management group. As long as management is located exclusively in one country, a global perspective is difficult to achieve. The global controversy was ignited by an article in 1983 by Theodore Levitt, professor of business administration and marketing at the Harvard Business School. Levitt argued that companies should operate as if there were only one global market. He suggested that people throughout the world were motivated by the same needs and desires and that differences should be ignored. Philip Kotler, marketing professor at Northwestern University, disagreed. He argued that existing successful global marketing was based on variations not offering the same product everywhere. Neither position seems totally correct. Global advertising is restricted by language, regulation, and lack of global media, but the direction is inescapably toward global. The challenge in advertising is the careful and sophisticated use of Kotler's "variations" nationally or regionally within a basic Levitt-style global plan.

The conflict between market freedom and regulation is accentuated as Eastern Europe moves to a market economy and the Common Market and North America impose or propose new regulations on products, marketing, and advertising. The changes in the communist bloc countries produced problems in international marketing and advertising as the formerly planned economies tried to move toward more competitive systems. In country after country the transition from planned to open economies was accompanied with major currency, inflationary, and other economic and political difficulties. As the Eastern bloc moved away from government regulation and interference, the opposite trend appeared in the Common Market and America. More regulations were proposed, and more restrictions were written into law. An international response to the problems was initiated by the International Advertising Association which was especially concerned by increasing restrictions on advertising in the international economy.

Internationalization of advertising requires new management tools. These tools include one common language, one control mechanism, and one strategic plan. Language affects the creation of the advertising in the range of available terms to express ideas, the amount of space needed, and the meaning of the message. In copywriting, the only reasonable solution to language problems is to employ bilingual copywriters who understand the full meaning of the English text and can capture the essence of the message in the second language. The budget has become almost another language -- one of budgetary control. Centralized companies typically distribute budget responsibility to branch operations. Local management negotiate final budgets. Finally, the strategic plan is developed in conjunction with the budget. Two models of assessing how to advertise in foreign cultures are used. The market-analysis model is based on the idea that markets share common characteristics. It uses two major variables, the share of market of brands within a category and the size of the category. The culture-oriented model emphasizes the cultural differences among people and nations. This model recognizes that all people share certain needs, but it also stresses that these needs are met differently in different cultures. For example, although the function of advertising is the same throughout the world, the expression of its message varies in different cultures. The major distinction is between high-context and low-context cultures. The high-context culture is one in which the meaning of a message can be understood only within a specific context. The low-context culture is one in which the message can be understood as an independent entity.

Although the United States accounts for approximately half of all advertising in the world, this percentage is dropping. Fewer than one-third of the highest-spending world advertisers are based in the United States. International advertisers organize their operations on the basis of their attitude toward centralization and the similarity of their brands as marketed worldwide. The more central the management and the more similar the products, the more common their advertising will be around the world. International agencies must organize to cope with the varying approaches of international advertisers. International agencies use one of three organizational options: tight central international control, centralized resources but moderate control, or matching individual client needs.

Although advertising campaigns can be created for worldwide exposure, the advertising is intended to persuade the customer to make a purchase that is usually completed at home, near home, or at least in the same country. For international advertising campaigns, the two basic starting points are: (1) success in one country; or (2) a centrally conceived strategy. Recent global launches may change these approaches. International media planning follows the same principles used for reaching a national target audience. The lack of global media forces advertisers to plan regionally or globally but to execute plans locally or regionally. The media planner might only be able to establish the media definition of the target audience, lay down a media strategy, and set the criteria for selecting media. Placement of international advertising can be supervised centrally or delegated according to a centrally approved plan. When advertising internationally, laws, customs, time constraints, and problems of inertia, resistance, rejection, and politics must be taken into account.

Key Terms and Concepts

culture-oriented model	The model for deciding how to advertise in foreign cultures that emphasizes the cultural differences among people and nations, that recognizes the sharing of universal needs but that also stresses that these needs are met differently in different cultures.
footprint	The coverage area of a satellite.
global brand	A brand that has the same name, same design and same creative strategy everywhere in the world.
global perspective	A corporate philosophy that directs products and advertising toward a worldwide, rather than a local or regional market.
high-context culture	Culture in which the meaning of a message can be understood only within a specific context.
international advertising	Advertising designed to promote the same product in different countries and cultures.
international brand	A brand or product that is available in most parts of the world.
local brand	A brand that is marketed in one specific country.
low-context culture	Culture in which the meaning of a message can be understood as an independent entity.
market-analysis model	The model for deciding how to advertise in foreign cultures that is based on the concept that markets share common characteristics and need to be analyzed to find local opportunities with focuses on market share and size of market.
regional brand	A brand that is available throughout an entire region.

True/False

Circle the appropriate letter.

T   **F**   1.   One of the main reasons that companies try to expand into foreign markets is to avoid high labor costs in the home-country.

T   F   2. The final step in the international expansion of marketing for a company and its products is coordinated global marketing.

T   F   3. Historically, when the emphasis in international trade changed from importing goods to exporting goods, the function advertising performed was to develop brand image in the home-country.

T   F   4. A company will seek to expand into foreign markets because of competitive pressures in the existing markets.

T   F   5. When advertising copy is to be used in another country, the copy developed for the second country should be re-written in the second country's language by a copywriter who is bilingual in the two languages.

T   F   6. The old axiom, "All business is local" should be modified in the international marketplace to state that all ideas are local.

T   F   7. A global brand and an international brand are the same thing.

T   F   8. A strong musical theme makes the transfer from a national campaign to an international campaign difficult because it can be almost impossible in another language to achieve the same meaning in the lyrics.

T   F   9. Media planning for an international campaign follows a completely different set of principles than those used to reach a national target audience.

T   F   10. If an international campaign involves a consumer product, local media planning and purchase are required.

T   F   11. A key decision in the development of a truly global perspective is the creation of a global headquarters with the separation of the North American and global operations.

T   F   12. Virtually every product category can be separated into local, regional, and international brands.

T   F   13. In the global controversy discussed in the text, Theodore Levitt argued that differences among nations and cultures should be ignored because people throughout the world are motivated by the same desires and wants.

T   F   14. While the communist bloc moves toward greater economic freedom, the Common Market and North America new restrictions on international economic activity are increasing.

T   F   15. English is usually the language of international management.

True/False Answers

1.	F	9.	F
2.	T	10.	T
3.	F	11.	T
4.	F	12.	T
5.	T	13.	T
6.	F	14.	T
7.	F	15.	T
8.	F		

Completion

Fill in the missing word or words in the blanks provided.

1. Historically, when the emphasis in international trade changed from importing goods to exporting goods, _____ emerged as an important element in international trade.

2. _____ is the first step in international marketing.

3. A corporate philosophy that directs products and advertising toward a worldwide, rather than a local or regional market is called _____.

4. _____ is almost always used as the example of a global brand.

5. A brand that has the same name, same design and same creative strategy everywhere in the world is called _____.

6. The text credits _____ with starting the controversy concerning the value of global marketing when it was argued that companies should operate as if there was only one global market.

7. _____ is where almost every successful global or international brand has come from.

8. The international media planner would not be able to _____ if an international campaign was to be locally funded.

9. To succeed within the company, and sometimes even to be hired into an internationalized company a person needs a working knowledge of the _____ language.

10. _____ is marketed in two or more of the four major regional market blocs: North America, Latin America, Europe, and Asia-Pacific.

11. _____ is second only to the United States in world advertising spending.

12. There are two major variables in the market-analysis model: the share of market of brands within a category and the _____.

13. Countries such as Japan, China, and Arabia would be classified as a _____ culture.

14. As far as language goes, English would be categorized as a _____.

15. The _____ language normally requires the least space in printed material or airtime.

Completion Answers

1. marketing
2. exporting
3. global perspective
4. Coca-Cola
5. global brand
6. Theodore Levitt
7. successful local brand
8. set media objectives
9. English
10. international brand
11. Japan
12. size of the category
13. high-context
14. low-context language
15. English

Matching

Match the terms and concepts with the appropriate statements. Each term or concept may be used only once; there are more terms and concepts than statements.

Terms and Concepts

a. corporate philosophy for a worldwide market
b. culture-oriented model
c. Dentsu
d. footprint
e. global brand
f. high-context culture
g. international advertising
h. international brand
i. lead agency
j. local brand
k. low-context culture
l. market-analysis model
m. Proctor & Gamble
n. regional brand
o. United States
p. advertising-analysis model
q. Johnson & Johnson
r. handprint

Statements

_____ 1. A brand that is marketed in one specific country.

_____ 2. A brand that is available throughout an entire region.

_____ 3. A brand or product that is available in most parts of the world.

_____ 4. Advertising designed to promote the same product in different countries and cultures.

_____ 5. A corporate philosophy that directs products and advertising toward a worldwide, rather than a local or regional market.

6. The model for deciding how to advertise in foreign cultures that is based on the concept that markets share common characteristics and need to be analyzed to find local opportunities with focuses on market share and size of market.

7. The model for deciding how to advertise in foreign cultures that emphasizes the cultural differences among people and nations, that recognizes the sharing of universal needs but that also stresses that these needs are met differently in different cultures.

8. When an international agency decentralizes the development of advertising campaigns and allows a local office to originate a campaign then serve as the coordinating point to develop all the necessary pattern elements and a standard manual for the international campaign, the local office.

9. The only major country in the world that still distinguishes between business and international business.

10. Culture in which the meaning of a message can be understood only within a specific context, this.

11. Culture in which the meaning of a message can be understood as an independent entity.

12. The coverage area of a satellite.

13. Company that had the largest worldwide advertising expenditures for 1989, according to Advertising Age.

14. Brand that has the same name, same design, and same creative strategy worldwide.

15. The largest international advertising agency (in terms of worldwide gross income in 1989), according to Advertising Age.

Matching Answers

1. j
2. n
3. h
4. g
5. a
6. l
7. b
8. i

9. o
10. f
11. k
12. d
13. m
14. e
15. c

Multiple Choice

Place the letter of the correct answer in the blank provided.

_____ 1. An international brand is a brand that:
   a. operates in one of the market blocs of North America, Europe, Latin America, or Asia-Pacific.
   b. is marketed in one specific country.
   c. is available in at least two or more of the four major regional blocs.
   d. has the same name, same design, and same strategy everywhere in the world.
   e. none of the above

_____ 2. What percentage of domestic production does international business and trade now account for in almost every industrialized country?
   a. 10%
   b. 25%
   c. 33%
   d. 50%
   e. 75%

_____ 3. In international marketing the communication of the benefits and characteristics of products in advertising is:
   a. unique to each country.
   b. not unique but very different for different countries.
   c. much the same from country to country.
   d. much the same within regions but very different between regions.
   e. none of the above

_____ 4. What is the dominant means for developing advertising on the international level?
   a. within the companies
   b. freelancers
   c. local retailers/resellers/wholesalers
   d. advertising agencies
   e. all of the above

_____ 5. Consumers within the regional blocs are:
   a. increasing in number.
   b. becoming more similar in tastes.
   c. decreasing in number.
   d. becoming more heterogeneous.
   e. becoming more different in tastes.

_____ 6. Which of the following is an example of a global brand?
   a. Coca-Cola
   b. IBM
   c. McDonald's
   d. Xerox
   e. all of the above

A global perspective is difficult to achieve as long as:
a. the headquarters is located in the United States.
b. English is the only language used by the organization.
c. management is located in one country.
d. local products form the basis of the company's product line.
e. all of the above

_____ 8. Which of the following is one of the factors that restricts global advertising?
a. culture
b. language
c. local media
d. regulation
e. all of the above

_____ 9. What has happened with foreign advertising billings in the seven years between 1984 to 1990 for U.S. advertising agencies involved in international advertising?
a. slight decrease
b. decreased significantly
c. slight increase
d. increased significantly
e. none of the above

_____ 10. Experience has shown that the only reasonable solution to language problems in international advertising is:
a. to employ bilingual copywriters who have a full understanding of English.
b. to use a back translation.
c. to employ retired school teachers to write the ads.
d. to use multiple back translations.
e. all of the above.

_____ 11. What are the two variables used in the market-analysis model for assessing how to advertise in foreign cultures?
a. restrictions of the political system and the type of language
b. share of market of brands within a category and size of the product category
c. nature of the language and the available media
d. share of market of brands within a category and nature of the language
e. population of the country and the available media

_____ 12. In a high-context culture, words:
a. can have more than one meaning depending on the preceding or following sentences.
b. have very clearly defined meanings.
c. can be understood as independent entities.
d. all of the above
e. none of the above.

13. According to an old axiom, "All business is:
    a. global."
    b. international."
    c. regional."
    d. local."
    e. none of the above.

14. All of the following are a starting point for international advertising campaigns **EXCEPT**:
    a. a centrally conceived new product or directive.
    b. success in one country.
    c. a centrally identified need.
    d. a centrally conceived strategy.
    e. none of the above

15. If the campaign is being handled by one of the international advertising agencies, the media orders will be placed in most cases:
    a. locally.
    b. globally.
    c. a minimum of 2 years prior to air date.
    d. via a member of the international advertising agency's headquarters only.
    e. none of the above.

Multiple Choice Answers

1.	c	9.	d
2.	a	10.	a
3.	c	11.	b
4.	d	12.	a
5.	b	13.	d
6.	e	14.	e
7.	c	15.	a
8.	e		

Career Exercise -- Professional Comments

The following are comments from professionals that have been gleaned from responses to career questionnaires and other sources. If you ask the pros in your career field, they will usually tell you straight up what they appreciate or don't and in the end what it takes to successfully market yourself.

The best advice I ever received about my career was READ! Read everything you can get your hands on every day of your career. Not only will this keep you from re-inventing the wheel, but you can go a long way toward solving many problems and developing many campaigns by knowing what has been done before.

interviewing an entry-level candidate, what impresses me most is honesty,
...eness, clear thinking, pleasant disposition, intellectual curiosity, high energy, openness,
...iveness, good judgment, and manners.

The best advice I ever received was to look for a mentor or a role model to work for -- ...eone about whom I could say, "When I grow up, I want to be just like him/her."

If I were planning my career today, I'd be more cautious in choosing the first position I ...tered into. The glamor and urgency of needing to get a position blinded me to certain things I ...ould have been more cautious about. For instance, the job description and title were great, but the leadership received from my boss was shallow. He actually found someone who eagerly did all of his work too.

When interviewing an entry-level candidate, what impresses me most is the "fire in the belly" -- an indication there is a special drive, an ability to succeed in adversity, a determination to overcome obstacles.

When interviewing an entry-level candidate, what impresses me most is to what extent this person is a self-starter, an entrepreneur who knows that the job in an agency is to build a business, not just one in which he/she practices a craft.

When interviewing an entry-level candidate, what impresses me most is someone who already knows what kind of work my agency does and doesn't have to have the business explained to him. I don't want to hear, "I like people," as the answer to "what are your biggest strengths?"

What impresses me most about an interview candidate are the questions he/she asks.

What impresses me most is someone who has gone the extra mile and gotten involved in extra-curricular activities for the experience. GPA isn't worth anything without real-life experience.

When interviewing an entry-level candidate, what impresses me most is their interest in our organization and what they can contribute rather than our benefits and what they can receive.

When interviewing entry-level candidates, what impresses me most is honesty on good and bad points.